RADICAL
POTHOLDER WEAVING

RADICAL
POTHOLDER WEAVING

Techniques and Inspiration for the Potholder Loom

DEBORAH JEAN COHEN

&

Mary Clarke • Christine Olsen Reis • Andréa Scheidler
• Kendal Rosenberger • Paula Royse

STACKPOLE
BOOKS

Essex, Connecticut
Blue Ridge Summit, Pennsylvania

STACKPOLE BOOKS

An imprint of Globe Pequot, the trade division of The Rowman & Littlefield
Publishing Group, Inc.
4501 Forbes Blvd., Ste. 200
Lanham, MD 20706
www.rowman.com

Distributed by NATIONAL BOOK NETWORK
800-462-6420

British Library Cataloguing in Publication Information available

Library of Congress Cataloging-in-Publication Data
Names: Cohen, Deborah Jean, author.
Title: Radical potholder weaving / Deborah Jean Cohen and Mary Clarke,
  Christine Olsen Reis, Andréa Scheidler, Kendal Rosenberger, Paula Royse.
Description: First edition. | Lanham, MD : Stackpole Books, [2024] |
  Summary: "Begin your radical potholder journey by trying the multitude
  of intriguing potholder designs presented in easy-to-follow charts. When
  you are ready to make your own designs, you'll find the advice on
  adapting an existing weaving draft to a potholder loom chart
  invaluable"— Provided by publisher.
Identifiers: LCCN 2023044605 (print) | LCCN 2023044606 (ebook) | ISBN
  9780811772747 (paperback) | ISBN 9780811772754 (epub)
Subjects: LCSH: Weaving—Patterns. | Potholders.
Classification: LCC TT848.7 .C622 2024 (print) | LCC TT848.7 (ebook) |
  DDC 746.1/4—dc23/eng/20240118
LC record available at https://lccn.loc.gov/2023044605
LC ebook record available at https://lccn.loc.gov/2023044606

Printed in India

First Edition

ONE HEART

Christine Reis
2023

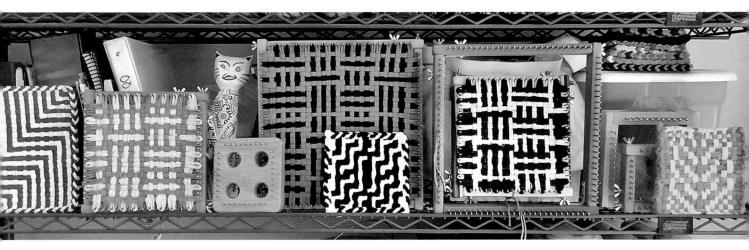

CONTENTS

INTRODUCTION

This book was originally born from the dearth of available potholder patterns; the lockdown of 2020; Noreen Crone-Findlay's original potholder pattern, Stepping Stones; and a promise. I admired Stepping Stones, and the proverbial lightbulb went off when I found a 4-harness weaving draft online. (That draft became Spiral Maze, shown on page 140.) I charted it for the potholder loom: it took a long time to chart, so I analyzed what was happening and developed a method to chart any draft. Suddenly there were unlimited possible potholder patterns. At the same time, Tertön Lama Hyolmo asked me to fundraise for a monastery being built in a remote area of Nepal: Illam. The monastery, Thegtse Sangyé Chöling, will be the source of education, community support, and senior care for the area, and it is Tertön Rinpoche's dream and promise to his teacher. The book you hold in your hands is the expanded and revised version of *In the Loop: Radical Potholder Patterns & Techniques. In the Loop* has brought the monastery's *gonpa* (main hall) to near completion, and this book, *Radical Potholder Weaving*, will continue to fund the effort. In these pages, you'll find the results of a group of dedicated, dynamic, and talented weavers and designers. Converted charts, original designs, and several strong classic potholder patterns are collected here for both your weaving library and your creative energy.

— Deborah Jean Cohen
Instagram: @deborahjeancohen

CHAPTER 1

HOW TO READ CHARTS; TIPS; SOURCES

Welcome to potholder weaving! In this chapter, you will find useful weaving tips, tricks, tools, sources, and some oddball techniques.

HOW TO READ CHARTS

Chart notation in this book follows this rule: "—" means weave your weft loop **over** the warp loop, and " | " means weave the weft loop **under** the warp loop. Warp column numbers are marked at the top and bottom of the chart, and weft rows at the left and right sides. Warp colors are at the top, and weft on the left side. The generic placeholders A and B are used for the colors. *A is always gray, and B is always white in all the charts.*

For plain weave charts, the Harrisville Designs Potholder Wizard convention is followed, except that here the lower right-hand square is marked with the beginning pick direction. In the example in figure 1.1, the first pick is under, so you would weave under/over until the row's end, and then over/under for the next row, and so on.

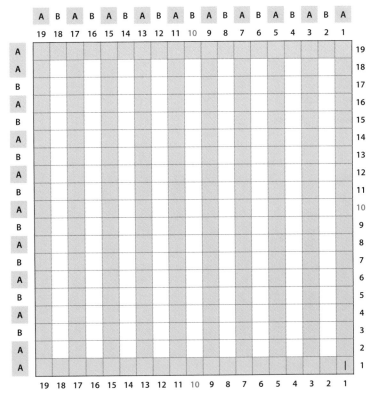

Figure 1.1. Weave II

Please note that patterns that are symmetrical around a column are charted for the 19- and 27-peg looms; those symmetrical around a line are charted for the 18- and 28-peg looms. If you have only the traditional 18- and 27-peg looms, drop a column and a row for those patterns that are charted for the 19- and 28-peg looms. Nonsymmetrical patterns are charted for the 18- and 27-peg loom sizes.

Basic Twill

Basic twill always has the warp all one color, and the weft all another. So, when the weft loop is woven under the warp loop, the warp color shows; when the weft loop is woven over the warp loop, the weft color shows. (In all the basic twill charts here, the under/over direction will be noted at the top.) In figure 1.2, you see that the first row is woven under/under, over/over, and so on until the end of the row. The next row reads first over, then under/under, over/over, until the last square, which is an under. This sequence tends to weave up very quickly, because your eye immediately translates the weaving direction into motion.

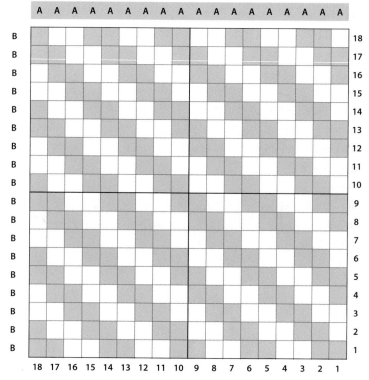

Figure 1.2. Basic twill

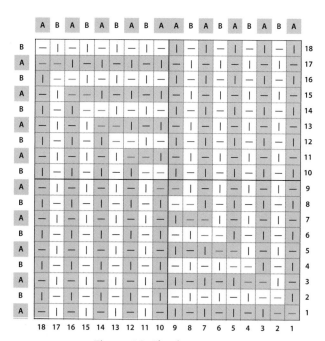

Figure 1.3. Shadow weave

The other pattern types in this book, shadow weave (figure 1.3) and predominantly twill (figure 1.4) structures (which I've placed in the twill chapter), are straightforward. Each square will contain the weaving direction "under" (|) or "over" (—). Note that 2- and 3-floats are bolded red, to make them easier to pick out; if they predominate, then single picks are bolded.

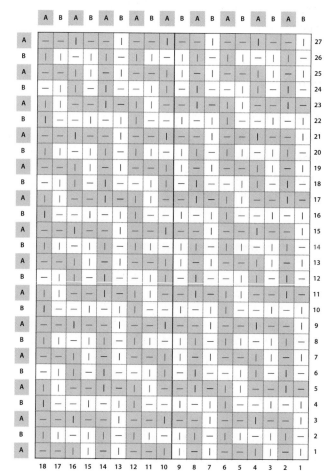

Figure 1.4. Predominantly twill

TIPS
Symmetry around a Column or around a Line

If a design is symmetrical around a column, it's charted for a loom with an odd number of pegs: the 19, 27, or 19 x 27. If a design is symmetrical around a line, or isn't symmetrical, it's charted for a loom with an even number of pegs: the 18, 28, or 18 x 27. Dropping a column and a row will fit a 19-peg design on an 18-peg loom, or a 28-peg design on a 27-peg loom, but symmetry is lost.

For those of you who might be unhappy with that situation, drop the first and last rows and the first and last columns of the chart (the blue areas in figure 1.5) and weave on 17 pegs of your 18-peg loom and 26 pegs of your 27-peg loom. In the example, the blue-shaded areas are the rows/columns to drop. Besides dropping rows and columns, you can increase the peg count on your loom to get symmetry. There are many ways to do this, but by far the neatest and easiest way is to use Andréa Scheidler's Convert-a-Loom Hack. Instructions follow.

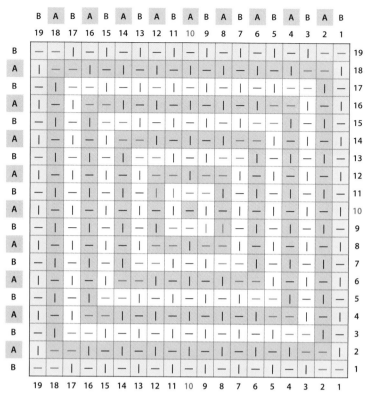
Figure 1.5. Square-in-a-Square

Weaving a 19-Peg Design on an 18-Peg Loom

Andréa Scheidler's Convert-a-Loom Hack can of course be used on any size loom: the principles are the same. Our example is Simple Meander (page 99), a 19-peg design that we'll weave on an 18-peg loom. In Simple Meander, both the center warp and the center weft colors are A; my A is a Wool Novelty Company loop dyed pink with Japanese mud dye.

1. Materials needed: 2 S hooks and some hair ties.

2. Select the loop color for your center warp and center weft and loop a hair tie at each end as shown.

3. Warp your loom with your chosen colors and lay the extra warp loop in the center spot. An 18-peg loom is symmetrical around a line, and that line is between the 9th and 10th pegs. That's your center.

4. Secure the ties to each other with an S hook at the back of the loom.

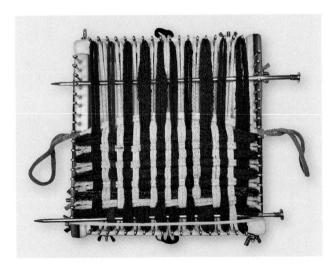

5. Weave as usual up to row 9; then weave in your center weft, hair ties and all.

6. Wrap the hair ties around your loom and secure at the back with an S hook.

7. When binding off, crochet up to the added warp/weft loop, remove the hair tie, and keep going.

8. Finished. This potholder is unblocked, just tugged into shape.

Weaving—Making a Shed, Evening Out Take-Up, and Straight Rows

If you weave first with a knitting needle, it's easy to slide your hook through the shed made by the needle (figure 1.6). It's faster to weave that way, and if you happen to put the wrong color loop in, or change your mind, you don't have to reweave.

Figure 1.6

Laying your loop in an arch within the shed evens out the take-up that occurs in the interlacing of warp and weft as you beat the weft down (figure 1.7). The weave will be more consistent, and the need for blocking reduced.

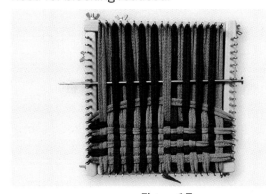

Figure 1.7

The knitting needle is also a good check for straight rows (figure 1.8)!

Figure 1.8

A knitting needle or chopstick across the bottom provides a strong base to keep rows straight as you beat them down (figure 1.9). This tip is from Christine, and I use it regularly. I sometimes add a gum band (rubber band to those who are not from western Pennsylvania), which holds the knitting needle firmly against the pegs.

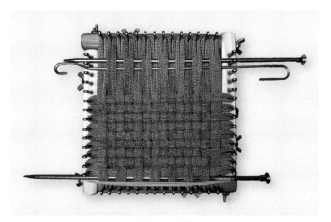

Figure 1.9

Maintaining Tension When Crocheting Off

It's far easier to crochet the potholder off the loom if the loops are tensioned. Use bullnose clips as you go along: loops won't pop off (figure 1.10). (Note the yarn tied around the loom at the bottom—I mark the middle of mine, on the bottom, and usually the right side. Others mark every so many pegs. This approach makes it easier to track row and column count.)

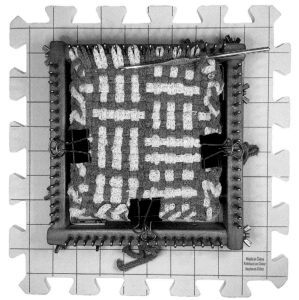

Figure 1.10

Blocking

Potholders straight off the loom aren't square. Several things can cause that result: uneven weaving; loops that are of different lengths, thicknesses, material, or springiness; the potholder pattern itself. You can mitigate this effect by careful weaving, matching the loops as best you can, and by stretching each loop well before placing on the warp pegs or weaving in the weft loop. I tug each Friendly Loom loop just until I hear the fabric crack (though not all of them will crack) and stretch each Wool Novelty Company loop until it is barely tensioned over the loom. I do the best I can with Pepperell—some stretch and some do not. Stretching allows the warp and weft room to interlace nicely, reducing take-up and allowing your fabric to lie flat. Still, even with nicely stretched and matched loops and careful weaving, potholders seldom come off the loom perfectly square. To me, this is just one of their endearing qualities, and I'm happy to give them a few tugs and call it a day. But if you want to give them as a gift, or you just have to have them as square as possible, you can block them.

Blocking is a method to adjust the shape of the finished piece, setting the final dimensions of the woven fabric. If you're a knitter, you'll be familiar with the idea; blocking potholders is very similar. There are many different ways to block.

- Press with a steam iron.
- Spray (or soak) with water, and pin to a grid (figure 1.11) until dry. You can use a ruler at the edges to keep them straight as you pin.
- Leave the potholder on the loom overnight.

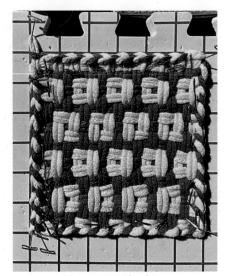

Figure 1.11. Blocking

There are some variations to the "leave it on the loom" method: I sometimes soak my potholders with very hot water while still on the loom, blot them, carefully dry the loom, and dry in front of a fan, generally overnight. Less difficult patterns are misted rather than soaked.

> Just like any fabric, loops will sometimes bleed. You generally won't even notice unless you use white loops, but if it happens, you can soak the potholder in OxiClean. This usually works. Then prewash whichever batch of loops bled before using them the next time, and you're all set.

SOURCES
Loops

Potholders made with loops owe their existence to the hosiery industry: sock mills produce huge amounts of cutoff strips, made as the sock tubing is cut. In the Depression-era 1930s, as a way to use this waste, mills would package these "loopers" with a loom and sell them to housewives. Today some loops still come from sock mills.

There are many resellers of loops, but listed here are the sources:

Harrisville Designs, Harrisville, New Hampshire

Harrisville Designs Friendly Loom custom-makes and dyes its loops from recycled yarn—they aren't sock mill waste. These are the most consistent loops on the market today, though variation still occurs: like yarn, color will not be exact from dye lot to dye lot, and loop stretchiness can also vary. Friendly Loom carries traditional loops and the larger PRO size, meant for a 10-inch loom. There's a wide selection of colors—32 plus black and white—in the Rainbow, Earthtones, Botanicals, and Neutrals lines. Excellent customer service. Friendly Loom loops are the basic tools in our loop tool kit: with their wonderful color palette and consistency, they're the go-to loop.

Wool Novelty Company, Levittown, New York

Wool Novelty Company (WNC) dyes and packages cotton loops from sock mills. These are sturdy loops, vary in size and color within each dye lot, and come in 10 colors (plus black and natural). Most will fit the traditional 7-inch loom; save the others for your 13- or 14-peg loom. Extraordinary customer

Figure 1.12. Mary Clarke's Fillet pattern (page 92), woven by her, in WNC brown, blue, and natural. *(left)*

Figure 1.13. The Broken Comb pattern (page 41), woven in Friendly Loom carnation and Pepperell shades of brown and orange. *(middle)*

Figure 1.14. This is Open Cross, which is simply the reverse side of Square-in-a-Square (page 117). It's woven in Friendly Loom black and Solmate colors on a 19-peg loom. *(right)*

service. We love these loops for their variation and wonderful saturated colors: their light greens can be an incredible acid color; the darker blues wonderful shades of denim; their black amazing (try a black-on-black pattern using both Friendly Loom and WNC blacks); their browns and natural often shot through with black or light Lycra. Use WNC with other brands' loops: adding a sturdier loop to your mix will stabilize the more complex patterns, often making the blocking step unnecessary. And mixing WNC with Pepperell or Hillcreek Fiber Studio's wool loops does much to cure take-up.

Pepperell Braiding Company, Pepperell, Massachusetts

Pepperell has three factories: in Pepperell, Massachusetts; Bradford, Pennsylvania; and Ningbo, China. They sell a 1-pound bag of "mixed artificial fibers," but the loops have a distinctly natural feel. I'm wondering whether some of them contain modal. The loops are all over the map—most fit the 7-inch traditional loom, others the 13- and 14-peg loom, and a very few are so tiny that I'm saving them for my 9-peg pin loom. The colors are random. You never know what you'll get—all variegated, some with shiny metallic threads mixed in. I absolutely love some of their shades and absolutely hate others (I overdye those). But many

A note about fiber content: The melting point of nylon is 515.9 degrees F. The melting point of polyester is 482 degrees F. Cotton does not melt, but it begins to decompose rapidly at 475 degrees F. So be careful. I don't ever use nylon loops but often mix cotton with polyester.

of my most favorite potholders are made with Pepperell loops: they're one of a kind.

Solmate Socks, Hickory, North Carolina

An obvious way to get your loops is from a sock mill. Solmate is a sock mill, and, as part of its sustainable production ethic, the mill washes the cotton loopers, masses of extraneous threads and all, and packs them into a 50-pound carton. Solmate will give it to you for postage. Colors are random: the waste from whatever sock run is happening. So I estimate that about one-third of my box contains white loops shot through with black Lycra; a good deal of the rest are dark loops (lots of charcoal gray), and the remainder various colors. Yavia's box was a majority red and blue. The loops are raggedy and rather thick, have lots of threads, and are a bit harder to weave with. However, they're worth the effort: they add texture, structure, and a different color palette to your work. Solmate has extraordinary customer service.

Now, if you for some strange reason don't want 50 pounds of loopers, you can get Solmate loops from:

Homestead Weaving Studio LLC, Columbus, Indiana

Homestead Weaving does the sorting and cleanup for you and packages traditional, jumbo, and baby Solmate loops in half-pound to 3-pound bags. Baby loops are available packed in a kit with a very well-made loom (12 pegs), custom built to accommodate Solmate's thicker width. It also sells kits with loops and looms in traditional (16-peg), jumbo (20-peg), and hybrid (16 x 20-peg) sizes and has added even more loom sizes. Plus, you can choose the colors you want: by individual color or custom blends. I have three of the kits and am happy with them. The pegs are cotter pins (more on cotter pins later). NOTE: You can weave Solmate loops on the more common 18- and 27-peg looms, so feel free to experiment.

As far as I know, these are the root sources of every cotton or mixed fiber loop in the United States. There's one source for wool loops:

Carol Leigh's Hillcreek Fiber Studio, Columbia, Missouri

In earlier literature that came along with one's Hillcreek order, Harrisville Designs is listed as the source of undyed wool loops, both traditional and PRO sized. My latest order didn't include that information, and Harrisville Designs does not offer wool loops to the general public. Carol Leigh is famous for her colorfast pokeberry dye recipe (colorfast it is; the wool I dyed using it is bright after 9 years). Carol dyes wool loops with poke and other natural dyestuff and provides undyed loops as well. They are expensive, but the price, considering the labor that goes along with dyeing naturally, is very fair. You can choose from 24 truly luscious shades or Carol's custom collections. Frankly, I love wool potholders. They weave up beautifully and have a wonderful hand. Wool, unlike cotton, has a memory, so take-up, or draw-in, is more pronounced, and your potholder will be distinctly smaller. Figure 1.15 shows a size comparison—cotton versus mostly wool. You can see the difference!

Looms

All the loop sources listed above carry looms. There are so many loom makers and resellers of metal looms that I can't list them all. I use wooden looms with cotter pin pegs: unlike metal looms, wood looms stand up well to the tension of loops strung across them, and they don't warp. The cotter pin pegs are long so that your loops don't randomly pop off; they're rounded, so they don't stab your wrists; and they're very sturdy and won't break like wood pegs or bend like nails. The infamous Last Row is much easier to weave: just push the loops up the pegs—your hook will slide right through. Homestead Weaving Studio and Cottage Looms Designs (Etsy) carries these looms. (If Cottage Looms' shop shows no stock, message them and they'll make it for you within a week. They'll make custom sizes too.) CinDwood makes sturdy looms with plastic pegs—also a good choice.

Figure 1.15. *Left:* Friendly Loom red and white. *Right:* WNC red and Hillcreek denim. WOVEN BY MARY CLARKE ON AN 18-PEG LOOM.

How to Make Your Own Loops from Socks

1. Cut the socks at the red lines.

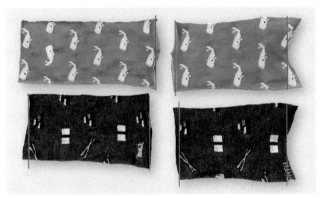

2. Trim them up so the tubes have straight edges.

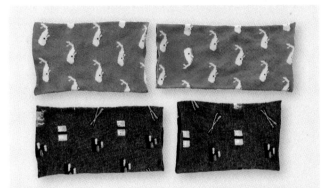

3. Then cut each tube into ⅜- to ½-inch strips.

4. They'll look like this when cut.

5. After cutting, the loops naturally curl up, with the inside of the sock showing.

6. Right Angles (page 96) woven with Friendly Loom turquoise and sock loops.

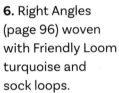

AN EXAMPLE OF TAKE-UP, AKA DRAW-IN

Each potholder in figure 1.16 is woven with Friendly Loom loops on an 18-peg loom. You can see how weaving over/under 2 and 3 warp loops results in progressively smaller potholders. These patterns are balanced: the floats occur evenly across the loom. When a pattern has 3-floats in only a few areas, draw-in can occur unevenly and may require blocking.

Figure 1.16. *Left:* Plain weave. *Center:* Twill (2-floats). *Right:* A 3-float basket weave.

FREESTYLE WEAVING

Above are examples of freestyle weaving, in which you're not following a specific pattern. You could make pairs in which one potholder is a formal pattern and the other is more abstract (Ladders paired with a random tabby, above), or grab a handful of loops and just see where they take you (the red/cream/black potholder). It's a nice respite—just play!

CHAPTER 2

TECHNIQUES: SPLIT LOOP AND CLASPED WEFT

SPLIT-LOOP TECHNIQUE

Normal potholder weaving views the warp loop as one unit, and you weave the weft under or over it: an 18-peg loom has 18 warp "threads." Split loop views each strand of the warp loop as an individual unit, and you weave the weft under and over accordingly. Looked at in this way, an 18-peg loom has 36 warp "threads." Using the technique, you can experiment with any of the weaving structures (plain weave, twill, etc.). It allows for a wonderful variety of interesting effects. Here are two to get you started.

Figure 2.2

Figure 2.3

Figure 2.1

Christine's Pebble Weave (Plain Weave)

When you use the split-loop technique with a plain weave structure, you simply weave under the first arm of the warp loop and over the next arm, continuing on in the normal plain weave pattern. This method gives a pebbly surface, which is greatly emphasized visually if you use three colors (figures 2.1, 2.2, and 2.3). It's a very tight weave.

Yavia's Half-Loopy Pattern (2 x 2 Twill), Plus Put a Ring on It!

Yavia's Half-Loopy Pattern

Row 1: Under 1/over 2/under 2.
Row 2: Over 1/under 2/over 2.
Repeat.

1. Warp in 2 colors.

2. Weave under the first thread.

Figure 2.4. Yavia's Half-Loopy Pattern with Ring
Figure 2.5. Yavia's Half-Loopy Pattern: Peas and Carrots

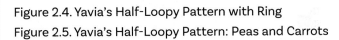

3. Weave over the next 2 threads.

4. Weave under the next 2 threads.

5. Continue weaving over 2, under 2 . . .

6. . . . until the end of the row. The last warp thread will be under.

7. Weave over the first thread and under the next 2 threads.

8. Weave over the next 2 threads; then continue weaving under 2/over 2 until the end of the row. The last warp thread will be over.

9. Repeat these 2-row steps . . .

10. . . . until you're done.

11. Crochet the potholder off the loom.

12. Here's how to put a ring on the last loop: Bring the loop through the ring from below.

13. Stretch the loop over the ring's top and pull through.

14. Voilà!

15. Voilà again!

CLASPED WEFT TECHNIQUE

The clasped weft method results in two or more completely different weaving areas within your loom. These can be triangles or rectangles, and each area can be a different weaving structure, pattern, and/or color(s). The technique is a lot of fun to explore, but it is better shown than explained, so what follows are examples of a few different ways to weave it.

Two-Triangle Clasped Weft

This is a very basic variation, a good weave for learning. In this example, the triangle in the upper right area will be yellow, and the lower left triangle will be blue.

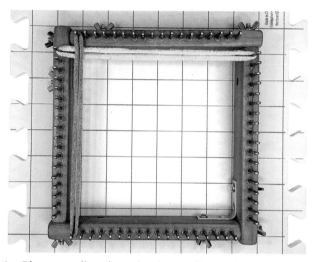

1a. Place a yellow loop horizontally on the top pegs; then lay a blue loop vertically over it.

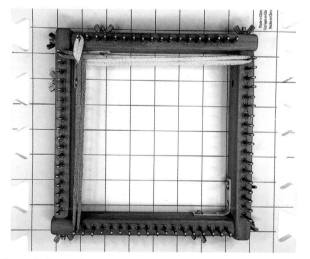

1b. Pull the yellow loop over the blue, to the right. Move the blue loop from the top left peg to the top side peg; then put the yellow loop where the blue loop was.

2a. Place a yellow loop horizontally on the next set of pegs, and lay a blue loop vertically over it.

2b. Pull the yellow loop over the blue, to the right (you don't have to use a hook—this is so you can clearly see what's happening)...

2c. ...and move the blue loop to the second peg. Weave the yellow loop under the loop above it; then place it over the now open second peg.

3a. Place a yellow loop horizontally on the next set of pegs, and lay a blue loop vertically over it.

3b. Pull the yellow loop over the blue, to the right . . .

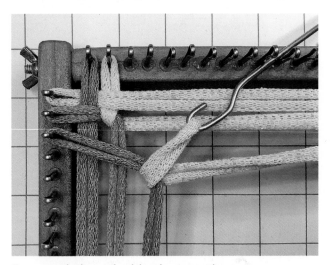

3c. . . . and place the blue loop on the next peg down.

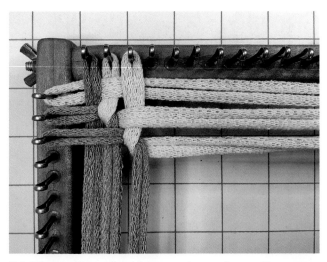

3d. Weave the yellow loop under and over the upper loops, and place on the next peg over.

3e. Then weave the blue loop over and under the blue loops to the left.

Continue on like this, placing the loops, twisting them around each other, and weaving them in.

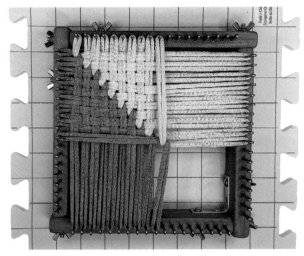

4. Adjust the diagonal as you go by making sure the columns and rows are straight, as you would in normal tabby weaving.

5. After the first 4 or so rows, I weave a few loops in each direction, adjust the twist (making sure my loops lie flat), and then finish weaving.

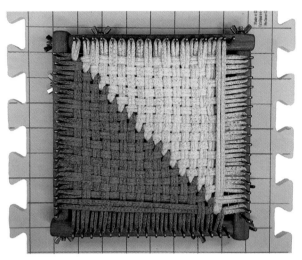

6. Almost done!

7. Bind off as usual! Voilà!

Figure 2.6. *Upper triangle:* Pinwheel (page 59), 2 blue, 2 white. *Lower triangle:* Stripes (page 37), 1 red, 1 white. *(left)*
Figure 2.7. *Upper triangle:* Pinwheel, 2 green, 2 carnation. *Lower triangle:* Confetti (page 55), 1 robin's egg, 2 yellow. *(middle)*
Figure 2.8. *Upper triangle:* Pinwheel, 2 orange, 2 white. *Lower triangle:* Stripes, 1 pink, 1 white. *(right)*

Four-Triangle Clasped Weft

For this method, begin at the center and weave outward within each section.

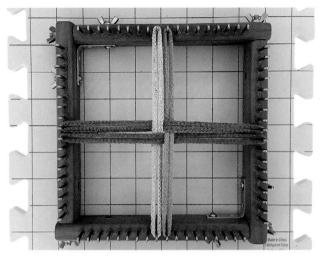

1a. Set up your first round like this. Brown will end up at the top, blue to the left, spice at the bottom, and leaf to the right.

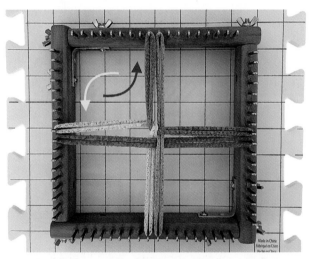

1b. Lift the brown loop over the blue to the right, and switch pegs: place the blue loop on brown's peg and fold the brown loop over the blue to blue's peg.

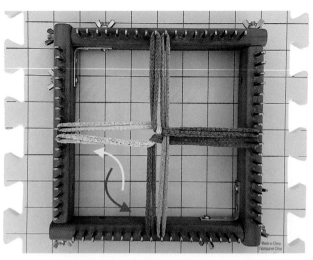

1c. Switch pegs: fold the blue loop over the spice toward the top, put the spice loop on blue's peg, and put blue on spice's peg.

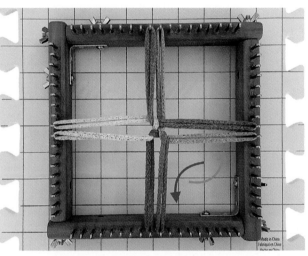

1d. Switch pegs: fold spice over leaf to the bottom, and leaf under spice to the right.

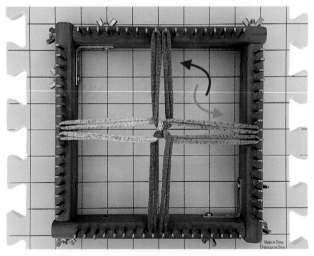

1e. Switch pegs: leaf is folded over brown to the right; brown goes under leaf to the top.

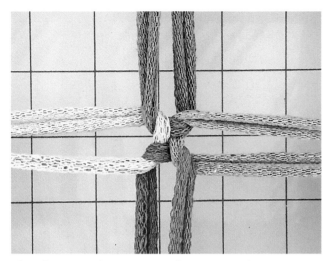

1f. Tighten up the center to form a neat knot.

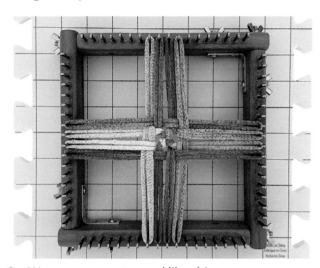

2a. Weave your next round like this.

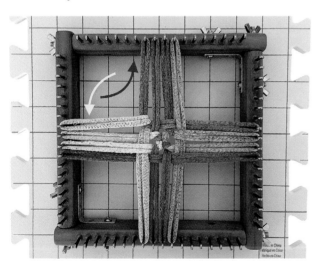

2b. Switch pegs: blue is folded over brown to the left, and brown under blue to the top.

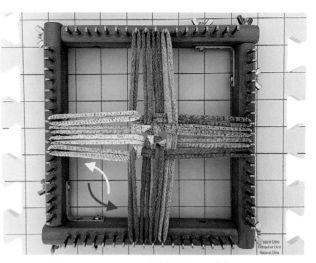

2c. Switch pegs: spice is folded over blue to the bottom, and blue under spice to the left.

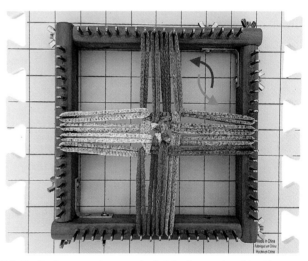

2d. Switch pegs: brown is folded over leaf to the top, and leaf under brown to the right.

2e. Switch pegs: leaf is folded over spice to the right, and spice under leaf to the bottom.

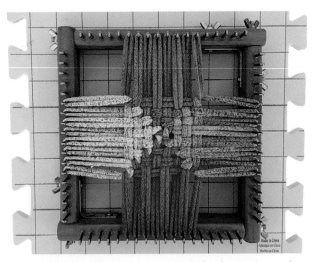

3. Continue on like this, weaving the loops in and switching the pegs, twisting the loops around each other.

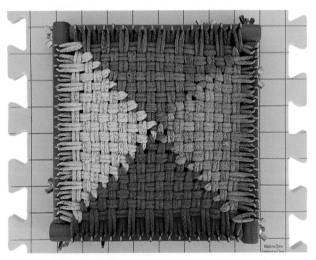

4. Bind off as usual . . .

5. . . . and you're done.

Figure 2.9. Examples of Four-Triangle Clasped Weft

Half-Quad Clasped Weft

This method divides a quadrangle into two sections. It's very easy, so we're going to mix it up a bit and weave some twill.

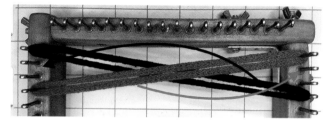

1a. Arrange your loops so black folds over red and red goes under black …

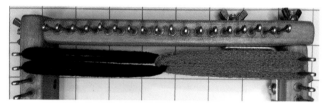

1b. … and switch pegs.

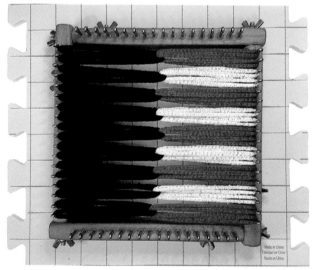

2. Continue warping, alternating red and white loops for the right-hand section.

3. Turn your loom so the black warp is on top; then begin at the base of that section and weave the 2 x 2 pattern in figure 2.10. Weave under gray and over white.

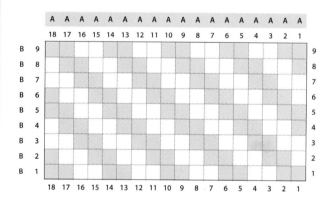

Figure 2.10. Left diagonals

4. Turn your loom so the red and white weft is on top and weave the Pinwheel pattern: in plain weave, repeat AABB until the end of the row. Begin at the bottom right with a weave under. (In this example, I switched the order, beginning with white, my B color, while my warp began with my A color, red.) Pinwheel is on page 59.

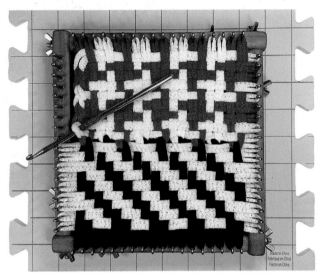

5. Bind off as usual.

6. Done.

Figure 2.11. In the potholder on the left, the Pinwheel weft began more properly with my A color (pink). The warp also begins with A. Notice how the overall pattern has shifted one row up from the potholder in step 6. Figure 2.12. The potholder on the right was woven using the left diagonals chart for one half (figure 2.10) and the right diagonals chart (figure 2.13) for the other.

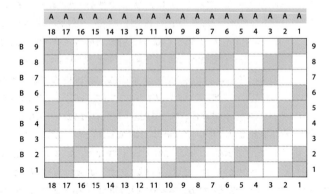

Figure 2.13. Right diagonals

Figure 2.14. Creative use of One Heart (page 188) in a potholder woven by Christine Olsen Reis

CHAPTER 3

HOW TO CHART A POTHOLDER FROM SCRATCH

There are several methods for charting a potholder, each dependent on the type of weave coupled with the pattern's source: another potholder, a weaving draft, or the weaver's original idea. Plain weave, shadow weave, and twill take different charting approaches, but the beginning point, drawing the pattern that you want to chart, is the same for each, and the techniques overlap. Plain weave and basic twill are simple to chart. Converting a weaving draft to suit the potholder loom is a bit more complex and, at times, more art than science.

Most potholder patterns are plain weave: you simply weave the weft loop over or under a warp loop, alternating weaving direction with each row. This process is so natural that we don't even think about it, let alone chart it in a potholder pattern.

So let's think about it. Plain weave is uniform, repetitious, and balanced. The pattern comes entirely from the weaver's choice of warp and weft colors, and their placement on the loom, and not at all from varying the weave structure. The weaver is bound by, and must take into account, the consistently alternating interlacing of the loops. In communicating a potholder pattern, we can write out the warp/weft sequences or we can chart them visually. For example, the chart in figure 3.1 is immediately understandable at a glance. It's Weave II, taken from Harrisville Designs' Potholder Wizard, but is more universally

known as the Log Cabin sequence ABABA/ABABA. (You can generate any Log Cabin by writing a sequence of two colors, repeating the sequence reversed, and repeating the whole for the width of your loom. The pattern here is for the 18-peg loom, so it is *almost* repeated twice: the last two colors in the second repetition are missing. To weave in Log Cabin, the weft sequence is the same as the warp.)

The plain weave pattern Weave II example is the most common kind of potholder chart. In

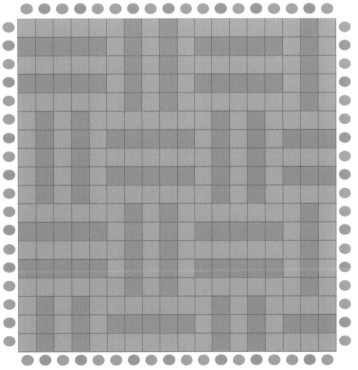

Figure 3.1. Weave II

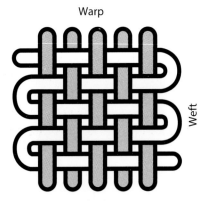

Warp

Weft

Figure 3.2

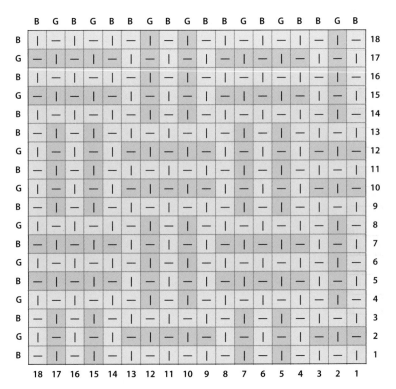

Figure 3.3

it, Harrisville Designs assumes that the weaver will know that they are to weave plain weave and that they will begin at the lower right corner by weaving "under" (see figure 3.2). (Thought experiment: What happens if they begin by weaving "over"?) It's assumed that the weaver knows that the color dots at the top and bottom represent the warp colors and sequence, and those on the sides represent the weft colors and sequence. And Harrisville Designs is correct: we know this.

The chart in figure 3.3 doesn't assume: it specifies the direction of each pick, over or under. The use of "−" for over and "|" for under mimics the way the weft looks in the fabric. Take a look at your potholder! You could, alternatively, use "o" for over and "u" for under. A method of specific charting is necessary for any potholder beyond plain weave or basic twill.

There isn't a huge catalog of potholder patterns, but there are close to 70,000 weaving drafts on Handweaving.net. We could convert one of these drafts, reverse engineer any potholder, or design our own. There are different ways to do all three, but each begins with the same step: transferring the pattern to graph paper or, if using an electronic device, a table or spreadsheet.

Draft 1 shown in figure 3.4 is a typical weaving draft. The top and sides give the threading and the treadling; the intersecting square in the upper left corner is the tie-up. If you are lucky, the weaving structure will be drawn in the draft (as

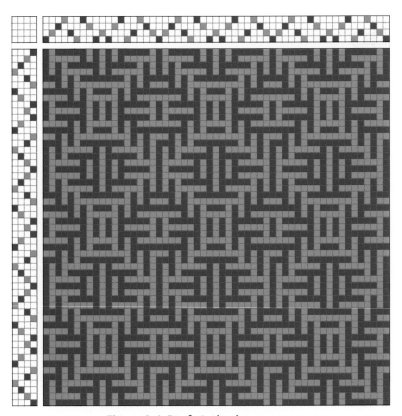

Figure 3.4. Draft 1: shadow weave

in draft 2, figure 3.5) and your work will be only to copy the pattern of over-and-under picks, but most will look flat, as if drawn on graph paper, like draft 1. In this most common case, the challenge is to chart

Figure 3.5. Draft 2: shadow weave

the weaving structure by using the pattern and the sequence of warp and weft colors.

Warp colors will be on the top or bottom of the weaving draft. Weft will be on the right or left side. In draft 1, the sequence of both warp and weft is dark blue/light blue, beginning and ending with dark blue. The colors move up and down the 4 rows of blocks, but if you collapse them onto one row, you get the sequence. Draft 2 illustrates this effect.

Both of these drafts are examples of shadow weave, with alternating warp and weft colors and a structure that combines plain weave with a twill step at pattern changes.

Draft 3 (figure 3.6) and draft 4 (figure 3.7) are twill: the weft passes over or under one or more warp loops, and has an offset between rows. Draft 3 is a basic twill: warp is one color and weft another, while draft 4 has, like shadow weave, alternating warp and weft colors. This difference is significant when charting. The following charting steps 1–3 don't apply to basic twill or plain weave: these are discussed at the chapter's end.

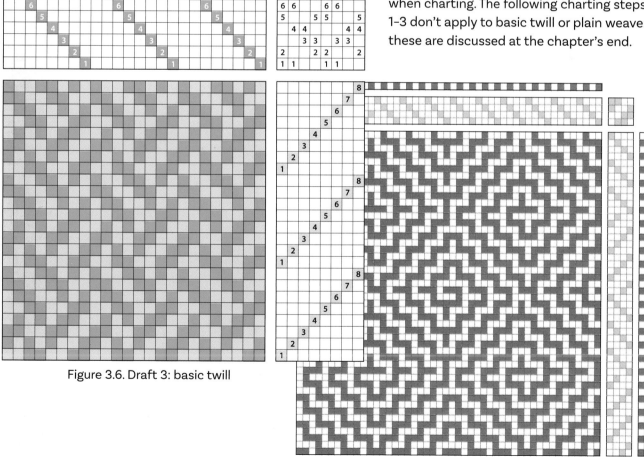

Figure 3.6. Draft 3: basic twill

Figure 3.7. Draft 4: twill

BASIC CHARTING STEPS

STEP 1 The first goal is to transfer the pattern from the draft to graph paper or, if using your laptop, tablet, or computer, into a table. Print out the draft, choose the block that fits your loom and clearly mark it off (figure 3.8).

Because the pattern is symmetrical around one central point, and I have a nice 19-peg loom, I've marked off a 19 x 19 block (figures 3.8 and 3.9). To fit the standard 18-peg loom, see "Tips" in chapter 1 on page 5.

Tip: For those of you with both 18- and 27-peg looms, chart the 27-peg first—it's easier to then size down for the smaller loom.

Transfer the pattern to a grid: graph paper and a pencil work perfectly. Alternately, use a table or Excel spreadsheet. Now look at the step 1 chart in figure 3.9. I mark the center square with an asterisk and then fill in the pattern. The warp and weft colors will be blue and white, so I've marked those at the top and side, referring to the draft to make sure the sequence begins and ends correctly. I number the rows and columns too.

STEP 2 Next, begin to chart the weaving structure. Look at the upper left side of the table in figure 3.10: in order to make the

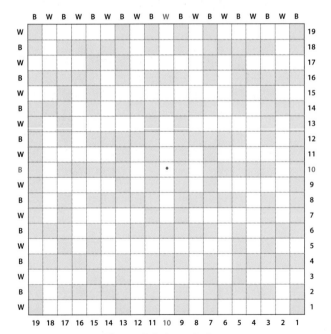

Figure 3.8

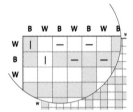

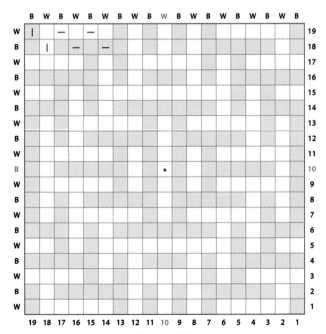

Figure 3.9. Step 1 chart

Figure 3.10

pattern, the white weft loop **must** go under the first blue warp loop and over the next 2 blue ones. In the same way, the blue weft **must** go under the first white warp loop and over the next 2 white warp loops. These picks are fixed and can't change.

At this point, the direction of the weave under or over those warp loops that are the same color as the weft isn't considered, because the pattern color at those picks remains the same either way.

Tip: When working in pencil, it helps at first to mark the chart in this first step with a different color, to make it clear that this notation can't be changed.

Take a close look at the step 2 chart in figure 3.11.

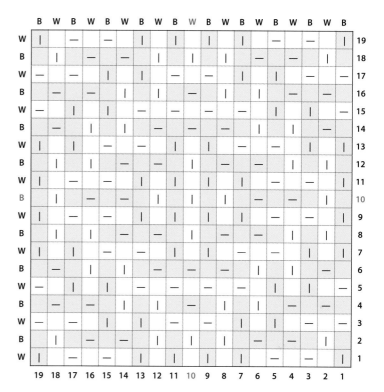

Figure 3.11. Step 2 notation is filled in

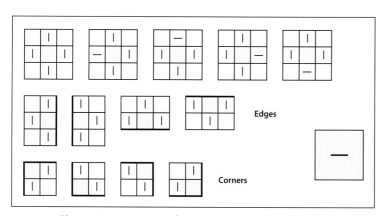

Figure 3.12. How to place step 3 "over" notation

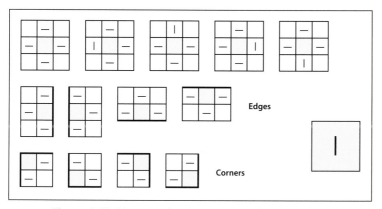

Figure 3.13. How to place step 3 "under" notation

STEP 3 Next, go through and look at each empty square and the pick notations surrounding it. If there are 3 or 4 "under" marks (|), then place an "over" (−) in the square. If there are 3 or 4 "over" marks, place an "under" in the square. Note that corners are the exception! Corners and edges can, if you want, wait to be filled in until the end. Depending on the pattern, this approach can be desirable, as it gives you more flexibility.

In figure 3.14, the top row, 4th square from the left is surrounded on each side and the bottom by "−" notation. We place a " | " there (figure 3.15). Similarly, in the 2nd row, 3rd square from the left, we place a " | ", as it's surrounded on 3 sides by "−" notation.

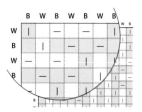

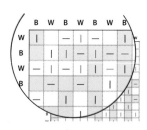

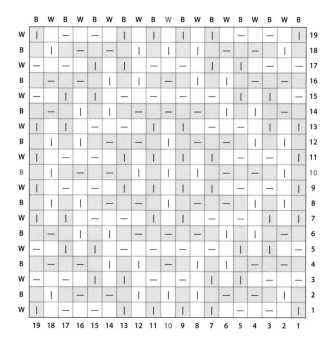

Figure 3.14

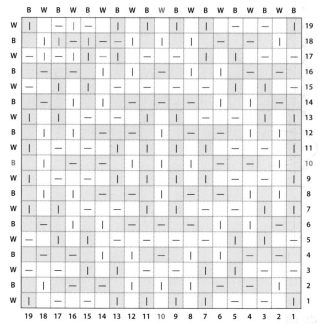

Figure 3.15

STEP 4 For the last few squares, the goal is to produce as balanced and tight a weave as possible. To do this, avoid 3 "under" (|) or "over" (—) floats in a row either horizontally or vertically. These potential long overshots are easy to spot. Three areas are circled in figure 3.16, and figure 3.17 shows the filled-in notation. There are a few more places where potential 3-floats exist: see whether you can find them.

In theory, 3-floats should be avoided in potholder charting. Because the loop floats over (or under) 3 others, it's not as stabilized by the weaving interlace, so the finished potholder will draw in more at that point, possibly distorting the fabric.

This being said, there are times when a 3-float is unavoidable and other times when it adds to the design. There are many patterns in this book that use them, as well as patterns in which 3-floats appear at the edges. So the 3-float rule is rather ambiguous: avoid them when you can, but don't worry if you can't.

When you have found the potential 3-floats, and avoided them, this pattern has no more empty

squares, and step 4 is finished; you're done charting. It's more often, though, not this easy. Next are more examples of what you might encounter, and how to chart, if after step 4 you are still left with blank squares.

HINT FOR SYMMETRICAL PATTERNS: Our example pattern is symmetrical along both axes: row 1 is the same as row 19; row 2 is the same as row 18; row 3 is the same as row 17; and on in the same way up to row 9 and row 11. Each row is also symmetrical within itself: row 1, column 1 is the same as row 1, column 19; row 1, column 2 is the same as row 1, column 18; and on until row 1, column 9 = row 1, column 11. If there were blank squares at any position, you'd look at the corresponding square in its row and use the same notation. This hint is for symmetrical patterns only, and usually it is needed only if you've missed a square.

HINT FOR DIAGONALS: Most often there are blank squares along several different diagonals. With these, you have more choice, as it generally

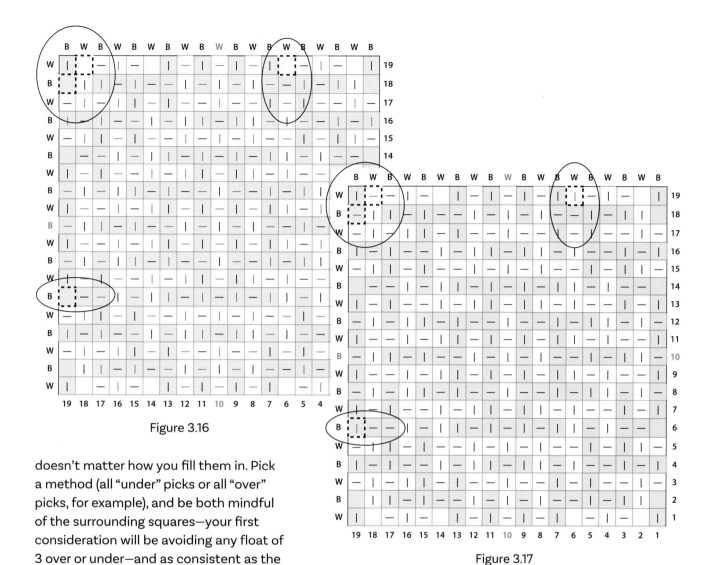

Figure 3.16

Figure 3.17

doesn't matter how you fill them in. Pick a method (all "under" picks or all "over" picks, for example), and be both mindful of the surrounding squares—your first consideration will be avoiding any float of 3 over or under—and as consistent as the surrounding squares allow.

From this point forward, charting is an art. Start with easier designs, and then explore: push the boundary of what you *think* will work. Experiment. You might discover your best designs in this way.

STACKED PAIRS: Figure 3.18 shows Mary Clarke's Straight-Edge Spiral (page 94)—a simple example of squares on diagonal runs. Note that blank squares are surrounded by 2 "under" (|) and 2 "over" (−) notations.

If you fill Straight-Edge Spiral's diagonals with all "over" (−) notations, you get the chart in figure 3.19. Stacked pairs of "under" (|) picks and "over" (−) picks are outlined in red. These don't happen to adversely affect the tightness of the weave and can be used as design elements. But, if you wanted, you could reduce the stacks, as in figure 3.20. Try it both ways, see how the weave looks, and decide.

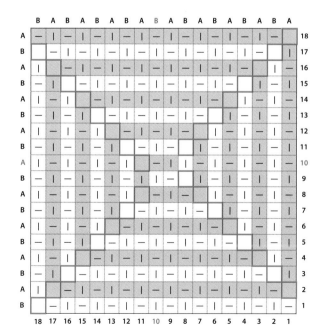

Figure 3.18. Straight-Edge Spiral

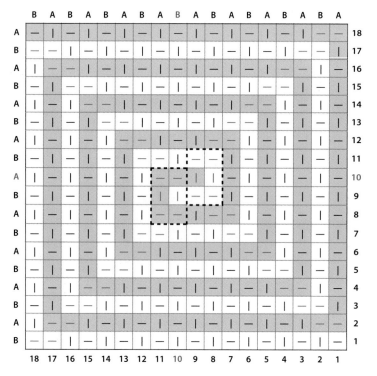

Figure 3.19

Figure 3.21 shows Mary's Fillet pattern (page 92). Stacked pairs of under and over picks flank either side of the central column and form a strong design element. Stacked pairs are stable.

SOMETIMES YOU MUST CHANGE THE PATTERN, OR NOT: Figure 3.22 shows an early version of a 2-pattern mashup that I have been playing with. Look at the squares within the red box: two opposing under picks and two opposing over picks. Both an under and an over in the center square will result in a 3-float. This configuration is a charting nemesis. The choices are to redesign the pattern or accept the 3-floats. My advice: Experiment. Try the floats and see what happens with the final structure. More often than not, the design will work.

At this point I want to add that not all weaving drafts are suited to a potholder loom conversion. There'll be drafts you think will surely work, but they won't. Never lose your sense of adventure, and keep trying—there are amazing patterns out there!

Figure 3.20

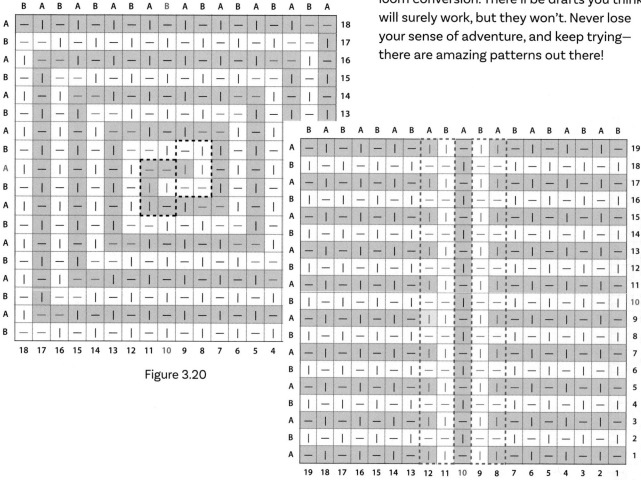

Figure 3.21. Mary's Fillet pattern

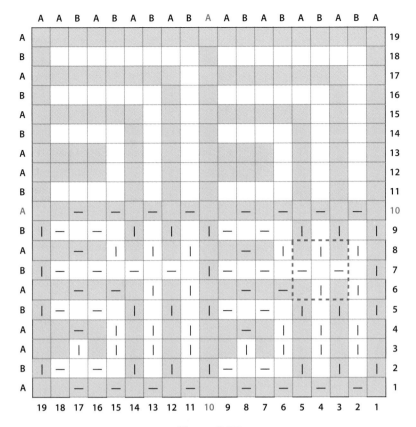

Figure 3.22

The charting steps 2–4 so far discussed apply to all weaves (as far as I know) except plain weave and basic twill. These two weaving structures are easy to chart.

CHARTING BASIC TWILL: Basic twill is simple to chart. In fact, no chart is needed. Look at the draft in figure 3.23: the warp is all green, the weft white. So, everywhere the green warp shows, the weft loop is woven under the warp loop. Everywhere the white weft shows, the weft loop is woven over the warp loop. So, looking at the magnifier in figure 3.23, the weft loop on the first row would be woven: over 2, under 1, over 2, under 1, over 2, and so on.

The second row would be woven: over 1, under 1, over 2, under 1, over 2, under 1, and so on. After step 1, there is really nothing more to do but weave. Try it with figure 3.23. (Note the 3-floats in this pattern: they work.)

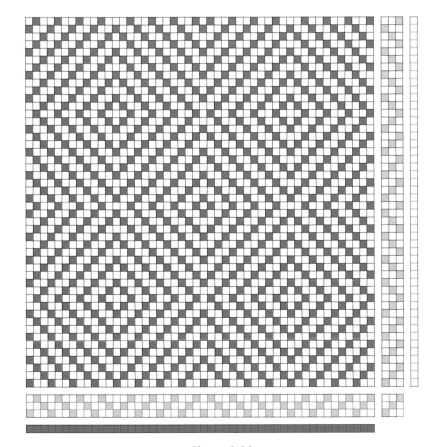
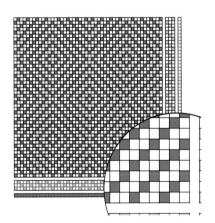

Figure 3.23

REVERSE ENGINEERING: To reverse engineer any existing plain weave potholder (actually any potholder!), just examine the warp and weft loops and transcribe their direction to your chart, noting the beginning weave direction at the bottom right. If it's not plain weave, use over and under notations throughout. Some people do this directly onto the loom, weaving as they go, and photograph the loom before crocheting the potholder off. The photo serves as your chart.

SUMMARY
For All Weaves Except Plain and Basic Twill

Step 1: Transfer the pattern to paper or digital media; make sure the warp and weft colors are properly charted.

Step 2: Fill in the notation for the required picks.

Step 3: Place the pick notation in the blank squares according to step 3's placement rules (see above).

Step 4: Fill in the remaining blank squares, avoiding 3-floats where possible.

For Basic Twill

Where the warp loop color shows, weave the weft loop under. Where the weft loop color shows, weave the weft loop over.

To Reverse Engineer

Transcribe the warp and weft colors, and direction of weave, to the chart by examining the weave structure. If plain weave, you only need to note the direction of the first pick.

There are so many exciting drafts on Handweaving .net, Pinterest, or a Google Images search. There's inspiration to be found in paintings, textiles, tiles, and nature. I wish you many happy hours making your unique potholder a reality.

Figure 3.25. A potholder woven from a chart made from figure 3.24 (see Shadow Fern, page 125)

Figure 3.24

CHAPTER 4

POTHOLDER PATTERNS: PLAIN WEAVE

Plain weave (also called tabby) is a basic weaving structure in which the weft is woven over or under each warp loop, alternating with each row. This approach produces a flat fabric with a checkered surface, which, because of the tight interlocking of thread, is very strong. The design can't take advantage of a varying weave, so it must depend on tabby's consistency coupled with the color and color sequence of warp and weft. Basket weave, in which threads (in our case, loops) are bundled together and woven as one, is a form of plain weave. You could play with design using basket weave, as well as thicker and thinner loops; you could play with color to create pattern.

Plain weave is the most common kind of potholder weaving, with tremendous variety and potential. Harrisville Designs has an online Potholder Wizard with which you can generate endless patterns using their color palette: it's a happy way to spend time, and you may find good, strong designs serendipitously. There are many patterns on the internet, in social media groups, and in a few books. The intention in this chapter is to gather together the strongest classic tabby designs all in one place, and you may find a few surprises as well.

Fun fact: The word "tabby" comes from a taffeta fabric of silk and cotton made in the 12th century in Attabiya, a district of Baghdad. It was called *attābī* and morphed through French as *tabis* to the English "tabby."

Ππ

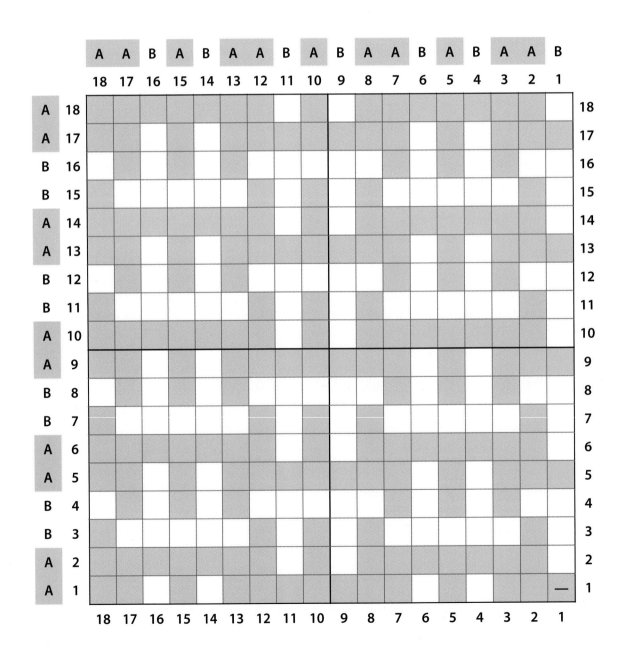

STRIPES
A FUNDAMENTAL WEAVING TECHNIQUE

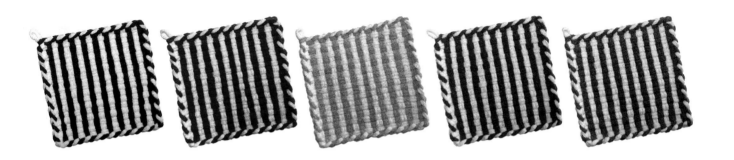

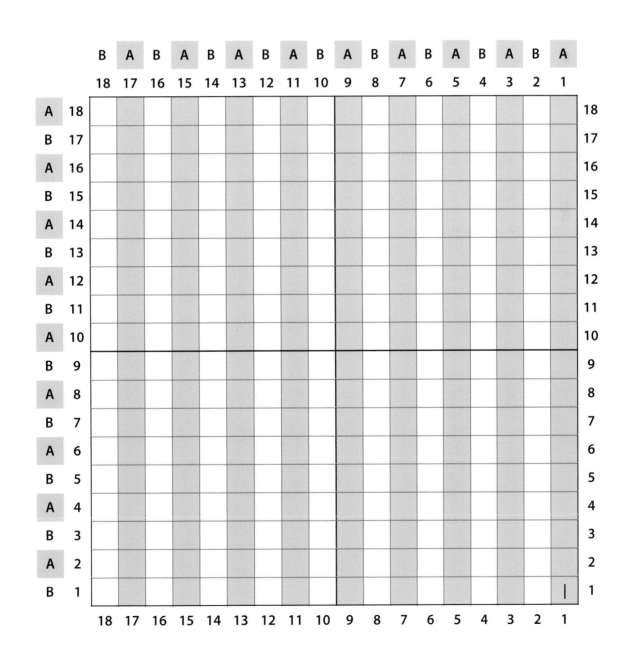

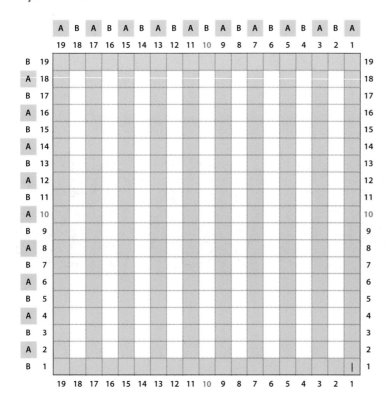

This Stripes with a Frame potholder is woven with Friendly Loom turquoise and loops cut from a sock.

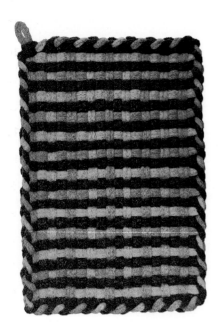

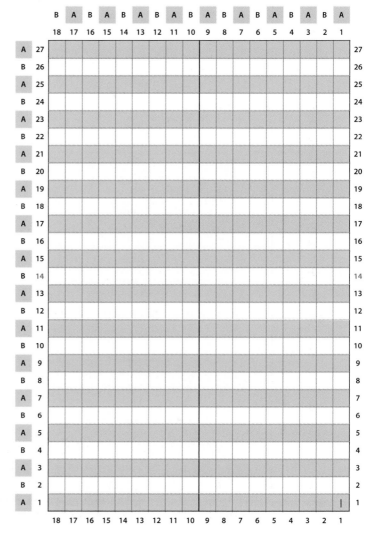

KANTHA

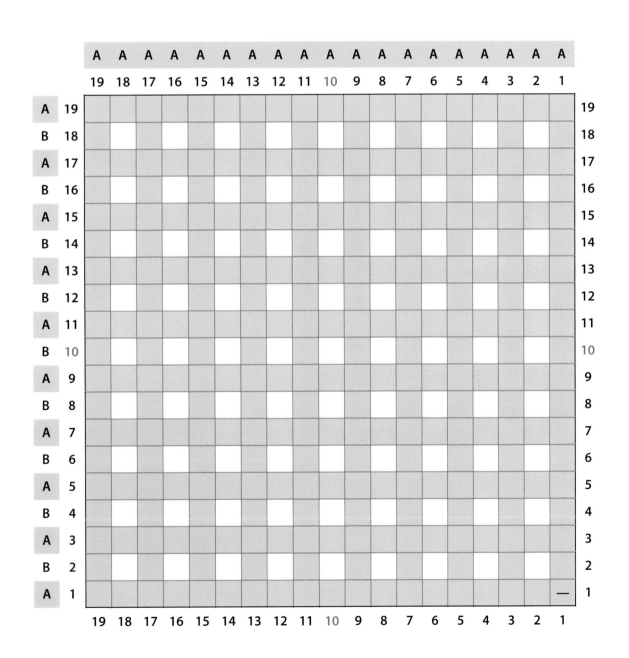

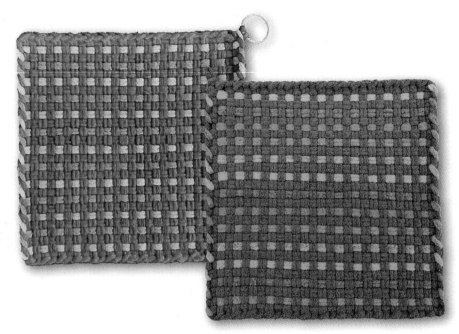

For any size loom, the warp and weft sequence is simply continued across the length and width of the loom. Here are two 27-peg examples.

A cheerful 18-peg Kantha from H. Michelle Spaulding in Friendly Loom colors.

Warp: White/Black across.

Weft, from bottom to top:

• Green	• Lime	• Plum
• Blue	• Carnation	• Pink
• Orange	• Yellow	• Turquoise
• Plum	• Green	• Lime
• Pink	• Blue	• Carnation
• Turquoise	• Salmon	• Yellow

BROKEN COMB

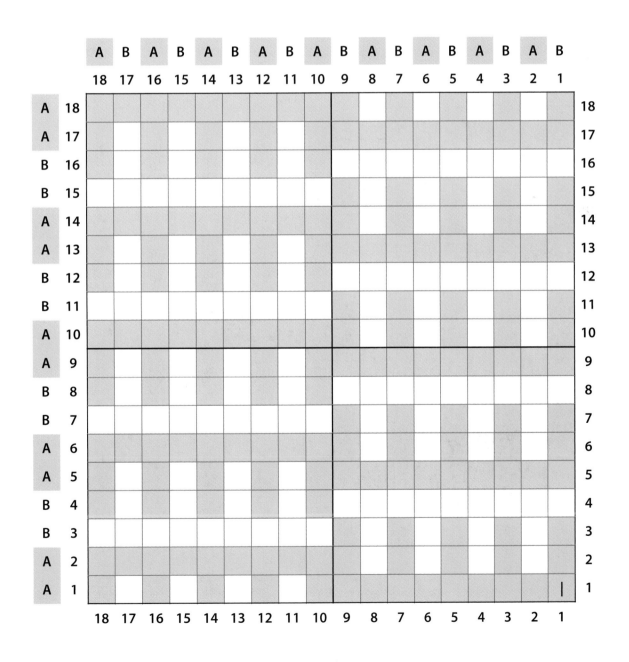

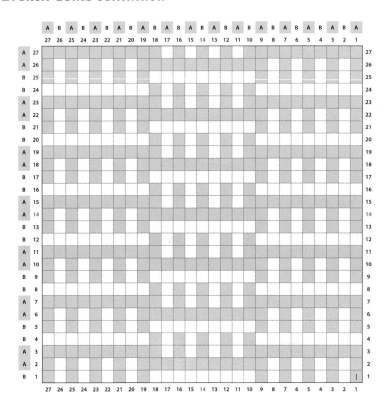

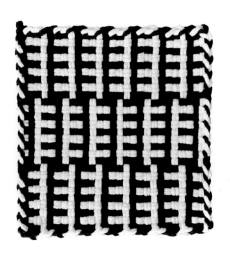

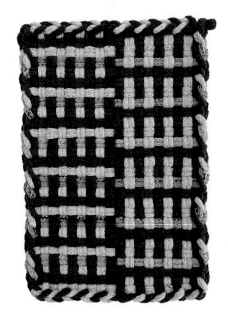

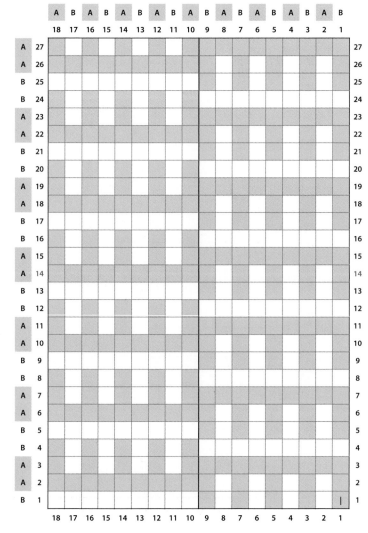

BROKEN LADDERS

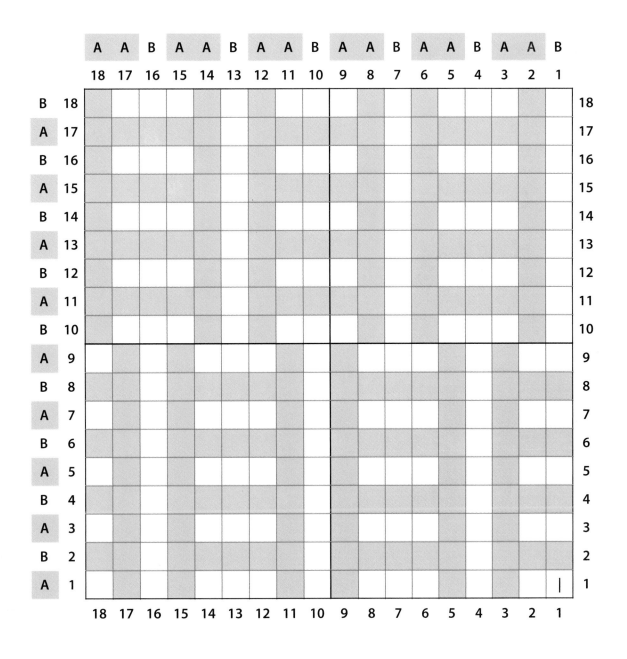

Broken Ladders *continued*

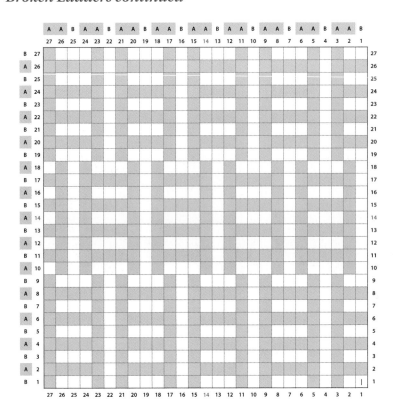

COMB

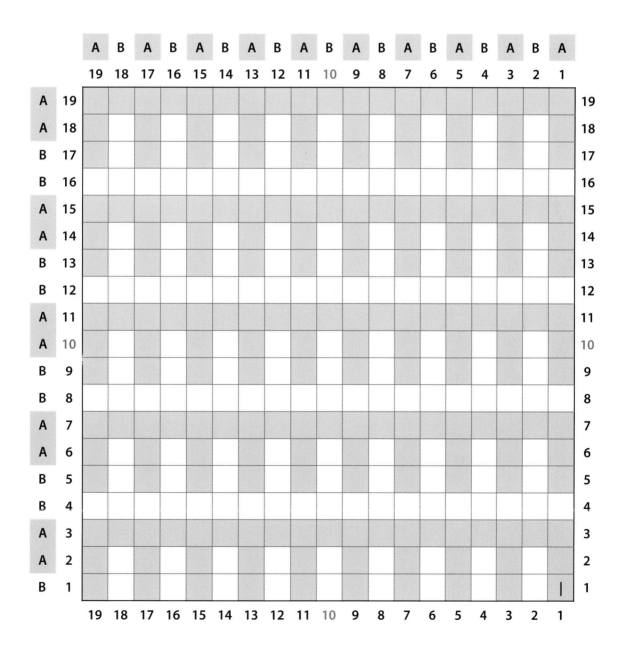

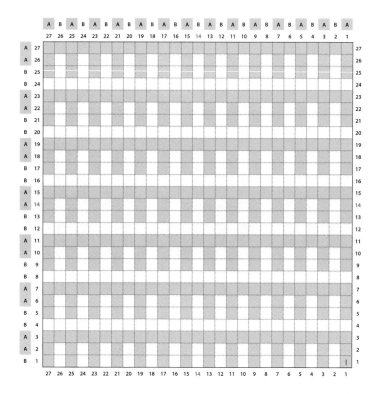

Woven on an 18 x 27-peg loom—
dropped a peg to fit the loom!

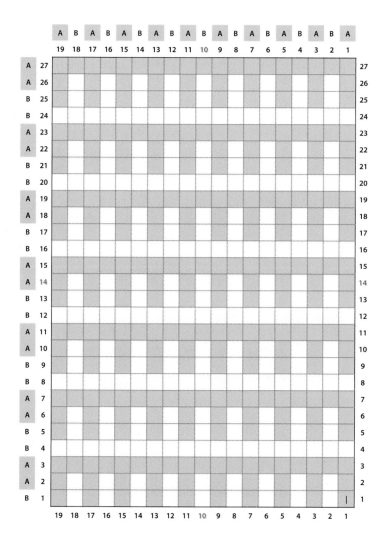

COMB VARIATION

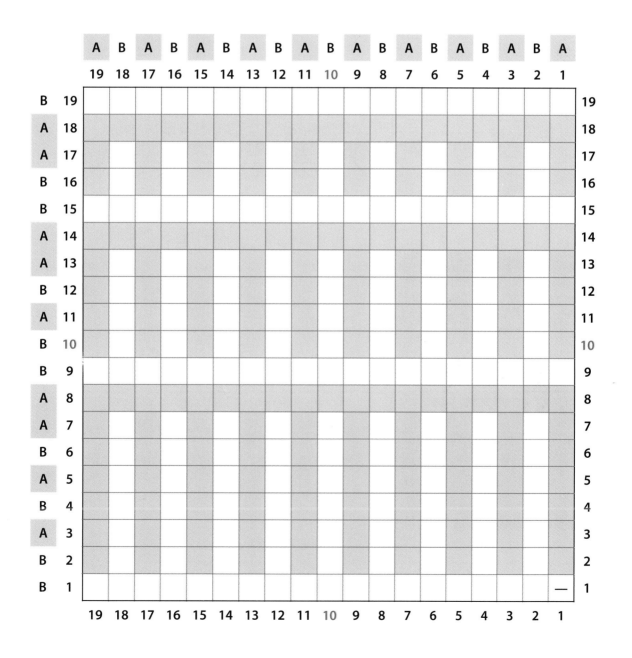

Comb Variation continued

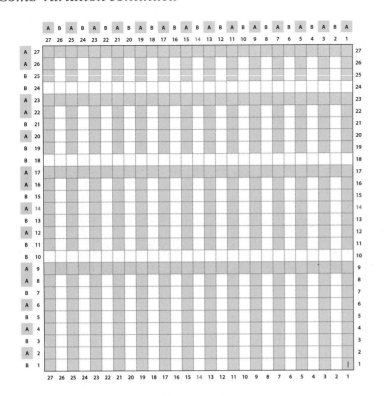

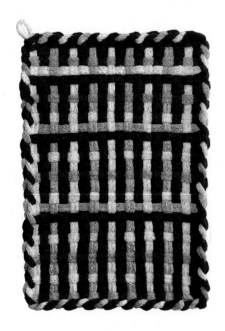

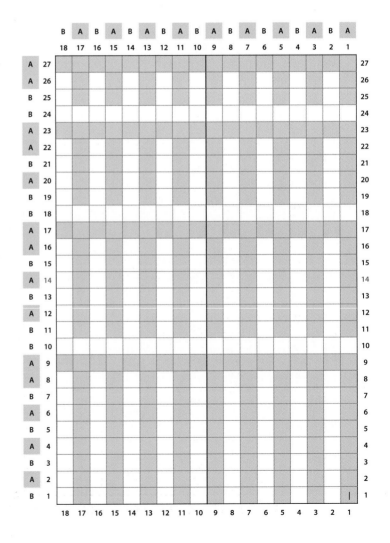

LADDERS

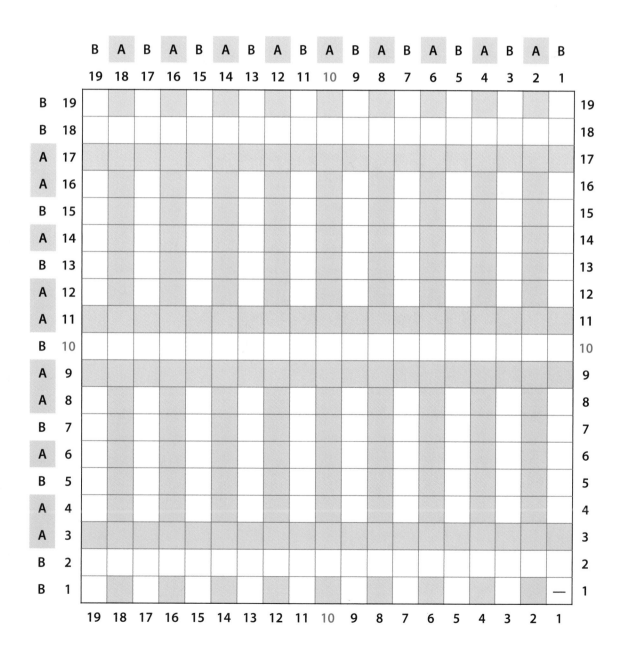

Ladders continued

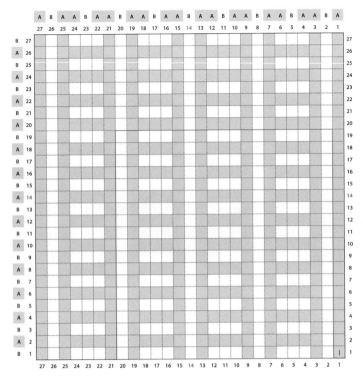

Top header row (warp colors): A B A A B A A B A A B A A B A A B A A B A A B A A B A

Columns: 27 26 25 24 23 22 21 20 19 18 17 16 15 14 13 12 11 10 9 8 7 6 5 4 3 2 1

Left side (weft colors, top to bottom): B 27, A 26, B 25, A 24, B 23, A 22, B 21, A 20, B 19, A 18, B 17, A 16, B 15, A 14, B 13, A 12, B 11, A 10, B 9, A 8, B 7, A 6, B 5, A 4, B 3, A 2, B 1

Woven black on black with
Friendly Loom and WNC blacks

This potholder is a 19-peg
version of the 27-peg
variation above. (It's outlined
in red for you to weave.) The
sequence: warp, from left top:
BAA repeated to end, ends
with B. Weft, from bottom: BA
repeated to end, ends with B.

Mary has camouflaged the
ladders by substituting two
similar shades (salmon and
pink) for A and black and
silver for B. Using color for the
ladders and a neutral for the
background makes the ladders
pop at the same time that the
4 colors break up the design:
delightfully interesting! This is
woven with the 19-peg pattern
above, using only 18 pegs.

LOG CABIN ABABAB

Centered

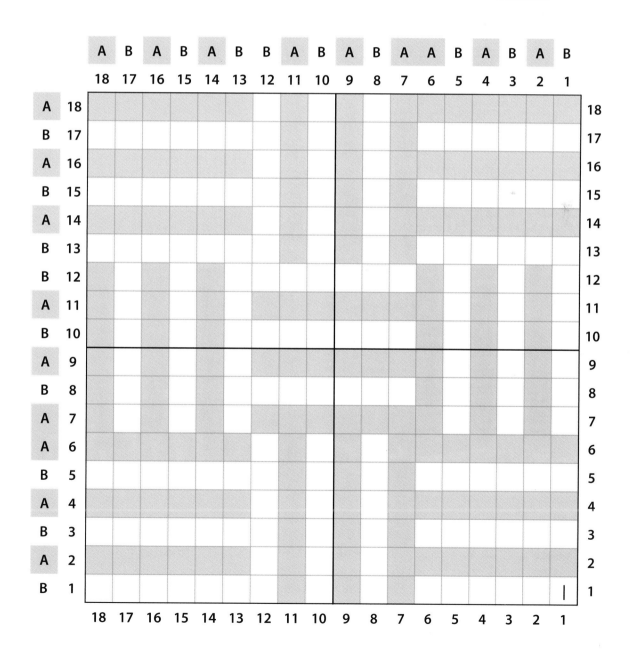

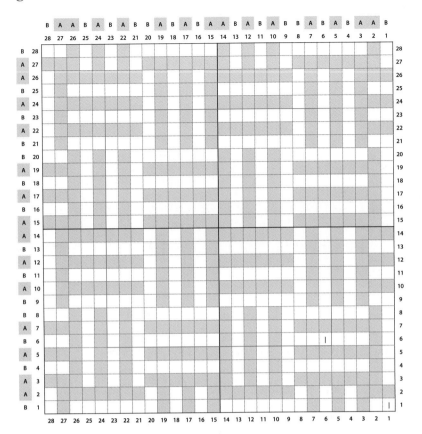

The Log Cabin Rule

Log Cabin is woven by warping a sequence of two alternating colors, repeating the sequence reversed, and repeating the whole for the width of your loom. Weft follows the warp sequence. The 28-peg chart for this pattern, ABABAB, is centered, so it begins with the end of the sequence. The centered 18-peg pattern is marked in red on the 28-peg chart for you to weave: look at the two centered examples.

You can weave Log Cabin on any size loom using this rule.

CATHERINE WHEEL

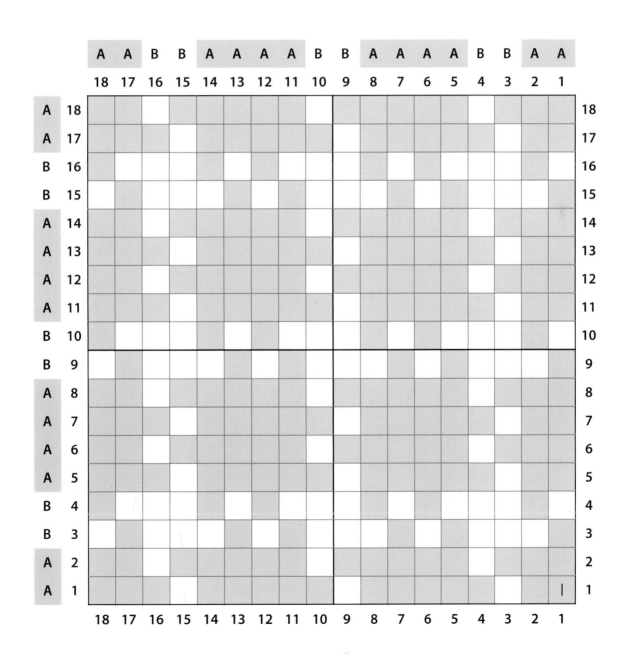

Catherine Wheel continued

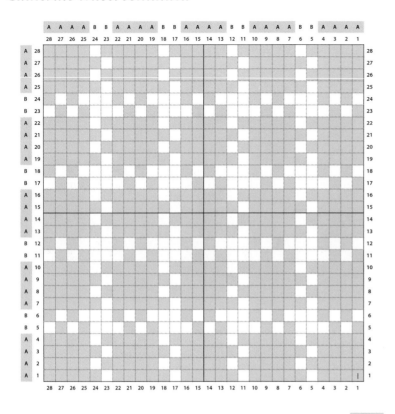

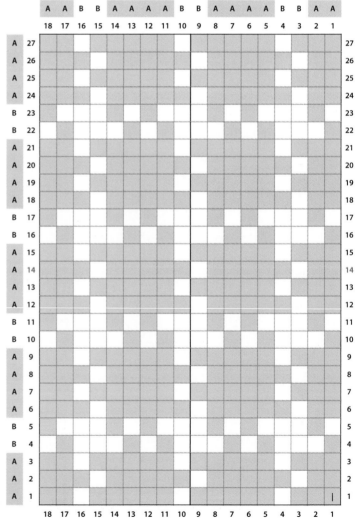

CONFETTI
LOG CABIN BABBAB

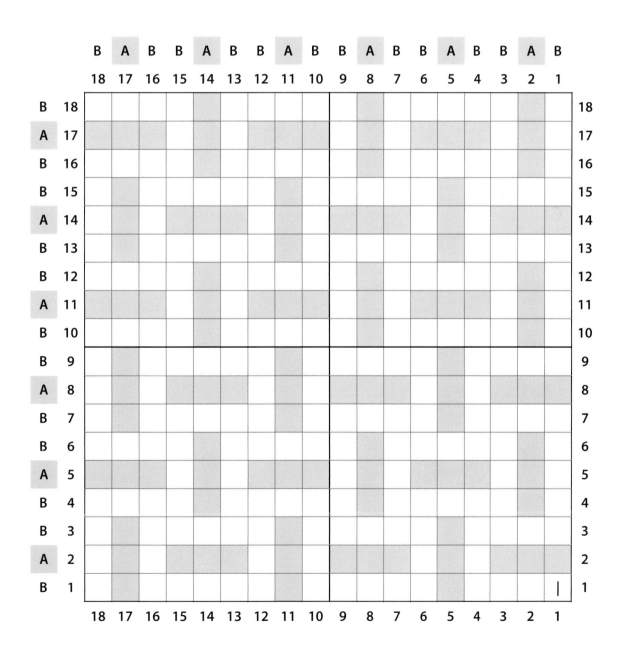

Confetti continued

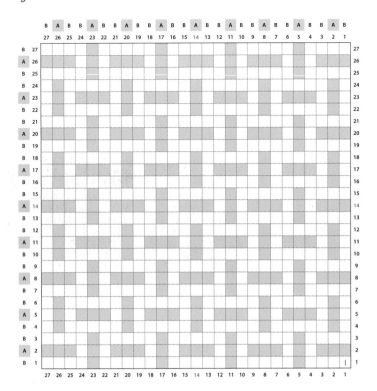

FILM STRIPS

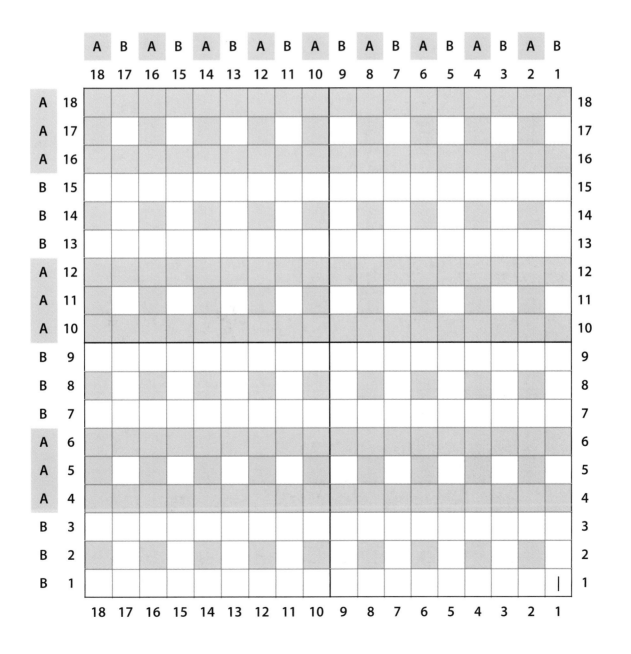

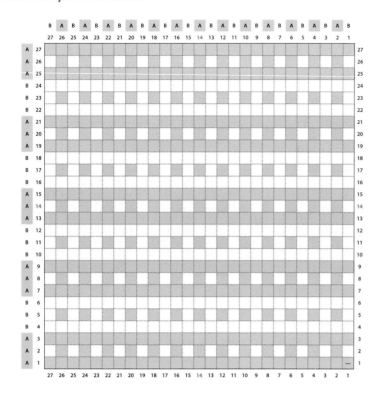

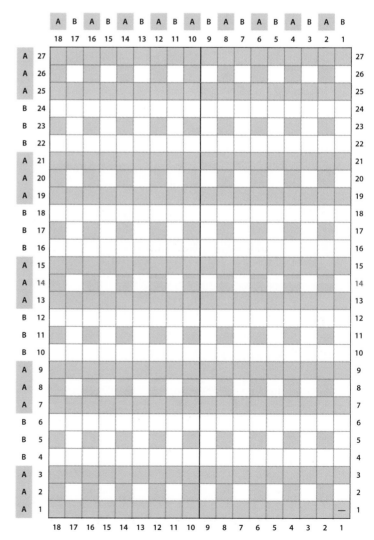

PINWHEEL AKA PUPPY TOOTH

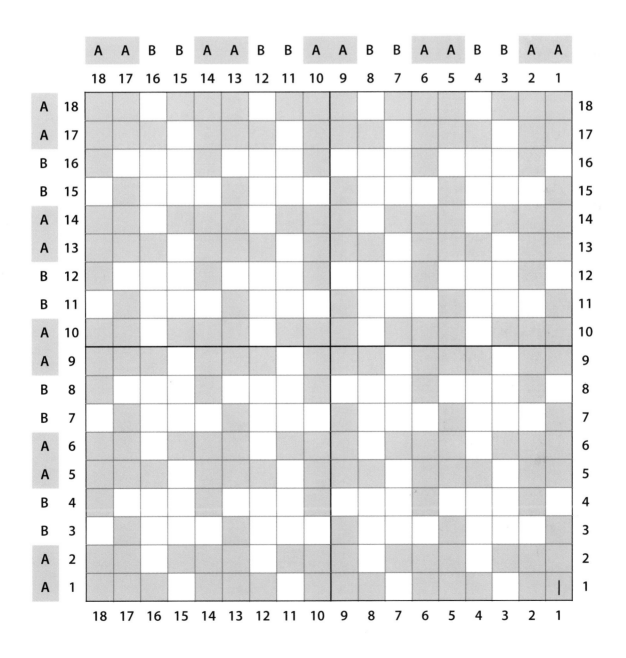

		A	A	B	B	A	A	B	B	A	A	B	B	A	A	B	B	A	A
		18	17	16	15	14	13	12	11	10	9	8	7	6	5	4	3	2	1

Pinwheel aka Puppy Tooth continued

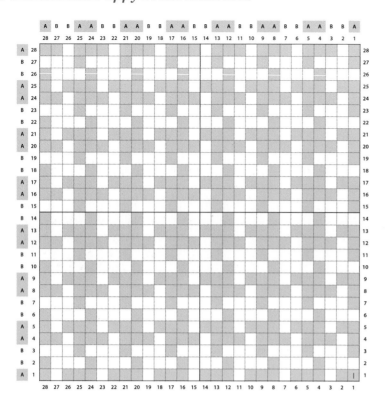

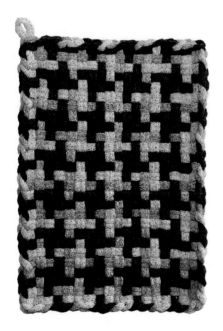

60 RADICAL POTHOLDER WEAVING

T

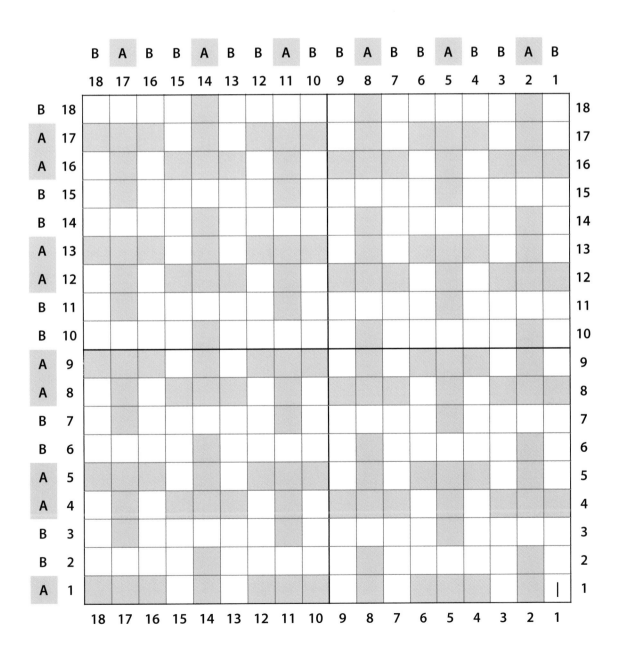

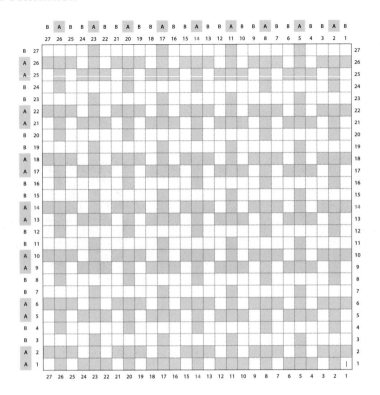

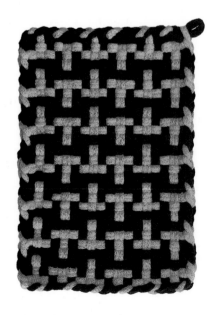

ZIPPER

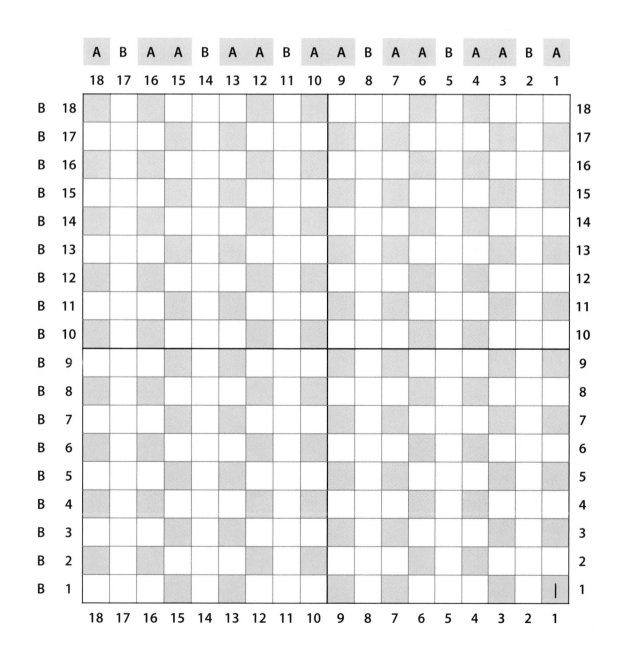

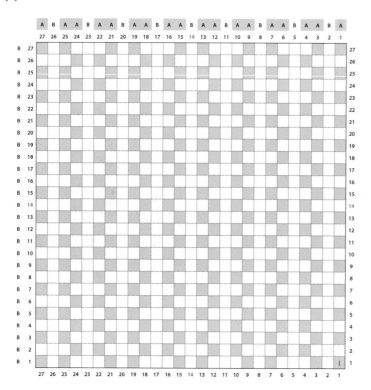

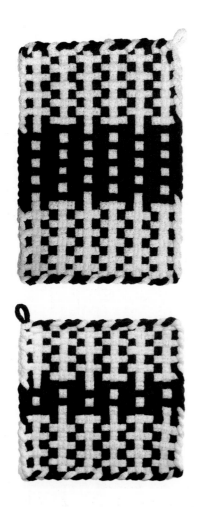

EQUALS
LOG CABIN ABABA/ABABA

Human Rights
Campaign

Pansexual

Transsexual

Gay Marriage
Equality

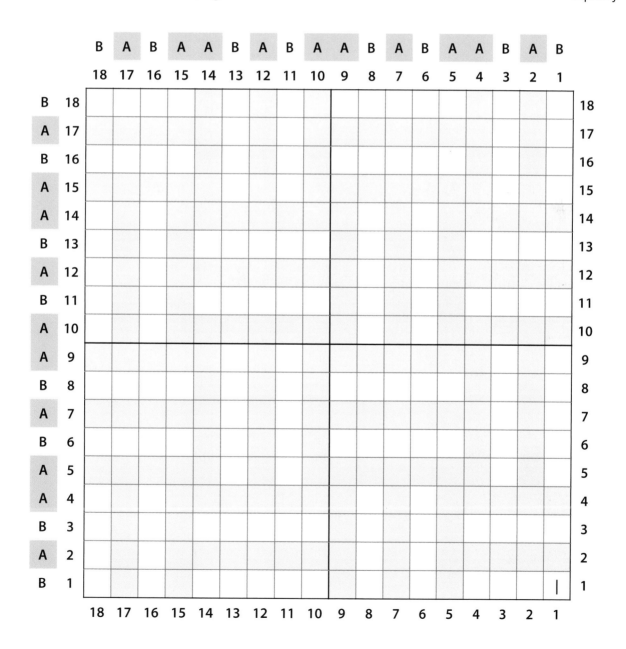

CHRISTINE'S GARDEN SAMPLER

Original design: Christine Olsen Reis

For the 27-peg loom, here are garden plans. Plain 18-peg potholders go well with this pattern as a set. Try a winter and fall (harvest) garden as well!

Warp and weft are the same color sequence: warp, and then follow the warp sequence from the bottom up for your weft.

Spring Garden

1 = Chocolate
2 = Leaf
3 = Flax
4 = Willow

Summer Garden

1 = Leaf
2 = Winter White
3 = Daffodil
4 = Willow

GINGHAM

Gingham is a cotton yarn-dyed fabric dating from the 17th century. Originally striped, we now recognize it as a two-toned check, generally in a bright color and white. On the loom, we can mimic a proper gingham with loops in three colors: two shades of one color, and white. The darker shade is alternated with white for the warp, and the lighter shade is used for the weft. But we don't have to be proper....

MUDCLOTH 1 AND MUDCLOTH 2 (AND REPEATS)

Original design: Deborah Jean Cohen

Many patterns can be fitted to different-sized looms by looking for and using the repeat. (A repeat on a textile is where an identical figure or pattern begins again.) To do this in plain weave, all you need to do is look at the color sequence of warp and weft, and follow them. Below are two examples: Mudcloth 1 and 2.

Mudcloth 1 has a 7-peg warp sequence of ABABABA. You'd warp your loom ABABABAABABABA, repeating until the end. The weft sequence is a 6-peg BAABAB, so you'd weave the weft rows BAABABBAABAB, repeating until finished. This method gives you a 7 x 6 pattern block.

Mudcloth 2 is a 7 x 12 block. The warp is the same as Mudcloth 1: ABABABA. The weft sequence is AAABABAABAAB. It's woven below on an 18-peg loom. Both warp and weft are centered.

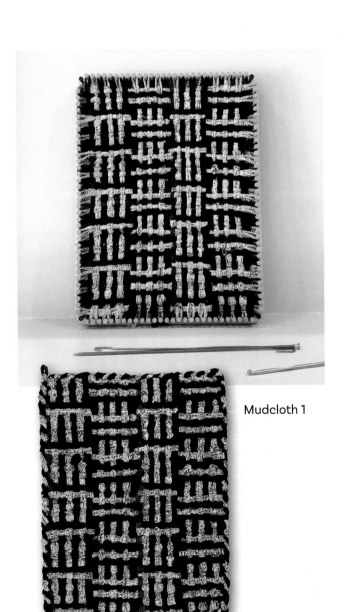

Mudcloth 1

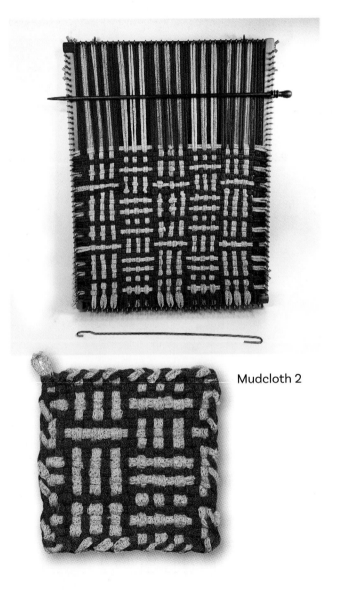

Mudcloth 2

How to Center a Sequence

The example in figure 4.1 isn't centered, so for the warp you have 2 pattern repeats, plus the first 4 of the sequence at the end to make up the 18 pegs. The weft fits evenly (3 x 6 = 18), so you just repeat the weft sequence as usual.

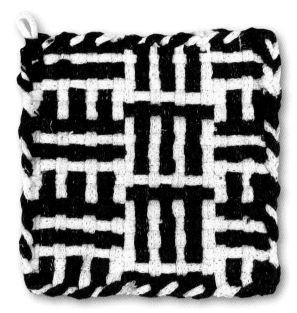

Figure 4.1. Mudcloth 1, uncentered

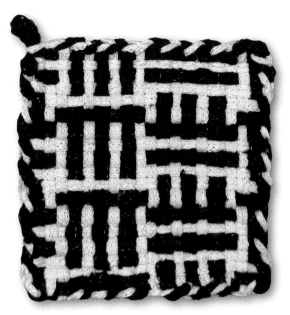

Figure 4.2. Mudcloth 2, centered

The example in figure 4.2 is centered. You know that 2 repeats cover 14 pegs, so you center them (figure 4.3).

		A	B	A	B	A	B	A	A	B	A	B	A	B	A		

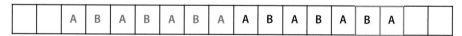

Figure 4.3

To make up the rest of the pegs, you'd need 2 on either end, but these must be in sequence. You'd use BA in the first 2 slots, because those would precede the first full repeat (figure 4.4).

		A	B	A	B	A	B	A	A	B	A	B	A	B	A		

Figure 4.4

You'd use AB in the last 2 slots, because those follow the last full repeat (figure 4.5).

B	A	A	B	A	B	A	B	A	A	B	A	B	A	B	A		

B	A	A	B	A	B	A	B	A	A	B	A	B	A	B	A	A	B

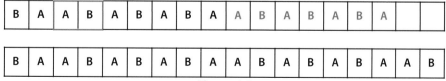

Figure 4.5

The weft fits evenly, so you simply repeat the row colors until finished (figure 4.6).

B	A	A	B	A	B	B	A	A	B	A	B	B	A	A	B	A	B

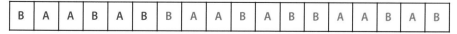

Figure 4.6

CHAPTER 5

POTHOLDER PATTERNS: SHADOW WEAVE

Shadow weave is a subset of the general category color-and-weave, in which the design is produced visually via the same alternating colors (or blocks of colors) in both warp and weft. Technically, shadow weave depends on two colors; Log Cabin is the simplest example of a shadow weave. The weaving structure is plain weave with a twill step at design changes. As you weave, you'll notice that rows will shadow each other in blocks of two: the second row will "shadow" the first, reversing the direction of the pick. Not surprisingly, this method produces a visual shadow effect in the fabric.

Shadow weave drafts seem to be well suited for conversion to potholder charts, and yet there are very few potholder patterns available in shadow weave. To change the few to many, this chapter is the largest of the three pattern chapters. It's been a heady experience to find, choose, and chart shadow weave drafts, and the by-product of this experience has been the emergence of original patterns. I hope that you'll find this a catalyst, as we have, opening an exciting creative door.

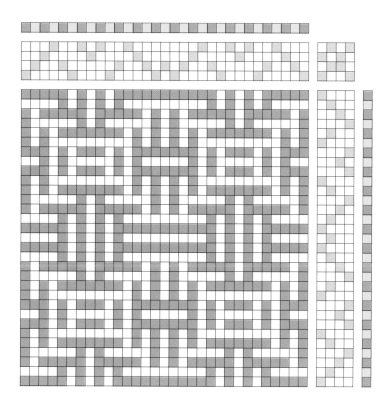

CORNERS

Original design: Deborah Jean Cohen

	A	B	A	B	A	B	A	B	A	B	A	B	A	B	A	B	A	B	A	
	19	18	17	16	15	14	13	12	11	10	9	8	7	6	5	4	3	2	1	
B 19	—	—	I	—	I	—	I	—	I	—	I	—	I	—	I	—	I	—	I	19
A 18	I	—	—	I	—	I	—	I	—	I	—	I	—	I	—	I	—	I	—	18
B 17	—	I	—	—	I	—	I	—	I	—	I	—	I	—	I	—	I	—	I	17
A 16	I	—	I	—	—	I	—	I	—	I	—	I	—	I	—	I	—	I	—	16
B 15	—	I	—	I	—	—	I	—	I	—	I	—	I	—	I	—	I	—	I	15
A 14	I	—	I	—	I	—	—	I	—	I	—	I	—	I	—	I	—	I	—	14
B 13	—	I	—	I	—	I	—	—	I	—	I	—	I	—	I	—	I	—	I	13
A 12	I	—	I	—	I	—	I	—	—	I	—	I	—	I	—	I	—	I	—	12
B 11	—	I	—	I	—	I	—	I	—	—	I	—	I	—	I	—	I	—	I	11
A 10	I	—	I	—	I	—	I	—	I	—	I	—	I	—	I	—	I	—	—	10
B 9	—	I	—	I	—	I	—	I	—	I	—	I	—	I	—	I	—	I	I	9
A 8	I	—	I	—	I	—	I	—	I	—	I	—	I	—	I	—	I	I	—	8
B 7	—	I	—	I	—	I	—	I	—	I	—	I	—	I	—	I	I	—	I	7
A 6	I	—	I	—	I	—	I	—	I	—	I	—	I	—	I	I	—	I	—	6
B 5	—	I	—	I	—	I	—	I	—	I	—	I	—	I	I	—	I	—	I	5
A 4	I	—	I	—	I	—	I	—	I	—	I	—	I	I	—	I	—	I	—	4
B 3	—	I	—	I	—	I	—	I	—	I	—	I	I	—	I	—	I	—	I	3
A 2	I	—	I	—	I	—	I	—	I	—	I	I	—	I	—	I	—	I	—	2
B 1	—	I	—	I	—	I	—	I	—	I	I	—	I	—	I	—	I	—	I	1
	19	18	17	16	15	14	13	12	11	10	9	8	7	6	5	4	3	2	1	

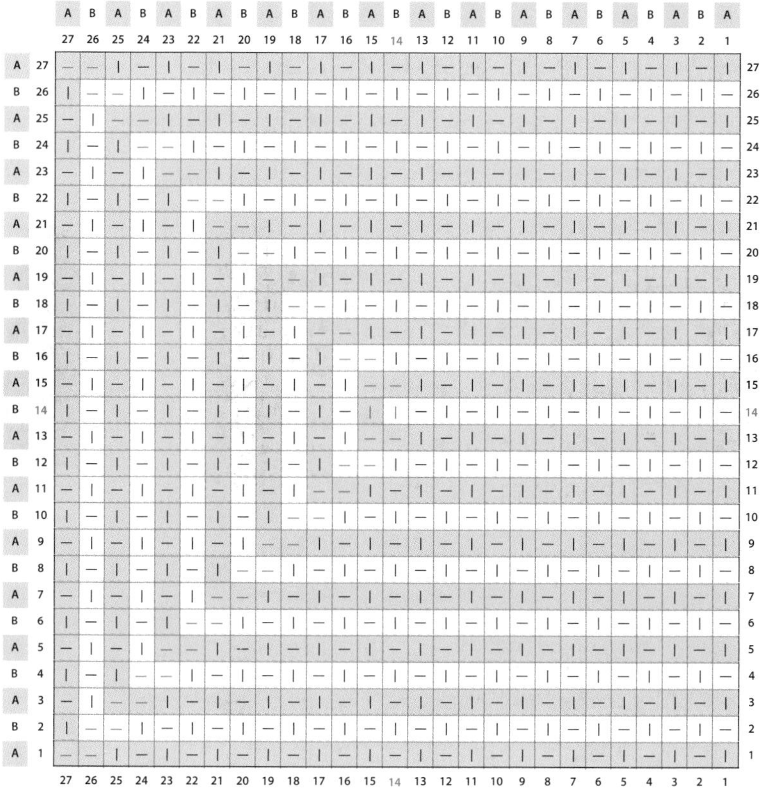

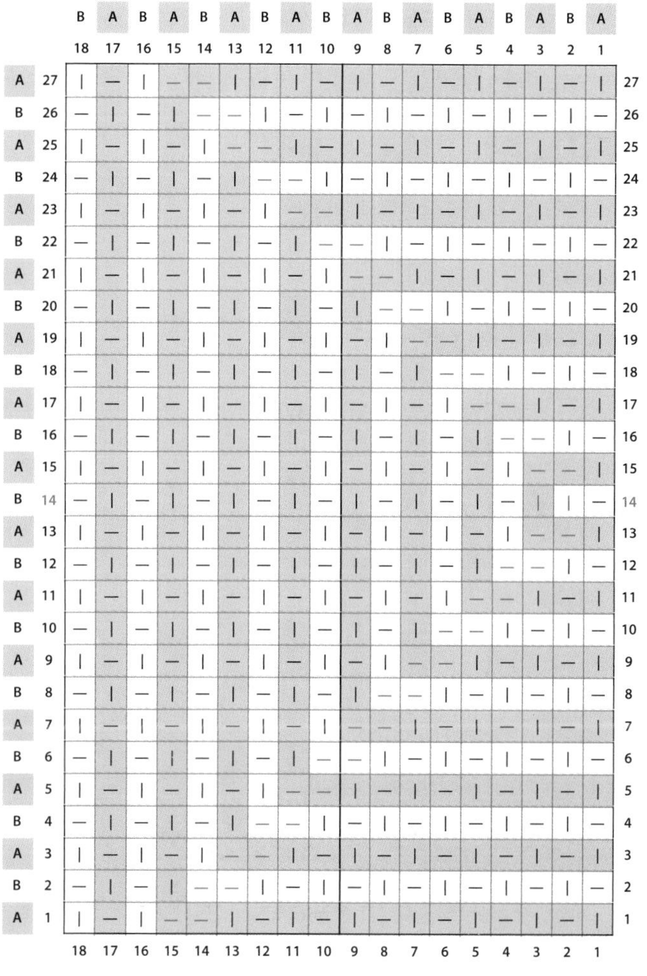

Top chart column headers:

| A | B | A | B | A | B | A | B | A | B | A | B | A | B | A | B | A | B | A | B | A | B | A | B | A | B | A |
| 27 | 26 | 25 | 24 | 23 | 22 | 21 | 20 | 19 | 18 | 17 | 16 | 15 | 14 | 13 | 12 | 11 | 10 | 9 | 8 | 7 | 6 | 5 | 4 | 3 | 2 | 1 |

Rows labeled (left and right): A 27, B 26, A 25, B 24, A 23, B 22, A 21, B 20, A 19, B 18, A 17, B 16, A 15, B 14, A 13, B 12, A 11, B 10, A 9, B 8, A 7, B 6, A 5, B 4, A 3, B 2, A 1

Bottom-right chart column headers:

| B | A | B | A | B | A | B | A | B | A | B | A | B | A | B | A | B | A |
| 18 | 17 | 16 | 15 | 14 | 13 | 12 | 11 | 10 | 9 | 8 | 7 | 6 | 5 | 4 | 3 | 2 | 1 |

Rows labeled (left and right): A 27, B 26, A 25, B 24, A 23, B 22, A 21, B 20, A 19, B 18, A 17, B 16, A 15, B 14, A 13, B 12, A 11, B 10, A 9, B 8, A 7, B 6, A 5, B 4, A 3, B 2, A 1

CORNER MEANDER
Original design: Deborah Jean Cohen

The second potholder from the right shows the back side of this pattern.

		B	A	B	A	B	A	B	A	B	A	B	A	B	A	B	A	B	A	B		
		19	18	17	16	15	14	13	12	11	10	9	8	7	6	5	4	3	2	1		
B	19	—	|	|	—	|	—	|	—	|	—	|	—	|	—	|	—	|	—	—	19
A	18	|	—	|	|	—	—	|	|	—	—	|	|	—	—	|	—	—	|	18
B	17	—	|	—	|	—	|	—	|	—	|	—	|	—	|	—	|	—	17
A	16	|	—	|	—	|	—	|	—	|	—	|	—	|	—	|	—	|	16
B	15	—	|	|	—	—	|	—	|	—	|	—	|	—	|	—	|	—	15
A	14	|	—	|	|	—	|	—	|	—	|	—	|	—	|	—	|	14
B	13	—	|	—	|	—	|	—	|	—	|	—	|	—	|	—	13
A	12	|	—	|	—	|	—	|	—	|	—	|	—	|	—	|	12
B	11	—	|	—	|	—	|	—	|	—	|	—	|	—	|	—	11
A	10	|	—	|	—	|	—	|	—	|	—	|	—	|	—	|	10
B	9	—	|	—	|	—	|	—	|	—	|	—	|	—	|	—	9
A	8	|	—	|	—	|	—	|	—	|	—	|	—	|	—	|	8
B	7	—	|	—	|	—	|	—	|	—	|	—	|	—	|	—	7
A	6	|	—	|	—	|	—	|	—	|	—	|	—	|	—	|	6
B	5	—	|	—	|	—	—	|	—	|	—	|	—	|	—	|	—	5
A	4	|	—	|	—	—	|	—	|	—	|	—	|	—	|	—	|	4
B	3	—	|	—	—	|	—	|	—	|	—	|	—	|	—	3
A	2	|	—	—	|	—	|	—	|	—	|	—	|	—	|	2
B	1	—	—	|	—	|	—	|	—	|	—	|	—	|	1

| | 19 | 18 | 17 | 16 | 15 | 14 | 13 | 12 | 11 | 10 | 9 | 8 | 7 | 6 | 5 | 4 | 3 | 2 | 1 |

CORNERS 2
Original design: Deborah Jean Cohen

		B	A	B	A	B	A	B	A	B	A	B	A	B	A	B	A	B	A	B	
		19	18	17	16	15	14	13	12	11	10	9	8	7	6	5	4	3	2	1	
B	19	—	—	|	—	|	—	|	—	|	—	|	—	|	—	|	—	|	—	—	19
A	18	|	—	—	|	—	|	—	—	|	—	|	—	|	—	|	—	—	|	|	18
B	17	—	|	—	|	—	|	—	|	—	|	—	|	—	|	—	|	—	|	—	17
A	16	|	—	|	—	|	—	|	—	|	—	|	—	|	—	|	—	|	—	|	16
B	15	—	|	—	|	—	|	—	|	—	|	—	|	—	|	—	|	—	|	—	15
A	14	|	—	|	—	|	—	|	—	|	—	|	—	|	—	|	—	|	—	|	14
B	13	—	|	—	—	|	—	|	—	|	—	|	—	|	—	|	—	|	—	—	13
A	12	|	—	|	—	|	—	|	—	|	—	|	—	|	—	|	—	|	—	|	12
B	11	—	|	—	|	—	|	—	|	—	|	—	|	—	|	—	|	—	|	—	11
A	10	|	—	|	—	|	—	|	—	|	—	|	—	|	—	|	—	|	—	|	10
B	9	—	|	—	|	—	|	—	|	—	—	|	—	|	—	|	—	|	—	—	9
A	8	|	—	|	—	|	—	|	—	—	|	—	—	|	—	|	—	|	—	|	8
B	7	—	|	—	|	—	|	—	—	|	—	|	—	|	—	|	—	|	—	|	7
A	6	|	—	|	—	|	—	|	—	|	—	|	—	|	—	|	—	|	—	|	6
B	5	—	|	—	|	—	|	—	|	—	|	—	|	—	|	—	|	—	|	—	5
A	4	|	—	|	—	|	—	|	—	|	—	|	—	|	—	|	—	|	—	|	4
B	3	—	|	—	|	—	|	—	|	—	|	—	|	—	|	—	|	—	|	—	3
A	2	|	—	—	|	—	|	—	|	—	|	—	|	—	|	—	—	|	—	|	2
B	1	—	—	|	—	|	—	|	—	|	—	|	—	|	—	|	—	|	—	—	1
		19	18	17	16	15	14	13	12	11	10	9	8	7	6	5	4	3	2	1	

GREEK KEY HICCUP, OR GREEK KEY GONE AWRY

Original design: Deborah Jean Cohen

		B	A	B	A	B	A	B	A	B	A	B	A	B	A	B	A	B	A	B		
		19	18	17	16	15	14	13	12	11	10	9	8	7	6	5	4	3	2	1		
A	19	−	|	−	|	−	|	−	|	−	|	−	|	−	|	−	|	−	|	−	19	
B	18	|	−	|	−	|	−	|	−	|	−	|	−	|	−	|	−	|	−	|	18	
A	17	|	|	−	|	−	|	−	−	|	−	−	|	|	−	|	−	|	|	−	17	
B	16	−	|	−	|	−	−	|	−	|	−	|	−	|	|	−	|	|	−	|	16	
A	15	|	−	|	|	−	−	|	|	−	|	−	|	|	−	|	|	−	|	|	15	
B	14	−	|	|	−	|	|	−	|	|	−	|	|	−	|	|	−	|	|	−	14	
A	13	|	|	−	|	|	−	|	−	|	−	|	−	|	−	|	−	|	|	−	13	
B	12	−	|	−	|	−	|	|	−	|	|	−	|	|	−	|	|	−	|	|	12	
A	11	|	−	|	−	|	|	−	|	−	|	|	−	|	−	|	|	−	|	|	11	
B	10	|	−	|	−	|	−	|	−	|	−	|	−	|	−	|	−	|	−	|	10	
A	9	|	|	−	|	−	|	−	|	|	−	|	−	−	|	−	|	|	−	−	9	
B	8	−	|	−	|	|	−	|	|	−	|	−	|	−	|	|	−	|	|	−	8	
A	7	|	−	|	−	|	−	|	−	|	|	−	−	|	−	|	−	|	−	|	7	
B	6	−	|	−	|	|	−	|	−	|	−	|	−	|	|	−	|	|	−	|	6	
A	5	|	−	|	−	|	−	|	|	−	|	−	|	|	−	|	−	|	−	|	5	
B	4	−	|	−	|	|	−	|	−	|	|	−	|	−	|	|	−	|	|	−	4	
A	3	−	−	|	|	|	−	−	|	|	−	|	|	−	|	−	−	|	|	|	3	
B	2	|	−	|	−	|	−	|	|	−	|	−	|	|	−	|	−	|	−	−	2	
A	1	−	|	−	|	−	|	−	|	−	|	−	|	−	|	−	|	−	|	|	1	
		19	18	17	16	15	14	13	12	11	10	9	8	7	6	5	4	3	2	1		

ESCAPE

Original design: Christine Olsen

		B	A	B	A	B	A	B	A	B	A	B	A	B	A	B	A	B	A	
		18	17	16	15	14	13	12	11	10	9	8	7	6	5	4	3	2	1	
A	18			−			−			−			−					−			−			−			−			−			−	18
B	17	−			−			−			−			−			−			−			−			−			−				17
A	16			−			−			−			−			−			−			−			−			−			−	16
B	15	−			−			−			−			−			−			−			−			−				15
A	14			−			−			−			−			−			−			−			−			−	14
B	13			−			−			−			−			−			−			−			−				13
A	12	−			−			−			−			−			−			−			−			−	12
B	11			−			−			−			−			−			−			−				11
A	10	−			−			−			−			−			−			−			−	10
B	9			−			−			−			−			−			−				9
A	8	−			−			−			−			−			−			−	8
B	7			−			−			−			−			−				7
A	6	−			−			−			−			−			−	6
A	5			−			−			−			−				5
B	4	−			−			−			−			−	4
A	3			−			−			−				3
B	2	−			−			−			−	2
A	1			−			−				1

	18	17	16	15	14	13	12	11	10	9	8	7	6	5	4	3	2	1

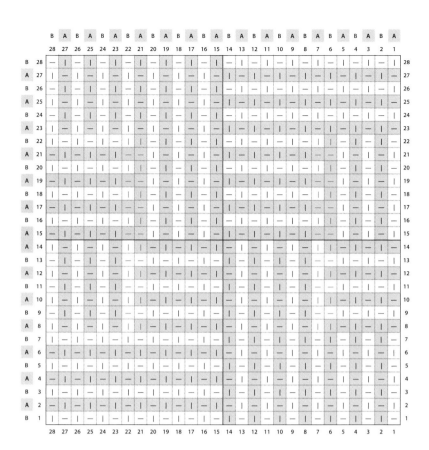

CONNECTING

Original design: Christine Olsen Reis

		A	B	A	B	A	B	A	B	A	B	A	B	A	B	A	B	A	B	A
		19	18	17	16	15	14	13	12	11	10	9	8	7	6	5	4	3	2	1
A	19																				19
B	18																				18
A	17																				17
B	16																				16
A	15																				15
B	14																				14
A	13																				13
B	12																				12
A	11																				11
B	10																				10
A	9																				9
B	8																				8
A	7																				7
B	6																				6
A	5																				5
B	4																				4
A	3																				3
B	2																				2
A	1																				1
		19	18	17	16	15	14	13	12	11	10	9	8	7	6	5	4	3	2	1

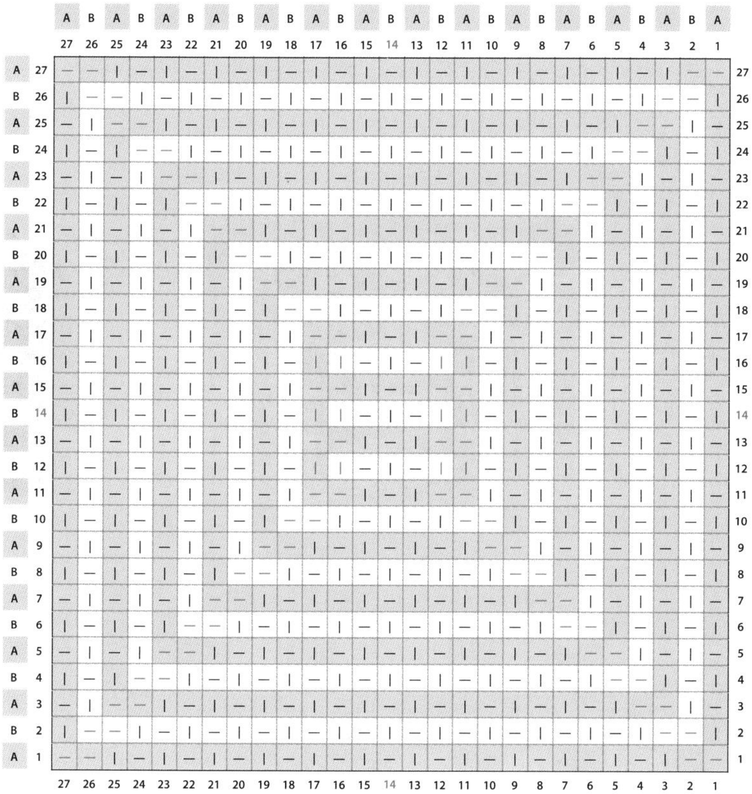
A B A B A B A B A B A B A B A B A B A B A B A B A B A
27 26 25 24 23 22 21 20 19 18 17 16 15 14 13 12 11 10 9 8 7 6 5 4 3 2 1
A 27, B 26, A 25, B 24, A 23, B 22, A 21, B 20, A 19, B 18, A 17, B 16, A 15, B 14, A 13, B 12, A 11, B 10, A 9, B 8, A 7, B 6, A 5, B 4, A 3, B 2, A 1

A B A B A B A B A B A B A B A B A B A
19 18 17 16 15 14 13 12 11 10 9 8 7 6 5 4 3 2 1
A 27, B 26, A 25, B 24, A 23, B 22, A 21, B 20, A 19, B 18, A 17, B 16, A 15, B 14, A 13, B 12, A 11, B 10, A 9, B 8, A 7, B 6, A 5, B 4, A 3, B 2, A 1

OPENING

Original design: Christine Olsen Reis

The second potholder from the left shows the back side of this pattern.

SEEKING

Original design: Christine Olsen Reis

		A	B	A	B	A	B	A	B	A	B	A	B	A	B	A	B	A	B	A	
		19	18	17	16	15	14	13	12	11	10	9	8	7	6	5	4	3	2	1	
A	19	—	|	—	|	—	|	—	|	—	|	—	|	—	|	—	|	—	—		19
B	18	|	—	—	|	—	|	—	|	—	|	—	|	—	|	—	|	—	—	|	18
A	17	—	|	—	—	|	—	|	—	|	—	|	—	|	—	|	—	—	|	—	17
B	16	|	—	—	|	—	|	—	|	—	|	—	|	—	|	—	—	|	—	|	16
A	15	—	|	—	|	—	|	—	|	—	|	—	|	—	|	—	|	—	|	—	15
B	14	|	—	|	—	|	—	|	—	|	—	|	—	|	—	|	—	|	—	|	14
A	13	—	|	—	|	—	|	—	|	—	|	—	|	—	|	—	|	—	|	—	13
B	12	|	—	|	—	|	—	|	—	|	—	|	—	|	—	|	—	|	—	|	12
A	11	—	|	—	|	—	|	—	|	—	|	—	|	—	|	—	|	—	|	—	11
B	10	|	—	|	—	|	—	|	—	|	—	|	—	|	—	|	—	|	—	|	10
A	9	—	|	—	|	—	|	—	|	—	|	—	|	—	|	—	|	—	|	—	9
B	8	|	—	|	—	|	—	|	—	|	—	|	—	|	—	|	—	|	—	|	8
A	7	—	|	—	|	—	|	—	|	—	|	—	|	—	|	—	|	—	|	—	7
B	6	|	—	|	—	|	—	|	—	|	—	|	—	|	—	|	—	|	—	|	6
A	5	—	|	—	|	—	|	—	|	—	|	—	|	—	|	—	|	—	|	—	5
B	4	|	—	|	—	—	|	—	|	—	|	—	|	—	|	—	—	|	—	|	4
A	3	—	|	—	—	|	—	|	—	|	—	|	—	|	—	|	—	—	|	—	3
B	2	|	—	—	|	—	|	—	|	—	|	—	|	—	|	—	|	—	—	|	2
A	1	—	|	—	|	—	|	—	|	—	|	—	|	—	|	—	|	—	|	—	1
		19	18	17	16	15	14	13	12	11	10	9	8	7	6	5	4	3	2	1	

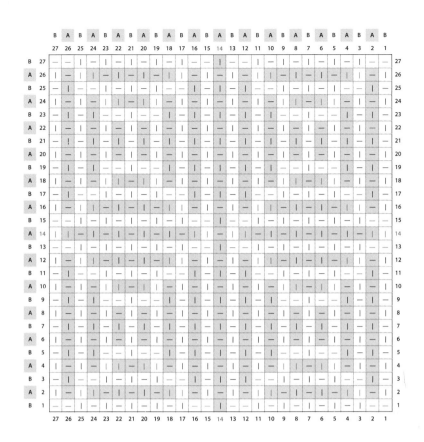

LOOP DE LOOP

Original design: Christine Olsen Reis

		A	A	B	A	B	A	B	A	B	A	A	B	A	B	A	B	A	B	A	
		19	18	17	16	15	14	13	12	11	10	9	8	7	6	5	4	3	2	1	
A	19	—	|	—	|	—	|	—	|	—	|	—	|	—	|	—	|	—	|	—	19
B	18	—	—	|	—	|	—	|	—	|	—	|	—	|	—	|	—	|	—	|	18
A	17	|	—	—	|	—	|	—	|	—	|	—	|	—	|	—	|	—	|	—	17
B	16	—	|	—	—	|	—	|	—	|	—	|	—	|	—	|	—	|	—	|	16
A	15	|	—	|	—	—	|	—	|	—	|	—	|	—	|	—	|	—	|	—	15
B	14	—	|	—	|	—	—	|	—	|	—	|	—	|	—	|	—	|	—	|	14
A	13	|	—	|	—	|	—	—	|	—	|	—	|	—	|	—	|	—	|	—	13
B	12	—	|	—	|	—	|	—	—	|	—	|	—	|	—	|	—	|	—	|	12
A	11	|	—	|	—	|	—	|	—	—	|	—	|	—	|	—	|	—	|	—	11
A	10	—	|	—	|	—	|	—	|	—	—	|	—	|	—	|	—	|	—	|	10
B	9	|	—	|	—	|	—	|	—	|	—	—	|	—	|	—	|	—	|	—	9
A	8	—	|	—	|	—	|	—	|	—	|	—	—	|	—	|	—	|	—	|	8
B	7	|	—	|	—	|	—	|	—	|	—	|	—	—	|	—	|	—	|	—	7
A	6	—	|	—	|	—	|	—	|	—	|	—	|	—	—	|	—	|	—	|	6
B	5	|	—	|	—	|	—	|	—	|	—	|	—	|	—	—	|	—	|	—	5
A	4	—	|	—	|	—	|	—	|	—	|	—	|	—	|	—	—	|	—	|	4
B	3	|	—	|	—	|	—	|	—	|	—	|	—	|	—	|	—	—	|	—	3
A	2	—	|	—	|	—	|	—	|	—	|	—	|	—	|	—	|	—	—	|	2
A	1	|	—	|	—	|	—	|	—	|	—	|	—	|	—	|	—	|	—	—	1
		19	18	17	16	15	14	13	12	11	10	9	8	7	6	5	4	3	2	1	

		A	A	B	A	B	A	B	A	B	A	B	A	B	A	A	B	A	B	A	B	A	B	A	B	A	B	A	
		27	26	25	24	23	22	21	20	19	18	17	16	15	14	13	12	11	10	9	8	7	6	5	4	3	2	1	
A	27	—	|	—	|	—	|	—	|	—	|	—	|	—	|	—	|	—	|	—	|	—	|	—	|	—	|	—	27
B	26	—	—	|	—	|	—	|	—	|	—	|	—	|	—	|	—	|	—	|	—	|	—	|	—	|	—	|	26
A	25	|	—	—	|	—	|	—	|	—	|	—	|	—	|	—	|	—	|	—	|	—	|	—	|	—	|	—	25
B	24	—	|	—	—	|	—	|	—	|	—	|	—	|	—	|	—	|	—	|	—	|	—	|	—	|	—	|	24
A	23	|	—	|	—	—	|	—	|	—	|	—	|	—	|	—	|	—	|	—	|	—	|	—	|	—	|	—	23
B	22	—	|	—	|	—	—	|	—	|	—	|	—	|	—	|	—	|	—	|	—	|	—	|	—	|	—	|	22
A	21	|	—	|	—	|	—	—	|	—	|	—	|	—	|	—	|	—	|	—	|	—	|	—	|	—	|	—	21
B	20	—	|	—	|	—	|	—	—	|	—	|	—	|	—	|	—	|	—	|	—	|	—	|	—	|	—	|	20
A	19	|	—	|	—	|	—	|	—	—	|	—	|	—	|	—	|	—	|	—	|	—	|	—	|	—	|	—	19
B	18	—	|	—	|	—	|	—	|	—	—	|	—	|	—	|	—	|	—	|	—	|	—	|	—	|	—	|	18
A	17	|	—	|	—	|	—	|	—	|	—	—	|	—	|	—	|	—	|	—	|	—	|	—	|	—	|	—	17
B	16	—	|	—	|	—	|	—	|	—	|	—	—	|	—	|	—	|	—	|	—	|	—	|	—	|	—	|	16
A	15	|	—	|	—	|	—	|	—	|	—	|	—	—	|	—	|	—	|	—	|	—	|	—	|	—	|	—	15
A	14	—	|	—	|	—	|	—	|	—	|	—	|	—	—	|	—	|	—	|	—	|	—	|	—	|	—	|	14
B	13	|	—	|	—	|	—	|	—	|	—	|	—	|	—	—	|	—	|	—	|	—	|	—	|	—	|	—	13
A	12	—	|	—	|	—	|	—	|	—	|	—	|	—	|	—	—	|	—	|	—	|	—	|	—	|	—	|	12
B	11	|	—	|	—	|	—	|	—	|	—	|	—	|	—	|	—	—	|	—	|	—	|	—	|	—	|	—	11
A	10	—	|	—	|	—	|	—	|	—	|	—	|	—	|	—	|	—	—	|	—	|	—	|	—	|	—	|	10
B	9	|	—	|	—	|	—	|	—	|	—	|	—	|	—	|	—	|	—	—	|	—	|	—	|	—	|	—	9
A	8	—	|	—	|	—	|	—	|	—	|	—	|	—	|	—	|	—	|	—	—	|	—	|	—	|	—	|	8
B	7	|	—	|	—	|	—	|	—	|	—	|	—	|	—	|	—	|	—	|	—	—	|	—	|	—	|	—	7
A	6	—	|	—	|	—	|	—	|	—	|	—	|	—	|	—	|	—	|	—	|	—	—	|	—	|	—	|	6
B	5	|	—	|	—	|	—	|	—	|	—	|	—	|	—	|	—	|	—	|	—	|	—	—	|	—	|	—	5
A	4	—	|	—	|	—	|	—	|	—	|	—	|	—	|	—	|	—	|	—	|	—	|	—	—	|	—	|	4
B	3	|	—	|	—	|	—	|	—	|	—	|	—	|	—	|	—	|	—	|	—	|	—	|	—	—	|	—	3
A	2	—	|	—	|	—	|	—	|	—	|	—	|	—	|	—	|	—	|	—	|	—	|	—	|	—	—	|	2
A	1	|	—	|	—	|	—	|	—	|	—	|	—	|	—	|	—	|	—	|	—	|	—	|	—	|	—	—	1
		27	26	25	24	23	22	21	20	19	18	17	16	15	14	13	12	11	10	9	8	7	6	5	4	3	2	1	

FACETS

Original design: Mary Clarke

		A	B	A	B	A	B	A	B	A	A	B	A	B	A	B	A	B	A	B	
		19	18	17	16	15	14	13	12	11	10	9	8	7	6	5	4	3	2	1	
A	19	—	—	|	—	|	—	|	—	|	—	|	—	|	—	|	—	|	—	|	19
B	18	|	—	—	|	—	|	—	|	—	|	—	|	—	|	—	|	—	|	—	18
A	17	—	|	—	—	|	—	|	—	|	—	|	—	|	—	|	—	|	—	|	17
B	16	|	—	|	—	—	|	—	|	—	|	—	|	—	|	—	|	—	|	—	16
A	15	—	|	—	|	—	—	|	—	|	—	|	—	|	—	|	—	|	—	|	15
B	14	|	—	|	—	|	—	—	|	—	|	—	|	—	|	—	|	—	|	—	14
A	13	—	|	—	|	—	|	—	—	|	—	|	—	|	—	|	—	|	—	|	13
B	12	|	—	|	—	|	—	|	—	—	|	—	|	—	|	—	|	—	|	—	12
A	11	—	|	—	|	—	|	—	|	—	—	|	—	|	—	|	—	|	—	|	11
A	10	|	—	|	—	|	—	|	—	|	—	—	|	—	|	—	|	—	|	—	10
B	9	—	|	—	|	—	|	—	|	—	|	—	—	|	—	|	—	|	—	|	9
A	8	|	—	|	—	|	—	|	—	|	—	|	—	—	|	—	|	—	|	—	8
B	7	—	|	—	|	—	|	—	|	—	|	—	|	—	—	|	—	|	—	|	7
A	6	|	—	|	—	|	—	|	—	|	—	|	—	|	—	—	|	—	|	—	6
B	5	—	|	—	|	—	|	—	|	—	|	—	|	—	|	—	—	|	—	|	5
A	4	|	—	|	—	|	—	|	—	|	—	|	—	|	—	|	—	—	|	—	4
B	3	—	|	—	|	—	|	—	|	—	|	—	|	—	|	—	|	—	—	|	3
A	2	|	—	|	—	|	—	|	—	|	—	|	—	|	—	|	—	|	—	—	2
B	1	—	|	—	|	—	|	—	|	—	|	—	|	—	|	—	|	—	|	—	1
		19	18	17	16	15	14	13	12	11	10	9	8	7	6	5	4	3	2	1	

<table>
<tr><td></td><td></td><td>A</td><td>B</td><td>A</td><td>B</td><td>A</td><td>B</td><td>A</td><td>B</td><td>A</td><td>B</td><td>A</td><td>B</td><td>A</td><td>A</td><td>B</td><td>A</td><td>B</td><td>A</td><td>B</td><td>A</td><td>B</td><td>A</td><td>B</td><td>A</td><td>B</td><td>A</td><td>B</td><td></td></tr>
<tr><td></td><td></td><td>27</td><td>26</td><td>25</td><td>24</td><td>23</td><td>22</td><td>21</td><td>20</td><td>19</td><td>18</td><td>17</td><td>16</td><td>15</td><td>14</td><td>13</td><td>12</td><td>11</td><td>10</td><td>9</td><td>8</td><td>7</td><td>6</td><td>5</td><td>4</td><td>3</td><td>2</td><td>1</td><td></td></tr>
<tr><td>A</td><td>27</td><td>—</td><td>—</td><td>|</td><td>—</td><td>|</td><td>—</td><td>|</td><td>—</td><td>|</td><td>—</td><td>|</td><td>—</td><td>|</td><td>—</td><td>|</td><td>—</td><td>|</td><td>—</td><td>|</td><td>—</td><td>|</td><td>—</td><td>|</td><td>—</td><td>|</td><td>—</td><td>|</td><td>27</td></tr>
<tr><td>B</td><td>26</td><td>|</td><td>—</td><td>—</td><td>|</td><td>—</td><td>|</td><td>—</td><td>|</td><td>—</td><td>|</td><td>—</td><td>|</td><td>—</td><td>|</td><td>—</td><td>|</td><td>—</td><td>|</td><td>—</td><td>|</td><td>—</td><td>|</td><td>—</td><td>|</td><td>—</td><td>|</td><td>—</td><td>26</td></tr>
<tr><td>A</td><td>25</td><td>—</td><td>|</td><td>—</td><td>—</td><td>|</td><td>—</td><td>|</td><td>—</td><td>|</td><td>—</td><td>|</td><td>—</td><td>|</td><td>—</td><td>|</td><td>—</td><td>|</td><td>—</td><td>|</td><td>—</td><td>|</td><td>—</td><td>|</td><td>—</td><td>|</td><td>—</td><td>|</td><td>25</td></tr>
<tr><td>B</td><td>24</td><td>|</td><td>—</td><td>|</td><td>—</td><td>—</td><td>|</td><td>—</td><td>|</td><td>—</td><td>|</td><td>—</td><td>|</td><td>—</td><td>|</td><td>—</td><td>|</td><td>—</td><td>|</td><td>—</td><td>|</td><td>—</td><td>|</td><td>—</td><td>|</td><td>—</td><td>|</td><td>—</td><td>24</td></tr>
<tr><td>A</td><td>23</td><td>—</td><td>|</td><td>—</td><td>|</td><td>—</td><td>—</td><td>|</td><td>—</td><td>|</td><td>—</td><td>|</td><td>—</td><td>|</td><td>—</td><td>|</td><td>—</td><td>|</td><td>—</td><td>|</td><td>—</td><td>|</td><td>—</td><td>|</td><td>—</td><td>|</td><td>—</td><td>|</td><td>23</td></tr>
<tr><td>B</td><td>22</td><td>|</td><td>—</td><td>|</td><td>—</td><td>|</td><td>—</td><td>—</td><td>|</td><td>—</td><td>|</td><td>—</td><td>|</td><td>—</td><td>|</td><td>—</td><td>|</td><td>—</td><td>|</td><td>—</td><td>|</td><td>—</td><td>|</td><td>—</td><td>|</td><td>—</td><td>|</td><td>—</td><td>22</td></tr>
<tr><td>A</td><td>21</td><td>—</td><td>|</td><td>—</td><td>|</td><td>—</td><td>|</td><td>—</td><td>—</td><td>|</td><td>—</td><td>|</td><td>—</td><td>|</td><td>—</td><td>|</td><td>—</td><td>|</td><td>—</td><td>|</td><td>—</td><td>|</td><td>—</td><td>|</td><td>—</td><td>|</td><td>—</td><td>|</td><td>21</td></tr>
<tr><td>B</td><td>20</td><td>|</td><td>—</td><td>|</td><td>—</td><td>|</td><td>—</td><td>|</td><td>—</td><td>—</td><td>|</td><td>—</td><td>|</td><td>—</td><td>|</td><td>—</td><td>|</td><td>—</td><td>|</td><td>—</td><td>|</td><td>—</td><td>|</td><td>—</td><td>|</td><td>—</td><td>|</td><td>—</td><td>20</td></tr>
<tr><td>A</td><td>19</td><td>—</td><td>|</td><td>—</td><td>|</td><td>—</td><td>|</td><td>—</td><td>|</td><td>—</td><td>—</td><td>|</td><td>—</td><td>|</td><td>—</td><td>|</td><td>—</td><td>|</td><td>—</td><td>|</td><td>—</td><td>|</td><td>—</td><td>|</td><td>—</td><td>|</td><td>—</td><td>|</td><td>19</td></tr>
<tr><td>B</td><td>18</td><td>|</td><td>—</td><td>|</td><td>—</td><td>|</td><td>—</td><td>|</td><td>—</td><td>|</td><td>—</td><td>—</td><td>|</td><td>—</td><td>|</td><td>—</td><td>|</td><td>—</td><td>|</td><td>—</td><td>|</td><td>—</td><td>|</td><td>—</td><td>|</td><td>—</td><td>|</td><td>—</td><td>18</td></tr>
<tr><td>A</td><td>17</td><td>—</td><td>|</td><td>—</td><td>|</td><td>—</td><td>|</td><td>—</td><td>|</td><td>—</td><td>|</td><td>—</td><td>—</td><td>|</td><td>—</td><td>|</td><td>—</td><td>|</td><td>—</td><td>|</td><td>—</td><td>|</td><td>—</td><td>|</td><td>—</td><td>|</td><td>—</td><td>|</td><td>17</td></tr>
<tr><td>B</td><td>16</td><td>|</td><td>—</td><td>|</td><td>—</td><td>|</td><td>—</td><td>|</td><td>—</td><td>|</td><td>—</td><td>|</td><td>—</td><td>—</td><td>|</td><td>—</td><td>|</td><td>—</td><td>|</td><td>—</td><td>|</td><td>—</td><td>|</td><td>—</td><td>|</td><td>—</td><td>|</td><td>—</td><td>16</td></tr>
<tr><td>A</td><td>15</td><td>—</td><td>|</td><td>—</td><td>|</td><td>—</td><td>|</td><td>—</td><td>|</td><td>—</td><td>|</td><td>—</td><td>|</td><td>—</td><td>—</td><td>|</td><td>—</td><td>|</td><td>—</td><td>|</td><td>—</td><td>|</td><td>—</td><td>|</td><td>—</td><td>|</td><td>—</td><td>|</td><td>15</td></tr>
<tr><td>A</td><td>14</td><td>|</td><td>—</td><td>|</td><td>—</td><td>|</td><td>—</td><td>|</td><td>—</td><td>|</td><td>—</td><td>|</td><td>—</td><td>|</td><td>—</td><td>—</td><td>|</td><td>—</td><td>|</td><td>—</td><td>|</td><td>—</td><td>|</td><td>—</td><td>|</td><td>—</td><td>|</td><td>—</td><td>14</td></tr>
<tr><td>B</td><td>13</td><td>—</td><td>|</td><td>—</td><td>|</td><td>—</td><td>|</td><td>—</td><td>|</td><td>—</td><td>|</td><td>—</td><td>|</td><td>—</td><td>|</td><td>—</td><td>—</td><td>|</td><td>—</td><td>|</td><td>—</td><td>|</td><td>—</td><td>|</td><td>—</td><td>|</td><td>—</td><td>|</td><td>13</td></tr>
<tr><td>A</td><td>12</td><td>|</td><td>—</td><td>|</td><td>—</td><td>|</td><td>—</td><td>|</td><td>—</td><td>|</td><td>—</td><td>|</td><td>—</td><td>|</td><td>—</td><td>|</td><td>—</td><td>—</td><td>|</td><td>—</td><td>|</td><td>—</td><td>|</td><td>—</td><td>|</td><td>—</td><td>|</td><td>—</td><td>12</td></tr>
<tr><td>B</td><td>11</td><td>—</td><td>|</td><td>—</td><td>|</td><td>—</td><td>|</td><td>—</td><td>|</td><td>—</td><td>|</td><td>—</td><td>|</td><td>—</td><td>|</td><td>—</td><td>|</td><td>—</td><td>—</td><td>|</td><td>—</td><td>|</td><td>—</td><td>|</td><td>—</td><td>|</td><td>—</td><td>|</td><td>11</td></tr>
<tr><td>A</td><td>10</td><td>|</td><td>—</td><td>|</td><td>—</td><td>|</td><td>—</td><td>|</td><td>—</td><td>|</td><td>—</td><td>|</td><td>—</td><td>|</td><td>—</td><td>|</td><td>—</td><td>|</td><td>—</td><td>—</td><td>|</td><td>—</td><td>|</td><td>—</td><td>|</td><td>—</td><td>|</td><td>—</td><td>10</td></tr>
<tr><td>B</td><td>9</td><td>—</td><td>|</td><td>—</td><td>|</td><td>—</td><td>|</td><td>—</td><td>|</td><td>—</td><td>|</td><td>—</td><td>|</td><td>—</td><td>|</td><td>—</td><td>|</td><td>—</td><td>|</td><td>—</td><td>—</td><td>|</td><td>—</td><td>|</td><td>—</td><td>|</td><td>—</td><td>|</td><td>9</td></tr>
<tr><td>A</td><td>8</td><td>|</td><td>—</td><td>|</td><td>—</td><td>|</td><td>—</td><td>|</td><td>—</td><td>|</td><td>—</td><td>|</td><td>—</td><td>|</td><td>—</td><td>|</td><td>—</td><td>|</td><td>—</td><td>|</td><td>—</td><td>—</td><td>|</td><td>—</td><td>|</td><td>—</td><td>|</td><td>—</td><td>8</td></tr>
<tr><td>B</td><td>7</td><td>—</td><td>|</td><td>—</td><td>|</td><td>—</td><td>|</td><td>—</td><td>|</td><td>—</td><td>|</td><td>—</td><td>|</td><td>—</td><td>|</td><td>—</td><td>|</td><td>—</td><td>|</td><td>—</td><td>|</td><td>—</td><td>—</td><td>|</td><td>—</td><td>|</td><td>—</td><td>|</td><td>7</td></tr>
<tr><td>A</td><td>6</td><td>|</td><td>—</td><td>|</td><td>—</td><td>|</td><td>—</td><td>|</td><td>—</td><td>|</td><td>—</td><td>|</td><td>—</td><td>|</td><td>—</td><td>|</td><td>—</td><td>|</td><td>—</td><td>|</td><td>—</td><td>|</td><td>—</td><td>—</td><td>|</td><td>—</td><td>|</td><td>—</td><td>6</td></tr>
<tr><td>B</td><td>5</td><td>—</td><td>|</td><td>—</td><td>|</td><td>—</td><td>|</td><td>—</td><td>|</td><td>—</td><td>|</td><td>—</td><td>|</td><td>—</td><td>|</td><td>—</td><td>|</td><td>—</td><td>|</td><td>—</td><td>|</td><td>—</td><td>|</td><td>—</td><td>—</td><td>|</td><td>—</td><td>|</td><td>5</td></tr>
<tr><td>A</td><td>4</td><td>|</td><td>—</td><td>|</td><td>—</td><td>|</td><td>—</td><td>|</td><td>—</td><td>|</td><td>—</td><td>|</td><td>—</td><td>|</td><td>—</td><td>|</td><td>—</td><td>|</td><td>—</td><td>|</td><td>—</td><td>|</td><td>—</td><td>|</td><td>—</td><td>—</td><td>|</td><td>—</td><td>4</td></tr>
<tr><td>B</td><td>3</td><td>—</td><td>|</td><td>—</td><td>|</td><td>—</td><td>|</td><td>—</td><td>|</td><td>—</td><td>|</td><td>—</td><td>|</td><td>—</td><td>|</td><td>—</td><td>|</td><td>—</td><td>|</td><td>—</td><td>|</td><td>—</td><td>|</td><td>—</td><td>|</td><td>—</td><td>—</td><td>|</td><td>3</td></tr>
<tr><td>A</td><td>2</td><td>|</td><td>—</td><td>|</td><td>—</td><td>|</td><td>—</td><td>|</td><td>—</td><td>|</td><td>—</td><td>|</td><td>—</td><td>|</td><td>—</td><td>|</td><td>—</td><td>|</td><td>—</td><td>|</td><td>—</td><td>|</td><td>—</td><td>|</td><td>—</td><td>|</td><td>—</td><td>—</td><td>2</td></tr>
<tr><td>B</td><td>1</td><td>—</td><td>|</td><td>—</td><td>|</td><td>—</td><td>|</td><td>—</td><td>|</td><td>—</td><td>|</td><td>—</td><td>|</td><td>—</td><td>|</td><td>—</td><td>|</td><td>—</td><td>|</td><td>—</td><td>|</td><td>—</td><td>|</td><td>—</td><td>|</td><td>—</td><td>|</td><td>—</td><td>1</td></tr>
<tr><td></td><td></td><td>27</td><td>26</td><td>25</td><td>24</td><td>23</td><td>22</td><td>21</td><td>20</td><td>19</td><td>18</td><td>17</td><td>16</td><td>15</td><td>14</td><td>13</td><td>12</td><td>11</td><td>10</td><td>9</td><td>8</td><td>7</td><td>6</td><td>5</td><td>4</td><td>3</td><td>2</td><td>1</td><td></td></tr>
</table>

RIGHT-ANGLE HITCH

Original design: Mary Clarke

		A	B	A	B	A	B	A	B	A	A	B	A	B	A	B	A	B	A	
		18	17	16	15	14	13	12	11	10	9	8	7	6	5	4	3	2	1	
B	18	—	I	—	I	—	I	—	I	—	I	—	I	—	I	—	I	—	I	18
A	17	—	—	I	—	I	—	I	—	I	—	I	—	I	—	I	—	I	—	17
B	16	I	—	—	I	—	I	—	I	—	I	—	I	—	I	—	I	—	I	16
A	15	—	I	—	—	I	—	I	—	I	—	I	—	I	—	I	—	I	—	15
B	14	I	—	I	—	—	I	—	I	—	I	—	I	—	I	—	I	—	I	14
A	13	—	I	—	I	—	—	I	—	I	—	I	—	I	—	I	—	I	—	13
B	12	I	—	I	—	I	—	—	I	—	I	—	I	—	I	—	I	—	I	12
A	11	—	I	—	I	—	I	—	—	I	—	I	—	I	—	I	—	I	—	11
B	10	I	—	I	—	I	—	I	—	—	I	—	I	—	I	—	I	—	I	10
A	9	—	I	—	I	—	I	—	I	—	I	—	I	—	I	—	I	—	—	9
B	8	I	—	I	—	I	—	I	—	I	—	—	I	—	I	—	I	—	I	8
A	7	—	I	—	I	—	I	—	I	—	I	—	—	I	—	I	—	I	—	7
B	6	I	—	I	—	I	—	I	—	I	—	I	—	—	I	—	I	—	I	6
A	5	—	I	—	I	—	I	—	I	—	I	—	I	—	—	I	—	I	—	5
B	4	I	—	I	—	I	—	I	—	I	—	I	—	I	—	—	I	—	I	4
A	3	—	I	—	I	—	I	—	I	—	I	—	I	—	I	—	—	I	—	3
B	2	I	—	I	—	I	—	I	—	I	—	I	—	I	—	I	—	—	I	2
A	1	—	I	—	I	—	I	—	I	—	I	—	I	—	I	—	I	—	—	1
		18	17	16	15	14	13	12	11	10	9	8	7	6	5	4	3	2	1	

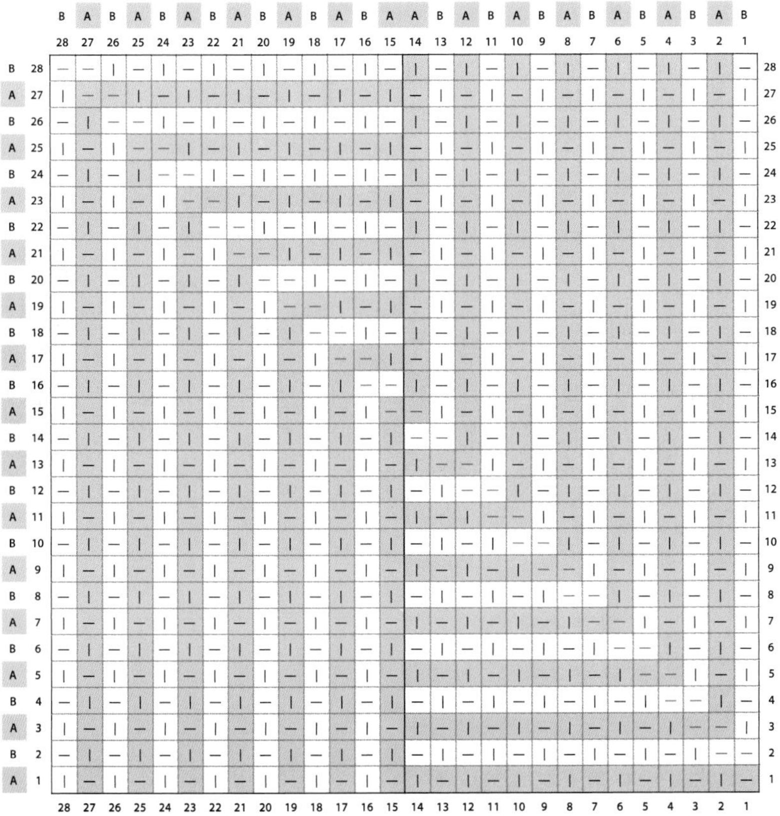

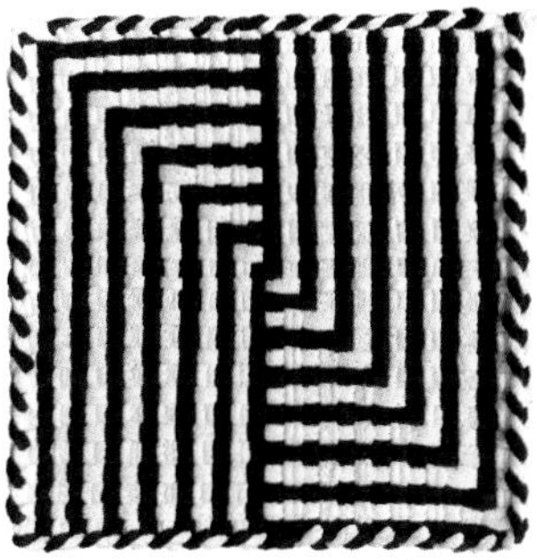

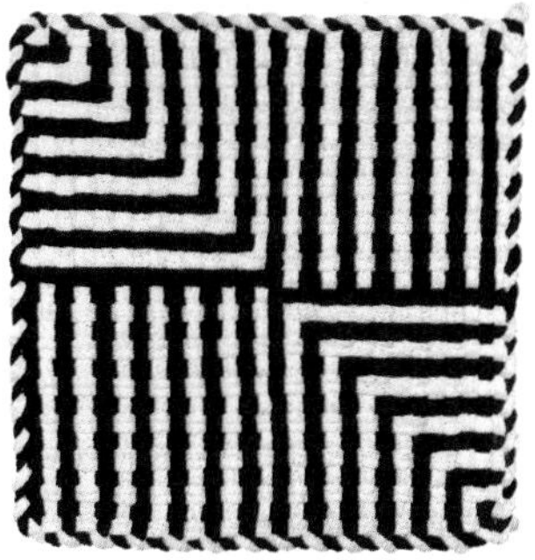

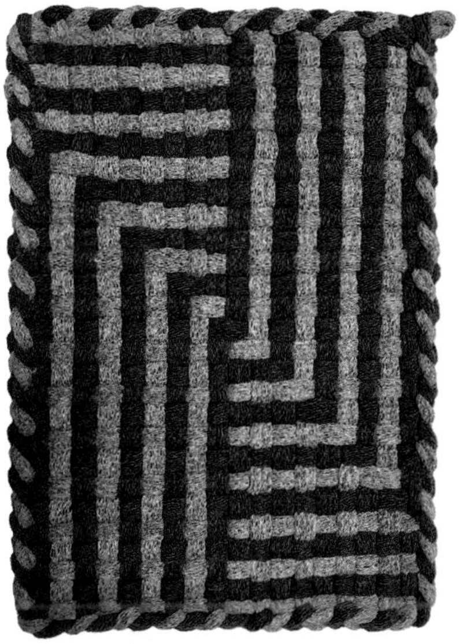

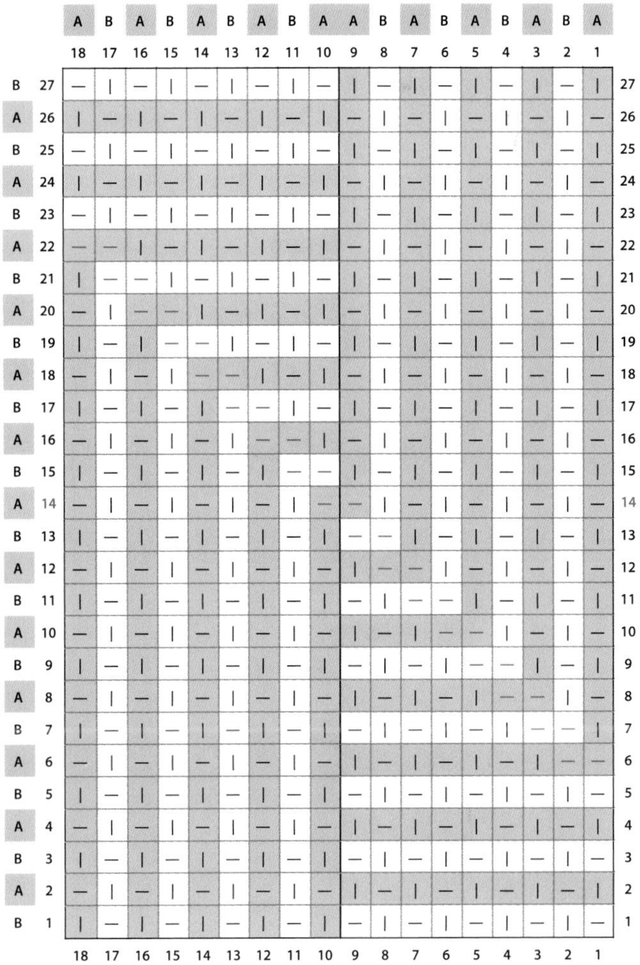

FILLET

Original design: Mary Clarke

Fillet is a straightforward design but contains possibilities far beyond the simplicity of its structure. Take a good look at the potholders on these two pages: they'll inspire you.

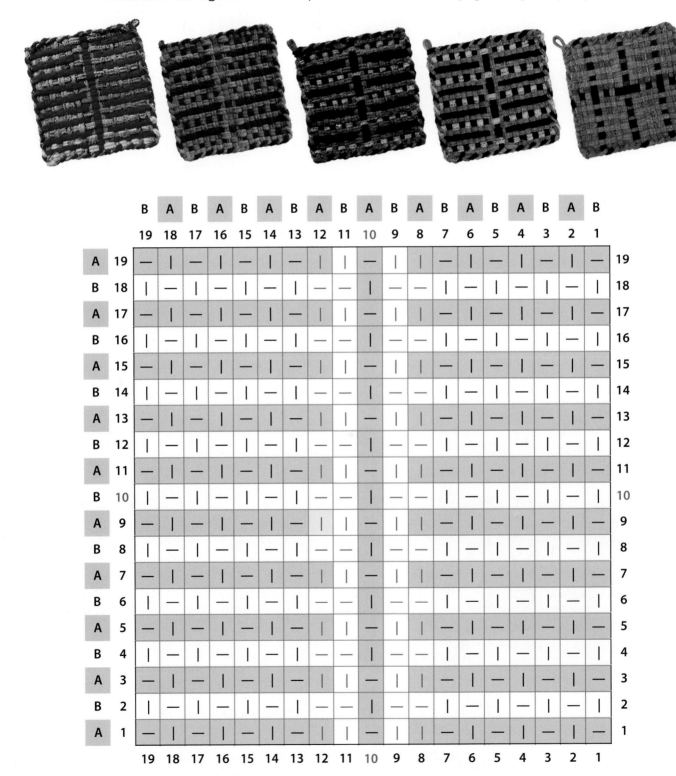

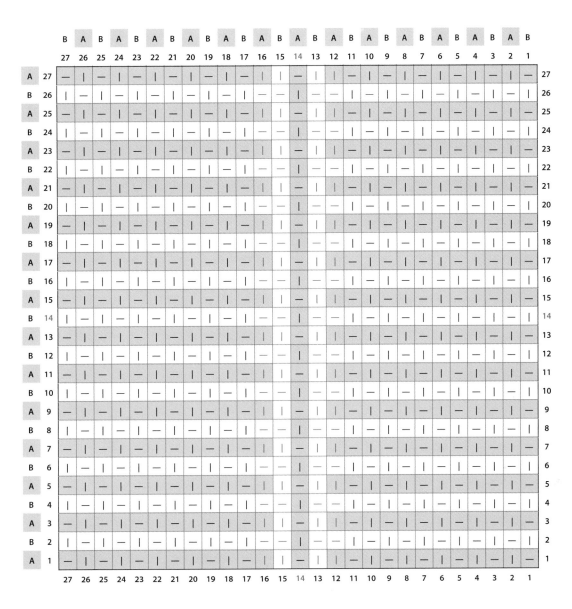

STRAIGHT-EDGE SPIRAL

Original design: Mary Clarke

		B	A	B	A	B	A	B	A	B	A	B	A	B	A	B	A	B	A	
		18	17	16	15	14	13	12	11	10	9	8	7	6	5	4	3	2	1	
A	18	—	I	—	I	—	I	—	I	—	I	—	I	—	I	—	I	—	—	18
B	17	—	—	I	—	I	—	I	—	I	—	I	—	I	—	I	—	—	I	17
A	16	I	—	—	I	—	I	—	I	—	I	—	I	—	I	—	—	I	—	16
B	15	—	I	—	—	I	—	I	—	I	—	I	—	I	—	I	—	—	I	15
A	14	I	—	I	—	—	I	—	I	—	I	—	I	—	I	—	—	I	—	14
B	13	—	I	—	I	—	—	I	—	I	—	I	—	—	I	—	I	—	I	13
A	12	I	—	I	—	I	—	—	I	—	I	—	I	—	I	—	I	—	I	12
B	11	—	I	—	I	—	—	—	I	—	I	I	—	I	—	I	—	I	—	11
A	10	I	—	I	—	I	—	I	—	—	I	—	I	—	I	—	I	—	—	10
B	9	—	I	—	I	—	I	—	I	I	—	—	I	—	I	—	I	—	I	9
A	8	I	—	I	—	I	—	I	—	I	—	I	—	I	—	I	—	I	—	8
B	7	—	I	—	I	—	I	—	I	—	I	—	I	—	I	—	I	—	I	7
A	6	I	—	I	—	I	—	I	—	I	—	I	—	I	—	I	—	I	—	6
B	5	—	I	—	I	—	I	—	I	—	I	—	I	—	I	—	I	—	I	5
A	4	I	—	I	—	I	—	I	—	I	—	I	—	I	—	I	—	I	—	4
B	3	—	I	—	—	I	—	I	—	I	—	I	—	I	—	I	—	—	I	3
A	2	I	—	—	I	—	I	—	I	—	I	—	I	—	I	—	I	—	—	2
B	1	—	—	I	—	I	—	I	—	I	—	I	—	I	—	I	—	I	—	1
		18	17	16	15	14	13	12	11	10	9	8	7	6	5	4	3	2	1	

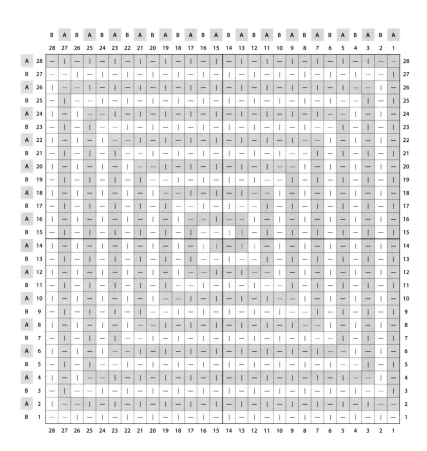

RIGHT ANGLES
Original design: Mary Clarke

		B	A	B	A	B	A	B	A	B	A	B	A	B	A	B	A	B	A	
		18	17	16	15	14	13	12	11	10	9	8	7	6	5	4	3	2	1	
B	18	—	—	I	—	I	—	I	—	I	—	I	—	I	—	I	—	I	—	18
A	17	I	—	—	I	—	I	—	I	—	I	—	I	—	I	—	I	—	I	17
B	16	—	I	—	—	I	—	I	—	I	—	I	—	I	—	I	—	I	—	16
A	15	I	—	I	—	—	I	—	I	—	I	—	I	—	I	—	I	—	I	15
B	14	—	I	—	I	—	—	I	—	I	—	I	—	I	—	I	—	I	—	14
A	13	I	—	I	—	I	—	—	I	—	I	—	I	—	I	—	I	—	I	13
B	12	—	I	—	I	—	I	—	—	I	—	I	—	I	—	I	—	I	—	12
A	11	I	—	I	—	I	—	I	—	—	I	—	I	—	I	—	I	—	I	11
B	10	—	I	—	I	—	I	—	I	—	—	I	—	I	—	I	—	I	—	10
A	9	I	—	I	—	I	—	I	—	I	—	—	I	—	I	—	I	—	I	9
B	8	—	I	—	I	—	I	—	I	—	I	—	—	I	—	I	—	I	—	8
A	7	I	—	I	—	I	—	I	—	I	—	I	—	—	I	—	I	—	I	7
B	6	—	I	—	I	—	I	—	I	—	I	—	I	—	—	I	—	I	—	6
A	5	I	—	I	—	I	—	I	—	I	—	I	—	I	—	—	I	—	I	5
B	4	—	I	—	I	—	I	—	I	—	I	—	I	—	I	—	—	I	—	4
A	3	I	—	I	—	I	—	I	—	I	—	I	—	I	—	I	—	—	I	3
B	2	—	I	—	I	—	I	—	I	—	I	—	I	—	I	—	I	—	—	2
A	1	I	—	I	—	I	—	I	—	I	—	I	—	I	—	I	—	I	—	1
		18	17	16	15	14	13	12	11	10	9	8	7	6	5	4	3	2	1	

Top-left chart

	B	A	B	A	B	A	B	A	B	A	B	A	B	A	B	A	B	A	B	A	B	A	B	A	B	A	B	
	27	26	25	24	23	22	21	20	19	18	17	16	15	14	13	12	11	10	9	8	7	6	5	4	3	2	1	

Row labels (left and right): B 27, A 26, B 25, A 24, B 23, A 22, B 21, A 20, B 19, A 18, B 17, A 16, B 15, A 14, B 13, A 12, B 11, A 10, B 9, A 8, B 7, A 6, B 5, A 4, B 3, A 2, B 1

Bottom-right chart

	A	B	A	B	A	B	A	B	A	B	A	B	A	B	A	B	A	B	
	18	17	16	15	14	13	12	11	10	9	8	7	6	5	4	3	2	1	

Row labels (left and right): A 27, B 26, A 25, B 24, A 23, B 22, A 21, B 20, A 19, B 18, A 17, B 16, A 15, B 14, A 13, B 12, A 11, B 10, A 9, B 8, A 7, B 6, A 5, B 4, A 3, B 2, A 1

FOUR CORNERS
A MASHUP OF RIGHT ANGLES AND BOXED ANGLES (DEBORAH JEAN COHEN)

		A	B	A	B	A	B	A	B	A	B	A	B	A	B	A	B	A	B	A	
		19	18	17	16	15	14	13	12	11	10	9	8	7	6	5	4	3	2	1	
B	19	—	l	—	l	—	l	—	l	—	—	l	—	l	—	l	—	l	—	—	19
A	18	l	—	l	—	l	—	l	—	l	—	l	—	l	—	l	—	—	l	18
B	17	—	l	—	l	—	l	l	—	l	—	l	—	l	—	l	—	l	—	17
A	16	l	—	l	—	l	—	l	—	l	—	l	—	l	—	l	—	l	—	l	16
B	15	—	l	—	l	—	l	—	l	—	l	—	l	—	l	—	l	—	l	15
A	14	l	—	l	—	l	—	l	—	l	—	l	—	l	—	l	—	l	14
B	13	—	l	—	l	—	l	—	l	—	l	—	l	—	l	—	l	13
A	12	l	—	—	l	—	l	—	l	—	l	—	l	—	l	—	l	12
B	11	—	l	—	l	—	l	—	l	—	l	—	l	—	l	—	11
A	10	—	l	—	l	—	l	—	—	l	—	l	—	l	—	—	—	10
B	9	l	—	l	—	l	—	l	—	l	—	l	—	l	—	—	l	9
A	8	—	l	—	l	—	l	—	l	—	l	—	l	—	—	l	—	8
B	7	l	—	l	—	l	—	l	—	l	—	l	—	—	l	—	l	7
A	6	—	l	—	l	—	l	—	l	—	l	—	l	—	l	6
B	5	l	—	l	—	—	l	—	l	—	l	—	l	—	l	5
A	4	—	l	—	l	—	l	—	l	—	l	—	l	4
B	3	l	—	—	l	—	l	—	l	—	l	—	l	3
A	2	—	l	—	l	—	l	—	l	—	l	2
B	1	—	l	—	l	—	l	—	l	—	l	1
		19	18	17	16	15	14	13	12	11	10	9	8	7	6	5	4	3	2	1	

SIMPLE MEANDER
Original design: Deborah Jean Cohen

		B	A	B	A	B	A	B	A	B	A	B	A	B	A	B	A	B	A	B		
		19	18	17	16	15	14	13	12	11	10	9	8	7	6	5	4	3	2	1		
B	19	—	|	—	—	|	—	|	—	|	—	|	—	|	—	|	—	|	—	—	19
A	18	|	—	|	—	—	|	|	—	—	|	|	—	—	|	|	—	—	|	|	18
B	17	—	|	—	|	—	|	—	|	—	|	—	|	—	|	—	|	—	|	—	17
A	16	|	—	|	—	|	—	|	—	|	—	|	—	|	—	|	—	|	—	|	16
B	15		|	—	|	—	|	—	|	—	|	—	|	—	|	—	|	—	|		15
A	14	|	—	|	—	|	—	|	—	|	—	|	—	|	—	|	—	|	—	|	14
B	13		|	—	|	—	|	—	|	—	|	—	|	—	|	—	|	—	|		13
A	12	|	—	|	—	|	—	|	—	|	—	|	—	|	—	|	—	|	—	|	12
B	11	—	|	—	|	—	|	—	|	—	|	—	|	—	|	—	|	—	|	—	11
A	10	|	—	|	—	|	—	|	—	|	—	|	—	|	—	|	—	|	—	|	10
B	9	—	|	—	|	—	|	—	|	—	|	—	|	—	|	—	|	—	|	—	9
A	8	|	—	|	—	|	—	|	—	|	—	|	—	|	—	|	—	|	—	|	8
B	7	—	|	—	|	—	|	—	|	—	|	—	|	—	|	—	|	—	|	—	7
A	6	|	—	|	—	|	—	|	—	|	—	|	—	|	—	|	—	|	—	|	6
B	5	—	|	—	|	—	|	—	|	—	|	—	|	—	|	—	|	—	|	—	5
A	4	|	—	|	—	|	—	|	—	|	—	|	—	|	—	|	—	|	—	|	4
B	3	—	|	—	|	—	|	—	|	—	|	—	|	—	|	—	|	—	|	—	3
A	2	|	—	—	|	—	—	|	—	—	|	—	—	|	—	—	|	—	|	|	2
B	1	—	|	—	|	—	|	—	|	—	|	—	|	—	|	—	|	—	|		1
		19	18	17	16	15	14	13	12	11	10	9	8	7	6	5	4	3	2	1		

SPIRAL HICCUP
(TWO AND THREE MEANDERS)

Original design: Deborah Jean Cohen

		A	B	A	B	A	B	A	B	A	B	A	B	A	B	A	B	A	B	A	
		19	18	17	16	15	14	13	12	11	10	9	8	7	6	5	4	3	2	1	
B	19	|	|	—	|	—	|	—	|	—	|	—	|	—	|	—	|	—	|	|	19
A	18	—	|	|	—	|	—	|	—	—	|	|	—	|	—	|	—	—	|	—	18
B	17	|	—	|	|	—	|	—	—	|	—	—	|	—	|	—	|	|	—	|	17
A	16	—	|	—	|	—	—	—	|	—	|	—	—	|	—	|	—	|	|	—	16
B	15	|	—	|	—	|	—	|	—	|	—	|	|	—	|	—	|	—	—	|	15
A	14	—	|	—	|	—	|	—	|	—	|	|	—	|	—	|	—	—	|	—	14
B	13	|	—	|	—	|	—	—	—	|	—	—	|	—	|	—	|	|	—	|	13
A	12	—	|	—	|	—	—	|	—	|	|	—	—	|	—	|	—	|	|	—	12
B	11	|	—	|	—	—	|	—	|	—	—	|	|	—	|	—	|	—	—	|	11
A	10	—	|	—	—	|	—	|	—	—	|	—	—	|	—	|	—	—	|	—	10
B	9	|	—	—	|	—	|	—	|	|	—	—	|	—	|	—	—	|	—	|	9
A	8	—	|	|	—	|	—	|	—	—	|	|	—	|	—	—	|	—	|	—	8
B	7	|	—	|	|	—	|	—	|	—	—	|	—	—	—	|	—	|	—	|	7
A	6	—	|	—	—	|	—	|	—	|	|	—	|	—	|	—	|	—	|	—	6
B	5	|	—	—	|	—	|	—	|	|	—	|	—	|	—	|	—	|	—	|	5
A	4	—	|	|	—	|	—	|	—	—	|	—	|	—	—	—	|	—	|	—	4
B	3	|	—	|	|	—	|	—	|	—	—	|	—	—	|	—	|	|	—	|	3
A	2	—	|	—	—	|	—	|	—	|	|	—	—	|	—	|	—	|	|	—	2
B	1	|	|	—	|	—	|	—	|	—	|	—	|	—	|	—	|	—	|	|	1
		19	18	17	16	15	14	13	12	11	10	9	8	7	6	5	4	3	2	1	

INSET SERIES: DIAGONAL

Original design: Deborah Jean Cohen

This is one of a series scattered throughout this book. I got the idea of insets from Op Art paintings, Handweaving.net's description of amalgams, and finally the Sol LeWitt (1928–2007) Wall Drawings. Notice that this is composed of a background of vertical stripes with a diagonal of horizontal stripes inset into it. These are a lot of fun to do: I'm still designing them.

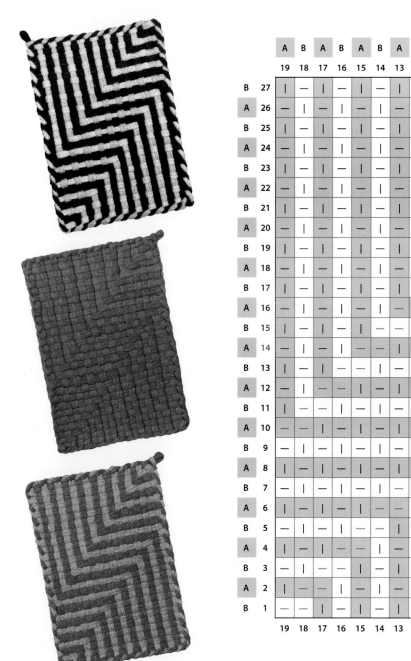

<table>
<tr><td></td><td></td><td>A</td><td>B</td><td>A</td><td>B</td><td>A</td><td>B</td><td>A</td><td>B</td><td>A</td><td>B</td><td>A</td><td>B</td><td>A</td><td>B</td><td>A</td><td>B</td><td>A</td><td>B</td><td>A</td><td></td></tr>
<tr><td></td><td></td><td>19</td><td>18</td><td>17</td><td>16</td><td>15</td><td>14</td><td>13</td><td>12</td><td>11</td><td>10</td><td>9</td><td>8</td><td>7</td><td>6</td><td>5</td><td>4</td><td>3</td><td>2</td><td>1</td><td></td></tr>
<tr><td>B</td><td>27</td><td>|</td><td>—</td><td>|</td><td>—</td><td>|</td><td>—</td><td>|</td><td>—</td><td>|</td><td>—</td><td>|</td><td>—</td><td>|</td><td>—</td><td>|</td><td>—</td><td>|</td><td>—</td><td>—</td><td>27</td></tr>
<tr><td>A</td><td>26</td><td>—</td><td>|</td><td>—</td><td>|</td><td>—</td><td>|</td><td>—</td><td>|</td><td>—</td><td>|</td><td>—</td><td>|</td><td>—</td><td>|</td><td>—</td><td>|</td><td>—</td><td>—</td><td>|</td><td>26</td></tr>
<tr><td>B</td><td>25</td><td>|</td><td>—</td><td>|</td><td>—</td><td>|</td><td>—</td><td>|</td><td>—</td><td>|</td><td>—</td><td>|</td><td>—</td><td>|</td><td>—</td><td>|</td><td>—</td><td>—</td><td>|</td><td>—</td><td>25</td></tr>
<tr><td>A</td><td>24</td><td>—</td><td>|</td><td>—</td><td>|</td><td>—</td><td>|</td><td>—</td><td>|</td><td>—</td><td>|</td><td>—</td><td>|</td><td>—</td><td>|</td><td>—</td><td>—</td><td>|</td><td>—</td><td>|</td><td>24</td></tr>
<tr><td>B</td><td>23</td><td>|</td><td>—</td><td>|</td><td>—</td><td>|</td><td>—</td><td>|</td><td>—</td><td>|</td><td>—</td><td>|</td><td>—</td><td>|</td><td>—</td><td>—</td><td>|</td><td>—</td><td>|</td><td>—</td><td>23</td></tr>
<tr><td>A</td><td>22</td><td>—</td><td>|</td><td>—</td><td>|</td><td>—</td><td>|</td><td>—</td><td>|</td><td>—</td><td>|</td><td>—</td><td>|</td><td>—</td><td>—</td><td>|</td><td>—</td><td>|</td><td>—</td><td>|</td><td>22</td></tr>
<tr><td>B</td><td>21</td><td>|</td><td>—</td><td>|</td><td>—</td><td>|</td><td>—</td><td>|</td><td>—</td><td>|</td><td>—</td><td>|</td><td>—</td><td>—</td><td>|</td><td>—</td><td>|</td><td>—</td><td>|</td><td>—</td><td>21</td></tr>
<tr><td>A</td><td>20</td><td>—</td><td>|</td><td>—</td><td>|</td><td>—</td><td>|</td><td>—</td><td>|</td><td>—</td><td>|</td><td>—</td><td>—</td><td>|</td><td>—</td><td>|</td><td>—</td><td>|</td><td>—</td><td>|</td><td>20</td></tr>
<tr><td>B</td><td>19</td><td>|</td><td>—</td><td>|</td><td>—</td><td>|</td><td>—</td><td>|</td><td>—</td><td>|</td><td>—</td><td>—</td><td>|</td><td>—</td><td>|</td><td>—</td><td>|</td><td>—</td><td>|</td><td>—</td><td>19</td></tr>
<tr><td>A</td><td>18</td><td>—</td><td>|</td><td>—</td><td>|</td><td>—</td><td>|</td><td>—</td><td>|</td><td>—</td><td>—</td><td>|</td><td>—</td><td>|</td><td>—</td><td>|</td><td>—</td><td>|</td><td>—</td><td>—</td><td>18</td></tr>
<tr><td>B</td><td>17</td><td>|</td><td>—</td><td>|</td><td>—</td><td>|</td><td>—</td><td>|</td><td>—</td><td>—</td><td>|</td><td>—</td><td>|</td><td>—</td><td>|</td><td>—</td><td>|</td><td>—</td><td>—</td><td>|</td><td>17</td></tr>
<tr><td>A</td><td>16</td><td>—</td><td>|</td><td>—</td><td>|</td><td>—</td><td>|</td><td>—</td><td>—</td><td>|</td><td>—</td><td>|</td><td>—</td><td>|</td><td>—</td><td>|</td><td>—</td><td>—</td><td>|</td><td>—</td><td>16</td></tr>
<tr><td>B</td><td>15</td><td>|</td><td>—</td><td>|</td><td>—</td><td>|</td><td>—</td><td>—</td><td>|</td><td>—</td><td>|</td><td>—</td><td>|</td><td>—</td><td>|</td><td>—</td><td>—</td><td>|</td><td>—</td><td>|</td><td>15</td></tr>
<tr><td>A</td><td>14</td><td>—</td><td>|</td><td>—</td><td>|</td><td>—</td><td>—</td><td>|</td><td>—</td><td>|</td><td>—</td><td>|</td><td>—</td><td>|</td><td>—</td><td>—</td><td>|</td><td>—</td><td>|</td><td>—</td><td>14</td></tr>
<tr><td>B</td><td>13</td><td>|</td><td>—</td><td>|</td><td>—</td><td>—</td><td>|</td><td>—</td><td>|</td><td>—</td><td>|</td><td>—</td><td>|</td><td>—</td><td>—</td><td>|</td><td>—</td><td>|</td><td>—</td><td>|</td><td>13</td></tr>
<tr><td>A</td><td>12</td><td>—</td><td>|</td><td>—</td><td>—</td><td>|</td><td>—</td><td>|</td><td>—</td><td>|</td><td>—</td><td>|</td><td>—</td><td>—</td><td>|</td><td>—</td><td>|</td><td>—</td><td>|</td><td>—</td><td>12</td></tr>
<tr><td>B</td><td>11</td><td>|</td><td>—</td><td>—</td><td>|</td><td>—</td><td>|</td><td>—</td><td>|</td><td>—</td><td>|</td><td>—</td><td>—</td><td>|</td><td>—</td><td>|</td><td>—</td><td>|</td><td>—</td><td>|</td><td>11</td></tr>
<tr><td>A</td><td>10</td><td>—</td><td>—</td><td>|</td><td>—</td><td>|</td><td>—</td><td>|</td><td>—</td><td>|</td><td>—</td><td>—</td><td>|</td><td>—</td><td>|</td><td>—</td><td>|</td><td>—</td><td>|</td><td>—</td><td>10</td></tr>
<tr><td>B</td><td>9</td><td>—</td><td>|</td><td>—</td><td>|</td><td>—</td><td>|</td><td>—</td><td>|</td><td>—</td><td>—</td><td>|</td><td>—</td><td>|</td><td>—</td><td>|</td><td>—</td><td>|</td><td>—</td><td>|</td><td>9</td></tr>
<tr><td>A</td><td>8</td><td>|</td><td>—</td><td>|</td><td>—</td><td>|</td><td>—</td><td>|</td><td>—</td><td>—</td><td>|</td><td>—</td><td>|</td><td>—</td><td>|</td><td>—</td><td>|</td><td>—</td><td>|</td><td>—</td><td>8</td></tr>
<tr><td>B</td><td>7</td><td>—</td><td>|</td><td>—</td><td>|</td><td>—</td><td>|</td><td>—</td><td>—</td><td>|</td><td>—</td><td>|</td><td>—</td><td>|</td><td>—</td><td>|</td><td>—</td><td>|</td><td>—</td><td>|</td><td>7</td></tr>
<tr><td>A</td><td>6</td><td>|</td><td>—</td><td>|</td><td>—</td><td>|</td><td>—</td><td>—</td><td>|</td><td>—</td><td>|</td><td>—</td><td>|</td><td>—</td><td>|</td><td>—</td><td>|</td><td>—</td><td>|</td><td>—</td><td>6</td></tr>
<tr><td>B</td><td>5</td><td>—</td><td>|</td><td>—</td><td>|</td><td>—</td><td>—</td><td>|</td><td>—</td><td>|</td><td>—</td><td>|</td><td>—</td><td>|</td><td>—</td><td>|</td><td>—</td><td>|</td><td>—</td><td>|</td><td>5</td></tr>
<tr><td>A</td><td>4</td><td>|</td><td>—</td><td>|</td><td>—</td><td>—</td><td>|</td><td>—</td><td>|</td><td>—</td><td>|</td><td>—</td><td>|</td><td>—</td><td>|</td><td>—</td><td>|</td><td>—</td><td>|</td><td>—</td><td>4</td></tr>
<tr><td>B</td><td>3</td><td>—</td><td>|</td><td>—</td><td>—</td><td>|</td><td>—</td><td>|</td><td>—</td><td>|</td><td>—</td><td>|</td><td>—</td><td>|</td><td>—</td><td>|</td><td>—</td><td>|</td><td>—</td><td>|</td><td>3</td></tr>
<tr><td>A</td><td>2</td><td>|</td><td>—</td><td>—</td><td>|</td><td>—</td><td>|</td><td>—</td><td>|</td><td>—</td><td>|</td><td>—</td><td>|</td><td>—</td><td>|</td><td>—</td><td>|</td><td>—</td><td>|</td><td>—</td><td>2</td></tr>
<tr><td>B</td><td>1</td><td>—</td><td>—</td><td>|</td><td>—</td><td>|</td><td>—</td><td>|</td><td>—</td><td>|</td><td>—</td><td>|</td><td>—</td><td>|</td><td>—</td><td>|</td><td>—</td><td>|</td><td>—</td><td>|</td><td>1</td></tr>
<tr><td></td><td></td><td>19</td><td>18</td><td>17</td><td>16</td><td>15</td><td>14</td><td>13</td><td>12</td><td>11</td><td>10</td><td>9</td><td>8</td><td>7</td><td>6</td><td>5</td><td>4</td><td>3</td><td>2</td><td>1</td><td></td></tr>
</table>

THREE DIAGONALS

Original design: Deborah Jean Cohen

INFINITE

Original design: Christine Olsen Reis

The second potholder from the left shows the back side of this pattern.

<table>
<tr><td></td><td></td><td>B</td><td>A</td><td>B</td><td>A</td><td>B</td><td>A</td><td>B</td><td>A</td><td>B</td><td>A</td><td>B</td><td>A</td><td>B</td><td>A</td><td>B</td><td>A</td><td>B</td><td>A</td><td>B</td><td></td></tr>
<tr><td></td><td></td><td>19</td><td>18</td><td>17</td><td>16</td><td>15</td><td>14</td><td>13</td><td>12</td><td>11</td><td>10</td><td>9</td><td>8</td><td>7</td><td>6</td><td>5</td><td>4</td><td>3</td><td>2</td><td>1</td><td></td></tr>
<tr><td>B</td><td>19</td><td>—</td><td>—</td><td>|</td><td>—</td><td>|</td><td>—</td><td>|</td><td>—</td><td>|</td><td>—</td><td>|</td><td>|</td><td>—</td><td>|</td><td>—</td><td>|</td><td>—</td><td>|</td><td>—</td><td>19</td></tr>
<tr><td>A</td><td>18</td><td>|</td><td>—</td><td>—</td><td>|</td><td>—</td><td>|</td><td>—</td><td>|</td><td>—</td><td>|</td><td>—</td><td>—</td><td>|</td><td>—</td><td>|</td><td>—</td><td>|</td><td>—</td><td>|</td><td>18</td></tr>
<tr><td>B</td><td>17</td><td>—</td><td>|</td><td>—</td><td>—</td><td>|</td><td>—</td><td>|</td><td>—</td><td>|</td><td>—</td><td>|</td><td>|</td><td>—</td><td>|</td><td>—</td><td>|</td><td>—</td><td>|</td><td>—</td><td>17</td></tr>
<tr><td>A</td><td>16</td><td>|</td><td>—</td><td>|</td><td>—</td><td>—</td><td>|</td><td>—</td><td>|</td><td>—</td><td>|</td><td>—</td><td>—</td><td>|</td><td>—</td><td>|</td><td>—</td><td>|</td><td>—</td><td>|</td><td>16</td></tr>
<tr><td>B</td><td>15</td><td>—</td><td>|</td><td>—</td><td>|</td><td>—</td><td>—</td><td>|</td><td>—</td><td>|</td><td>—</td><td>|</td><td>|</td><td>—</td><td>|</td><td>—</td><td>|</td><td>—</td><td>|</td><td>—</td><td>15</td></tr>
<tr><td>A</td><td>14</td><td>|</td><td>—</td><td>|</td><td>—</td><td>|</td><td>—</td><td>—</td><td>|</td><td>—</td><td>|</td><td>—</td><td>—</td><td>|</td><td>—</td><td>|</td><td>—</td><td>|</td><td>—</td><td>|</td><td>14</td></tr>
<tr><td>B</td><td>13</td><td>—</td><td>|</td><td>—</td><td>|</td><td>—</td><td>|</td><td>—</td><td>—</td><td>|</td><td>—</td><td>|</td><td>|</td><td>—</td><td>|</td><td>—</td><td>|</td><td>—</td><td>|</td><td>—</td><td>13</td></tr>
<tr><td>A</td><td>12</td><td>|</td><td>—</td><td>|</td><td>—</td><td>|</td><td>—</td><td>|</td><td>—</td><td>—</td><td>|</td><td>—</td><td>—</td><td>|</td><td>—</td><td>|</td><td>—</td><td>|</td><td>—</td><td>|</td><td>12</td></tr>
<tr><td>B</td><td>11</td><td>—</td><td>|</td><td>—</td><td>|</td><td>—</td><td>|</td><td>—</td><td>|</td><td>|</td><td>—</td><td>|</td><td>|</td><td>—</td><td>|</td><td>—</td><td>|</td><td>—</td><td>|</td><td>—</td><td>11</td></tr>
<tr><td>A</td><td>10</td><td>|</td><td>—</td><td>|</td><td>—</td><td>|</td><td>—</td><td>|</td><td>—</td><td>—</td><td>|</td><td>—</td><td>—</td><td>|</td><td>—</td><td>|</td><td>—</td><td>|</td><td>—</td><td>|</td><td>10</td></tr>
<tr><td>B</td><td>9</td><td>—</td><td>|</td><td>—</td><td>|</td><td>—</td><td>|</td><td>—</td><td>|</td><td>|</td><td>—</td><td>|</td><td>|</td><td>—</td><td>|</td><td>—</td><td>|</td><td>—</td><td>|</td><td>—</td><td>9</td></tr>
<tr><td>A</td><td>8</td><td>|</td><td>—</td><td>|</td><td>—</td><td>|</td><td>—</td><td>|</td><td>—</td><td>—</td><td>|</td><td>—</td><td>—</td><td>|</td><td>—</td><td>|</td><td>—</td><td>|</td><td>—</td><td>|</td><td>8</td></tr>
<tr><td>B</td><td>7</td><td>—</td><td>|</td><td>—</td><td>|</td><td>—</td><td>|</td><td>—</td><td>|</td><td>|</td><td>—</td><td>|</td><td>—</td><td>—</td><td>|</td><td>—</td><td>|</td><td>—</td><td>|</td><td>—</td><td>7</td></tr>
<tr><td>A</td><td>6</td><td>|</td><td>—</td><td>|</td><td>—</td><td>|</td><td>—</td><td>|</td><td>—</td><td>—</td><td>|</td><td>—</td><td>|</td><td>—</td><td>—</td><td>|</td><td>—</td><td>|</td><td>—</td><td>|</td><td>6</td></tr>
<tr><td>B</td><td>5</td><td>—</td><td>|</td><td>—</td><td>|</td><td>—</td><td>|</td><td>—</td><td>|</td><td>|</td><td>—</td><td>|</td><td>—</td><td>|</td><td>—</td><td>—</td><td>|</td><td>—</td><td>|</td><td>—</td><td>5</td></tr>
<tr><td>A</td><td>4</td><td>|</td><td>—</td><td>|</td><td>—</td><td>|</td><td>—</td><td>|</td><td>—</td><td>—</td><td>|</td><td>—</td><td>|</td><td>—</td><td>|</td><td>—</td><td>—</td><td>|</td><td>—</td><td>|</td><td>4</td></tr>
<tr><td>B</td><td>3</td><td>—</td><td>|</td><td>—</td><td>|</td><td>—</td><td>|</td><td>—</td><td>|</td><td>|</td><td>—</td><td>|</td><td>—</td><td>|</td><td>—</td><td>|</td><td>—</td><td>—</td><td>|</td><td>—</td><td>3</td></tr>
<tr><td>A</td><td>2</td><td>|</td><td>—</td><td>|</td><td>—</td><td>|</td><td>—</td><td>|</td><td>—</td><td>—</td><td>|</td><td>—</td><td>|</td><td>—</td><td>|</td><td>—</td><td>|</td><td>—</td><td>—</td><td>|</td><td>2</td></tr>
<tr><td>B</td><td>1</td><td>—</td><td>|</td><td>—</td><td>|</td><td>—</td><td>|</td><td>—</td><td>|</td><td>|</td><td>—</td><td>|</td><td>—</td><td>|</td><td>—</td><td>|</td><td>—</td><td>|</td><td>—</td><td>—</td><td>1</td></tr>
<tr><td></td><td></td><td>19</td><td>18</td><td>17</td><td>16</td><td>15</td><td>14</td><td>13</td><td>12</td><td>11</td><td>10</td><td>9</td><td>8</td><td>7</td><td>6</td><td>5</td><td>4</td><td>3</td><td>2</td><td>1</td><td></td></tr>
</table>

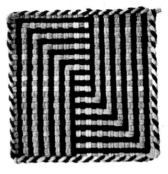

SHADOW CROSS

Draft charted by Christine Olsen Reis

RIPPLE

Original design: Christine Olsen Reis

		B	B	A	B	A	B	A	B	A	A	B	A	B	A	B	A	B	B	
		18	17	16	15	14	13	12	11	10	9	8	7	6	5	4	3	2	1	
B	18	—	|	|	—	|	|	—	|	|	—	|	|	—	|	|	—	|	|	18
B	17	|	—	|	|	—	|	|	—	|	|	—	|	|	—	|	|	—	|	17
A	16	|	|	—	|	|	—	|	|	—	|	|	—	|	|	—	|	|	—	16
B	15	—	|	|	—	|	|	—	|	|	—	|	|	—	|	|	—	|	|	15
A	14	|	—	|	|	—	|	|	—	|	|	—	|	|	—	|	|	—	|	14
B	13	|	|	—	|	|	—	|	|	—	|	|	—	|	|	—	|	|	—	13
A	12	—	|	|	—	|	|	—	|	|	—	|	|	—	|	|	—	|	|	12
B	11	|	—	|	|	—	|	|	—	|	|	—	|	|	—	|	|	—	|	11
A	10	|	|	—	|	|	—	|	|	—	|	|	—	|	|	—	|	|	—	10
A	9	—	|	|	—	|	|	—	|	|	—	|	|	—	|	|	—	|	|	9
B	8	|	—	|	|	—	|	|	—	|	|	—	|	|	—	|	|	—	|	8
A	7	|	|	—	|	|	—	|	|	—	|	|	—	|	|	—	|	|	—	7
B	6	—	|	|	—	|	|	—	|	|	—	|	|	—	|	|	—	|	|	6
A	5	|	—	|	|	—	|	|	—	|	|	—	|	|	—	|	|	—	|	5
B	4	|	|	—	|	|	—	|	|	—	|	|	—	|	|	—	|	|	—	4
A	3	—	|	|	—	|	|	—	|	|	—	|	|	—	|	|	—	|	|	3
B	2	|	—	|	|	—	|	|	—	|	|	—	|	|	—	|	|	—	|	2
B	1	|	|	—	|	|	—	|	|	—	|	|	—	|	|	—	|	|	—	1
		18	17	16	15	14	13	12	11	10	9	8	7	6	5	4	3	2	1	

RAMBLE

Original design: Mary Clarke

		B	A	B	A	B	A	B	A	B	A	B	A	B	A	B	A	B	A	
		18	17	16	15	14	13	12	11	10	9	8	7	6	5	4	3	2	1	
A	18	I	—	I	—	I	—	I	—	I	—	I	—	I	—	I	—	I	—	18
B	17	—	I	—	—	I	—	I	—	I	I	—	I	—	I	—	I	—	I	17
A	16	I	—	I	—	—	I	—	I	—	I	—	I	—	I	—	I	—	16
B	15	—	I	—	I	—	—	I	—	I	—	I	—	I	—	I	—	I	15
A	14	I	—	I	—	I	—	—	I	—	I	—	I	—	I	—	I	—	14
B	13	—	I	—	I	—	I	I	—	I	—	I	—	I	—	I	—	I	13
A	12	I	—	I	—	I	—	—	I	—	I	—	I	—	I	—	I	—	12
B	11	—	I	—	I	—	I	—	I	—	—	I	—	I	—	I	—	I	11
A	10	I	—	I	—	I	—	I	—	I	—	I	—	I	—	I	—	I	10
B	9	—	I	—	I	—	I	—	I	—	I	—	I	—	I	—	I	9
A	8	I	I	—	I	—	I	—	I	—	I	—	I	—	I	8
B	7	—	—	I	—	I	—	I	—	I	—	I	—	I	—	I	7
A	6	I	—	I	—	I	—	I	—	I	—	I	—	I	6
B	5	—	I	—	I	—	I	—	I	—	I	—	I	—	I	5
A	4	I	—	I	I	—	I	—	I	—	I	—	I	—	I	4
B	3	—	I	—	I	—	I	—	I	—	I	—	I	—	I	3
A	2	I	—	—	I	—	I	—	I	—	I	—	I	—	I	—	2
B	1	—	—	I	—	I	—	I	—	I	—	I	—	I	I	1
		18	17	16	15	14	13	12	11	10	9	8	7	6	5	4	3	2	1	

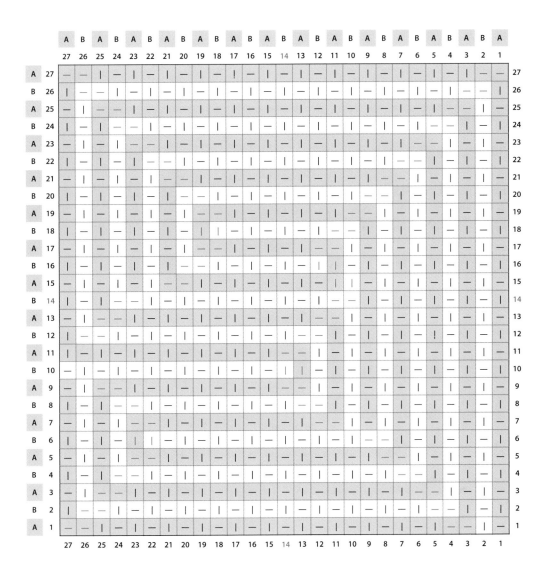

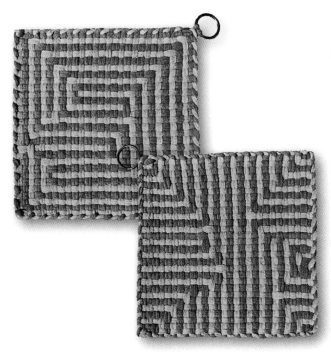

The original Green-and-Black Weirdo, which became Ramble.

TRIAD
Original design: Mary Clarke

The second potholder from the right shows the back side of this pattern.

		A	B	A	B	A	B	A	B	A	B	A	B	A	B	A	B	A	B	A	
		19	18	17	16	15	14	13	12	11	10	9	8	7	6	5	4	3	2	1	
B	19	—	I	—	I	—	I	—	I	—	I	—	I	—	I	—	I	—	I	—	19
A	18	I	—	I	—	I	—	I	—	I	—	I	—	I	—	I	—	I	—	I	18
B	17	I	—	I	—	I	—	—	—	I	—	I	—	I	—	I	—	I	—	I	17
A	16	—	I	—	I	—	I	—	I	—	I	—	I	—	I	—	I	—	I	—	16
B	15	I	—	I	—	I	—	I	—	I	—	I	—	I	—	I	—	I	—	I	15
A	14	I	—	I	—	I	—	I	—	I	—	I	—	I	—	I	—	I	—	I	14
B	13	—	I	—	I	—	I	—	I	—	—	I	—	I	—	I	—	I	—	I	13
A	12	I	—	I	—	I	—	I	—	I	—	I	—	I	—	I	—	I	—	I	12
B	11	I	—	I	—	I	—	I	—	—	—	I	—	I	—	I	—	I	—	I	11
A	10	—	I	—	I	—	I	—	I	—	I	—	I	—	I	—	I	—	I	—	10
B	9	I	—	I	—	I	—	I	—	I	—	I	—	I	—	I	—	I	—	I	9
A	8	I	—	I	—	I	—	I	—	I	—	I	—	I	—	I	—	I	—	I	8
B	7	—	I	—	I	—	I	—	I	—	I	—	I	—	I	—	I	—	I	—	7
A	6	I	—	I	—	I	—	I	—	I	—	I	—	I	—	I	—	I	—	I	6
B	5	I	—	I	—	I	—	I	—	I	—	I	—	I	—	I	—	I	—	I	5
A	4	—	I	—	I	—	I	—	I	—	I	—	I	—	I	—	I	—	I	—	4
B	3	I	—	I	—	I	—	I	—	I	—	I	—	I	—	I	—	I	—	I	3
A	2	I	—	I	—	I	—	I	—	I	—	I	—	I	—	I	—	I	—	I	2
B	1	—	I	—	I	—	I	—	I	—	I	—	I	—	I	—	I	—	I	—	1
		19	18	17	16	15	14	13	12	11	10	9	8	7	6	5	4	3	2	1	

SWELL

Original design: Mary Clarke

		B	A	B	A	B	A	B	A	B	A	B	A	B	A	B	A	B	A	B	
		19	18	17	16	15	14	13	12	11	10	9	8	7	6	5	4	3	2	1	
A	19	—	I	—	I	—	I	—	I	—	I	—	I	—	I	—	I	—	I	—	19
B	18	I	—	I	—	I	—	I	—	I	—	I	—	I	—	I	—	I	—	I	18
A	17	I	—	I	—	I	—	I	—	I	—	I	—	I	—	I	—	I	—	I	17
B	16	—	I	—	I	—	I	I	—	I	—	I	—	I	—	I	—	I	—	—	16
A	15	I	—	I	—	I	—	—	I	—	I	—	I	—	I	—	I	—	—	I	15
B	14	—	—	I	—	I	—	I	—	I	—	I	—	I	—	I	—	I	—	I	14
A	13	—	I	—	I	—	I	—	I	—	I	—	I	—	I	—	I	—	I	—	13
B	12	I	—	I	—	I	—	I	—	I	—	I	—	I	—	I	—	I	—	I	12
A	11	I	—	I	—	I	—	I	—	I	—	I	—	I	—	I	—	—	I	11
B	10	—	I	—	I	—	I	—	I	—	I	—	I	—	I	—	I	—	I	—	10
A	9	I	—	I	—	I	—	I	—	I	—	I	—	I	—	I	—	I	—	I	9
B	8	I	—	I	—	I	—	I	—	I	—	I	—	I	—	I	—	I	—	I	8
A	7	—	I	—	I	—	I	—	I	—	I	—	I	—	I	—	I	—	I	—	7
B	6	I	—	I	—	I	—	I	—	I	—	I	—	I	—	I	—	I	—	I	6
A	5	I	—	I	—	I	—	I	—	I	—	I	—	I	—	I	—	I	—	I	5
B	4	—	I	—	I	—	I	—	I	—	I	—	I	—	I	—	I	—	I	—	4
A	3	I	—	I	—	I	—	I	—	I	—	I	—	I	—	I	—	I	—	I	3
B	2	I	—	I	—	I	—	I	—	I	—	I	—	I	—	I	—	I	—	I	2
A	1	—	I	—	I	—	I	—	I	—	I	—	I	—	I	—	I	—	I	—	1
		19	18	17	16	15	14	13	12	11	10	9	8	7	6	5	4	3	2	1	

VERSO

Original design: Mary Clarke

		B	A	B	A	B	A	B	A	B	A	B	A	B	A	B	A	B	A	B	
		19	18	17	16	15	14	13	12	11	10	9	8	7	6	5	4	3	2	1	
A	19	|	—	—	|	—	—	|	—	—	|	—	—	|	—	—	|	—	—	|	19
B	18	—	|	|	—	|	|	—	|	|	—	|	|	—	|	|	—	|	|	—	18
A	17	|	—	|	|	—	|	|	—	|	|	—	|	|	—	|	|	—	|	|	17
B	16	—	|	|	—	|	|	—	|	|	—	|	|	—	|	|	—	|	|	—	16
A	15	|	—	|	|	—	|	|	—	|	|	—	|	|	—	|	|	—	|	|	15
B	14	—	|	|	—	|	|	—	|	|	—	|	|	—	|	|	—	|	|	—	14
A	13	|	—	|	|	—	|	|	—	|	|	—	|	|	—	|	|	—	|	|	13
B	12	—	|	|	—	|	|	—	|	|	—	|	|	—	|	|	—	|	|	—	12
A	11	|	—	|	|	—	|	|	—	|	|	—	|	|	—	|	|	—	|	|	11
B	10	—	|	|	—	|	|	—	|	|	—	|	|	—	|	|	—	|	|	—	10
A	9	|	—	|	|	—	|	|	—	|	|	—	|	|	—	|	|	—	|	|	9
B	8	—	|	|	—	|	|	—	|	|	—	|	|	—	|	|	—	|	|	—	8
A	7	|	—	|	|	—	|	|	—	|	|	—	|	|	—	|	|	—	|	|	7
B	6	—	|	|	—	|	|	—	|	|	—	|	|	—	|	|	—	|	|	—	6
A	5	|	—	|	|	—	|	|	—	|	|	—	|	|	—	|	|	—	|	|	5
B	4	—	|	—	|	|	—	|	—	|	|	—	|	—	|	—	|	—	|	—	4
A	3	|	—	|	—	|	|	—	|	|	—	|	|	—	|	|	—	|	—	|	3
B	2	—	|	—	|	—	|	—	|	—	|	—	|	—	|	—	|	—	|	—	2
A	1	|	—	|	—	|	|	—	|	|	—	|	|	—	|	—	|	—	|	|	1
		19	18	17	16	15	14	13	12	11	10	9	8	7	6	5	4	3	2	1	

RECTO

Original design: Mary Clarke

		B	A	B	A	B	A	B	A	B	A	B	A	B	A	B	A	B	A	B		
		19	18	17	16	15	14	13	12	11	10	9	8	7	6	5	4	3	2	1		
A	19	—	|	—	|	—	|	—	|	—	|	—	|	—	|	—	|	—	|	—	19	A
B	18	|	—	—	|	—	—	|	|	—	—	|	—	—	|	|	—	—	|	|	18	B
A	17	|	—	|	—	|	—	|	—	|	—	|	—	|	—	|	—	|	—	|	17	A
B	16	—	|	|	—	|	—	|	|	—	|	—	|	|	—	|	|	—	|	—	16	B
A	15	|	—	|	—	|	—	|	—	|	—	|	—	|	—	|	—	|	—	|	15	A
B	14	—	|	|	—	|	—	|	|	—	|	—	|	|	—	|	|	—	|	—	14	B
A	13	|	—	|	—	|	—	|	—	|	—	|	—	|	—	|	—	|	—	|	13	A
B	12	—	|	|	—	|	—	|	|	—	|	—	|	|	—	|	|	—	|	—	12	B
A	11	|	—	|	—	|	—	|	—	|	—	|	—	|	—	|	—	|	—	|	11	A
B	10	—	—	|	—	|	—	|	—	|	—	|	—	|	—	|	—	|	—	—	10	B
A	9	|	—	—	|	—	|	—	—	|	—	|	—	—	|	|	—	—	|	|	9	A
B	8	—	|	—	|	—	|	—	|	—	|	—	|	—	|	—	|	—	|	—	8	B
A	7	|	—	|	—	|	—	|	—	|	—	|	—	|	—	|	—	|	—	|	7	A
B	6	—	|	—	|	—	|	—	|	—	|	—	|	—	|	—	|	—	|	—	6	B
A	5	|	—	|	—	|	—	|	—	|	—	|	—	|	—	|	—	|	—	|	5	A
B	4	—	|	—	|	—	|	—	|	—	|	—	|	—	|	—	|	—	|	—	4	B
A	3	|	—	|	—	|	—	|	—	|	—	|	—	|	—	|	—	|	—	|	3	A
B	2	|	—	|	—	|	—	|	|	—	—	|	—	—	|	—	—	|	—	|	2	B
A	1	—	|	|	—	|	—	|	—	|	—	|	—	|	—	|	—	|	—	—	1	A
		19	18	17	16	15	14	13	12	11	10	9	8	7	6	5	4	3	2	1		

SCRIBBLE

Original design: Mary Clarke

		B	A	B	A	B	A	B	A	B	A	B	A	B	A	B	A	B	A	B	
		19	18	17	16	15	14	13	12	11	10	9	8	7	6	5	4	3	2	1	
A	19	I	—	—	I	—	I	—	I	—	I	—	I	—	I	—	I	—	—	I	19
B	18	—	I	—	I	I	—	I	I	—	I	I	—	I	I	—	I	—	I	—	18
A	17	I	—	I	—	I	—	I	—	I	—	I	I	—	I	—	I	—	I	I	17
B	16	—	I	—	I	—	I	—	I	—	I	—	I	—	I	—	I	—	I	I	16
A	15	I	I	—	I	—	I	—	I	—	I	—	I	I	—	I	—	I	—	I	15
B	14	—	I	I	—	I	—	I	—	I	—	I	—	I	I	—	I	—	I	I	14
A	13	I	I	—	I	—	I	—	I	—	I	—	I	—	I	—	I	I	—	I	13
B	12	—	I	—	I	—	I	—	I	—	I	—	I	—	I	—	I	I	—	I	12
A	11	I	I	—	—	I	—	I	—	I	—	I	—	I	—	I	I	—	—	I	11
B	10	—	—	I	—	I	—	I	—	I	—	I	—	I	—	I	—	I	—	—	10
A	9	I	I	—	I	—	I	—	I	—	I	—	I	—	I	—	I	—	I	I	9
B	8	—	I	I	—	I	—	I	—	I	—	I	—	I	—	I	—	I	—	—	8
A	7	I	I	—	—	I	—	I	—	I	—	I	—	I	—	I	—	I	I	I	7
B	6	—	I	—	I	—	I	—	I	—	I	—	I	—	I	—	I	I	I	—	6
A	5	I	I	—	I	—	I	—	I	—	I	—	I	—	I	—	I	—	—	I	5
B	4	—	I	I	—	I	—	I	—	I	—	I	—	I	—	I	—	I	—	—	4
A	3	I	—	I	—	I	—	I	—	I	—	I	—	I	—	I	—	I	I	I	3
B	2	—	—	I	—	I	—	I	—	I	—	I	—	I	—	I	—	I	I	—	2
A	1	I	I	—	I	—	I	—	I	—	I	—	I	—	I	—	I	—	I	I	1
		19	18	17	16	15	14	13	12	11	10	9	8	7	6	5	4	3	2	1	

SEMPERVIRENS

Original design: Mary Clarke

Top edge: B A B A B A B A B A B A B A B A B A B

19 18 17 16 15 14 13 12 11 10 9 8 7 6 5 4 3 2 1

Left	#		#
B	19	*(pattern grid)*	19
A	18		18
B	17		17
A	16		16
B	15		15
A	14		14
B	13		13
A	12		12
B	11		11
A	10		10
B	9		9
A	8		8
B	7		7
A	6		6
B	5		5
A	4		4
B	3		3
A	2		2
B	1		1

Bottom edge: 19 18 17 16 15 14 13 12 11 10 9 8 7 6 5 4 3 2 1

Sempervirens continued

B	A	B	A	B	A	B	A	B	A	B	A	B	A	B	A	B	A	B	A	B	A	B	A	B	A	B
27	26	25	24	23	22	21	20	19	18	17	16	15	14	13	12	11	10	9	8	7	6	5	4	3	2	1

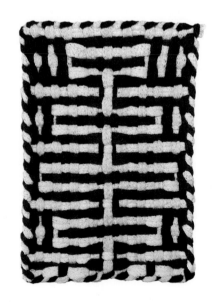

B	A	B	A	B	A	B	A	B	A	B	A	B	A	B	A	B	A	B
19	18	17	16	15	14	13	12	11	10	9	8	7	6	5	4	3	2	1

TWO DOTS

Original design: Deborah Jean Cohen

		A	B	A	B	A	B	A	B	A	A	B	A	B	A	B	A	B	A		
		18	17	16	15	14	13	12	11	10	9	8	7	6	5	4	3	2	1		
A	27	—	|	—	|	—	|	—	|	—	|	—	|	—	|	—	|	—	—	27
B	26	|	—	|	—	|	—	|	|	—	—	|	—	|	—	|	—	—	|	26
A	25	—	|	—	|	—	|	—	—	|	|	—	|	—	|	—	|	—	—	25
B	24	|	—	|	—	|	—	|	—	|	—	|	—	|	—	—	|	—	|	24
A	23	—	|	—	|	—	—	|	—	|	|	—	|	—	—	|	—	|	—	23
B	22	|	—	|	—	—	|	—	|	—	|	—	|	|	—	|	—	—	|	22
A	21	—	|	—	—	|	—	|	—	|	—	|	—	|	—	|	—	|	—	21
B	20	|	—	—	|	—	|	—	|	—	|	—	|	—	|	|	—	—	|	20
A	19	—	—	|	—	|	—	|	—	—	|	—	|	—	|	—	|	|	—	19
A	18	—	|	—	|	—	|	—	|	—	|	—	|	—	|	—	—	|	—	18
B	17	|	—	|	—	|	—	|	—	—	|	—	|	—	|	—	—	|	|	17
A	16	—	|	—	|	—	|	—	—	|	|	—	|	—	|	—	—	|	—	16
B	15	|	—	|	—	|	—	—	|	—	|	—	|	—	|	—	|	—	|	15
A	14	—	|	—	|	—	—	|	—	|	|	—	|	—	|	—	|	—	—	14
B	13	|	—	|	—	—	|	—	|	—	|	—	|	—	—	|	—	|	|	13
A	12	—	|	—	—	|	—	|	—	|	—	|	—	|	—	|	—	|	—	12
B	11	|	—	—	|	—	|	—	|	—	|	—	|	—	|	—	|	—	|	11
A	10	—	—	|	—	|	—	|	—	|	|	—	|	—	|	—	|	—	—	10
A	9	—	|	—	|	—	|	—	|	—	|	—	|	—	|	—	|	—	—	9
B	8	|	—	|	—	|	—	|	—	—	|	—	|	—	|	—	—	|	|	8
A	7	—	|	—	|	—	|	—	|	—	|	—	|	—	|	—	—	|	—	7
B	6	|	—	|	—	|	—	|	—	|	—	|	—	|	—	|	—	—	|	6
A	5	—	|	—	|	—	|	—	—	|	|	—	|	—	|	—	|	—	—	5
B	4	|	—	|	—	|	—	|	—	|	—	|	—	|	—	|	—	—	|	4
A	3	—	|	—	|	—	|	—	|	—	|	—	|	—	|	—	|	—	—	3
B	2	|	—	—	|	—	|	—	|	—	|	|	—	|	—	|	—	—	|	2
A	1	—	—	|	—	|	—	|	—	|	—	|	—	|	—	|	—	|	—	1
		18	17	16	15	14	13	12	11	10	9	8	7	6	5	4	3	2	1		

WHIRLING LOGS

Original design: Deborah Jean Cohen

SHADOW AZTEC

Draft charted by Deborah Jean Cohen

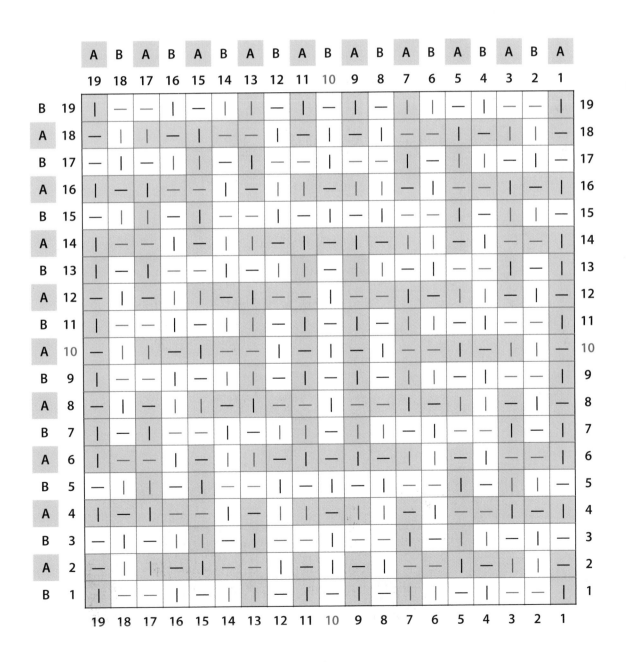

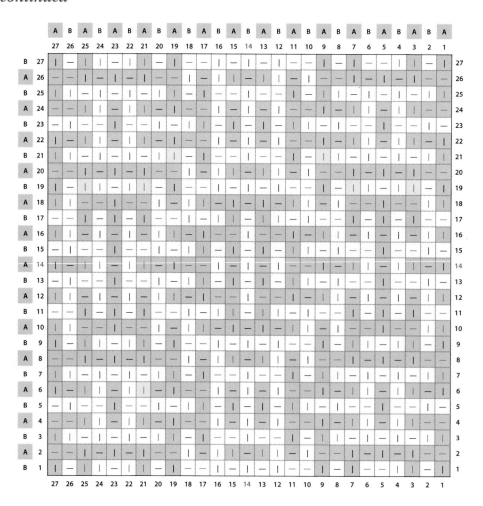

Woven with
the weft colors
reversed

Woven with weft
colors reversed
and multiple
colors for B

SHADOW X

Draft (opgang from Handweaving.net) charted by Deborah Jean Cohen

*The second potholder from the left shows the back side of this pattern.

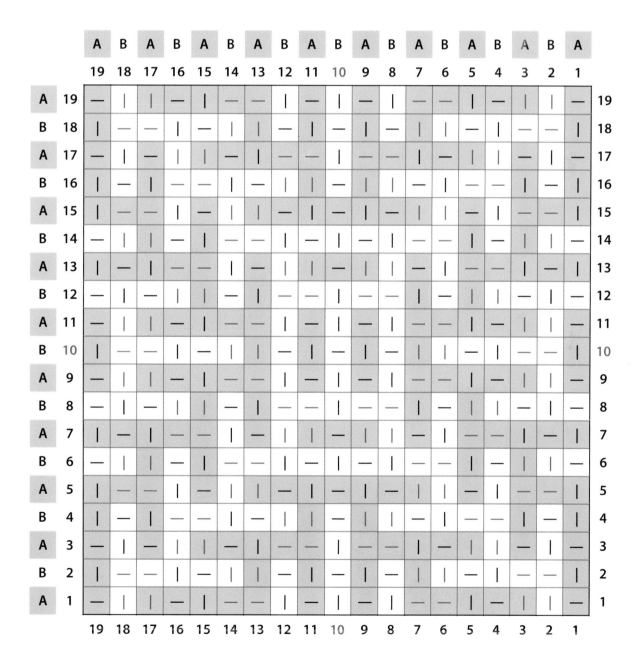

		A	B	A	B	A	B	A	B	A	B	A	B	A	B	A	B	A	B	A	B	A	B	A	B	A	B	A	
		27	26	25	24	23	22	21	20	19	18	17	16	15	14	13	12	11	10	9	8	7	6	5	4	3	2	1	
A	27	—	|	|	—	|	—	—	|	—	|	|	—	|	—	|	—	|	|	—	|	—	—	|	—	|	|	—	27
B	26	|	—	—	|	—	|	|	—	|	—	—	|	—	|	—	|	—	—	|	—	|	|	—	|	—	—	|	26
A	25	—	|	—	|	|	—	|	—	—	|	—	|	|	—	|	|	—	|	—	—	|	—	|	|	—	|	—	25
B	24	|	—	|	—	—	|	—	|	|	—	|	—	—	|	—	—	|	—	|	|	—	|	—	—	|	—	|	24
A	23	|	—	—	|	—	|	|	—	|	—	—	|	—	|	—	|	—	—	|	—	|	|	—	|	—	—	|	23
B	22	—	|	|	—	|	—	—	|	—	|	|	—	|	—	|	—	|	|	—	|	—	—	|	—	|	|	—	22
A	21	|	—	|	—	—	|	—	|	|	—	|	—	—	|	—	—	|	—	|	|	—	|	—	—	|	—	|	21
B	20	—	|	—	|	|	—	|	—	—	|	—	|	|	—	|	|	—	|	—	—	|	—	|	|	—	|	—	20
A	19	—	|	|	—	|	—	—	|	—	|	|	—	|	—	|	—	|	|	—	|	—	—	|	—	|	|	—	19
B	18	|	—	—	|	—	|	|	—	|	—	—	|	—	|	—	|	—	—	|	—	|	|	—	|	—	—	|	18
A	17	—	|	—	|	|	—	|	—	—	|	—	|	|	—	|	|	—	|	—	—	|	—	|	|	—	|	—	17
B	16	|	—	|	—	—	|	—	|	|	—	|	—	—	|	—	—	|	—	|	|	—	|	—	—	|	—	|	16
A	15	|	—	—	|	—	|	|	—	|	—	—	|	—	|	—	|	—	—	|	—	|	|	—	|	—	—	|	15
B	14	—	|	|	—	|	—	—	|	—	|	|	—	|	—	|	—	|	|	—	|	—	—	|	—	|	|	—	14
A	13	|	—	—	|	—	|	|	—	|	—	—	|	—	|	—	|	—	—	|	—	|	|	—	|	—	—	|	13
B	12	|	—	|	—	—	|	—	|	|	—	|	—	—	|	—	—	|	—	|	|	—	|	—	—	|	—	|	12
A	11	—	|	—	|	|	—	|	—	—	|	—	|	|	—	|	|	—	|	—	—	|	—	|	|	—	|	—	11
B	10	|	—	—	|	—	|	|	—	|	—	—	|	—	|	—	|	—	—	|	—	|	|	—	|	—	—	|	10
A	9	—	|	|	—	|	—	—	|	—	|	|	—	|	—	|	—	|	|	—	|	—	—	|	—	|	|	—	9
B	8	—	|	—	|	|	—	|	—	—	|	—	|	|	—	|	|	—	|	—	—	|	—	|	|	—	|	—	8
A	7	|	—	|	—	—	|	—	|	|	—	|	—	—	|	—	—	|	—	|	|	—	|	—	—	|	—	|	7
B	6	—	|	|	—	|	—	—	|	—	|	|	—	|	—	|	—	|	|	—	|	—	—	|	—	|	|	—	6
A	5	|	—	—	|	—	|	|	—	|	—	—	|	—	|	—	|	—	—	|	—	|	|	—	|	—	—	|	5
B	4	|	—	|	—	—	|	—	|	|	—	|	—	—	|	—	—	|	—	|	|	—	|	—	—	|	—	|	4
A	3	—	|	—	|	|	—	|	—	—	|	—	|	|	—	|	|	—	|	—	—	|	—	|	|	—	|	—	3
B	2	|	—	—	|	—	|	|	—	|	—	—	|	—	|	—	|	—	—	|	—	|	|	—	|	—	—	|	2
A	1	—	|	|	—	|	—	—	|	—	|	|	—	|	—	|	—	|	|	—	|	—	—	|	—	|	|	—	1
		27	26	25	24	23	22	21	20	19	18	17	16	15	14	13	12	11	10	9	8	7	6	5	4	3	2	1	

The design looks like this if you reverse the weft colors. Here, the warp A is red, and B is carnation. The weft is A carnation and B red.

SHADOW FERN

Draft charted by Deborah Jean Cohen

**The second potholder from the left shows the back side of this pattern.*

		B	A	B	A	B	A	B	A	B	A	B	A	B	A	B	A	B	A	
		18	17	16	15	14	13	12	11	10	9	8	7	6	5	4	3	2	1	
B	18	|	—	|	—	|	—	|	—	—	|	—	|	—	|	—	|	—	|	18
A	17	—	|	—	|	—	|	|	—	|	—	|	—	|	—	|	—	—	|	17
B	16	|	—	|	—	|	—	—	|	—	|	—	|	—	|	—	|	|	—	16
A	15	—	|	—	|	|	—	|	—	|	—	|	—	|	—	—	|	—	|	15
B	14	|	—	|	—	—	|	—	|	—	|	—	|	—	|	|	—	|	—	14
A	13	—	|	|	—	|	—	|	—	|	—	|	—	—	|	—	|	—	|	13
B	12	|	—	—	|	—	|	—	|	—	|	—	|	|	—	|	—	|	—	12
A	11	|	—	|	—	|	—	|	—	—	|	—	|	—	|	—	|	—	|	11
B	10	—	|	—	|	—	|	—	|	|	—	|	—	|	—	|	—	|	—	10
A	9	|	—	|	—	|	—	|	—	—	|	—	|	—	|	—	|	—	|	9
B	8	—	|	—	|	—	|	—	|	|	—	|	—	|	—	|	—	|	—	8
A	7	|	—	|	—	|	—	—	|	—	|	—	|	—	|	—	|	|	—	7
B	6	—	|	—	|	—	|	|	—	|	—	|	—	|	—	|	—	—	|	6
A	5	|	—	|	—	—	|	—	|	—	|	—	|	—	|	|	—	|	—	5
B	4	—	|	—	|	|	—	|	—	|	—	|	—	|	—	—	|	—	|	4
A	3	|	—	—	|	—	|	—	|	—	|	—	|	|	—	|	—	|	—	3
B	2	—	|	|	—	|	—	|	—	|	—	|	—	—	|	—	|	—	|	2
A	1	—	|	—	|	—	|	—	|	|	—	|	—	|	—	|	—	|	—	1
		18	17	16	15	14	13	12	11	10	9	8	7	6	5	4	3	2	1	

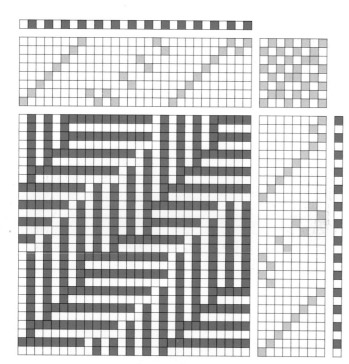

The original draft

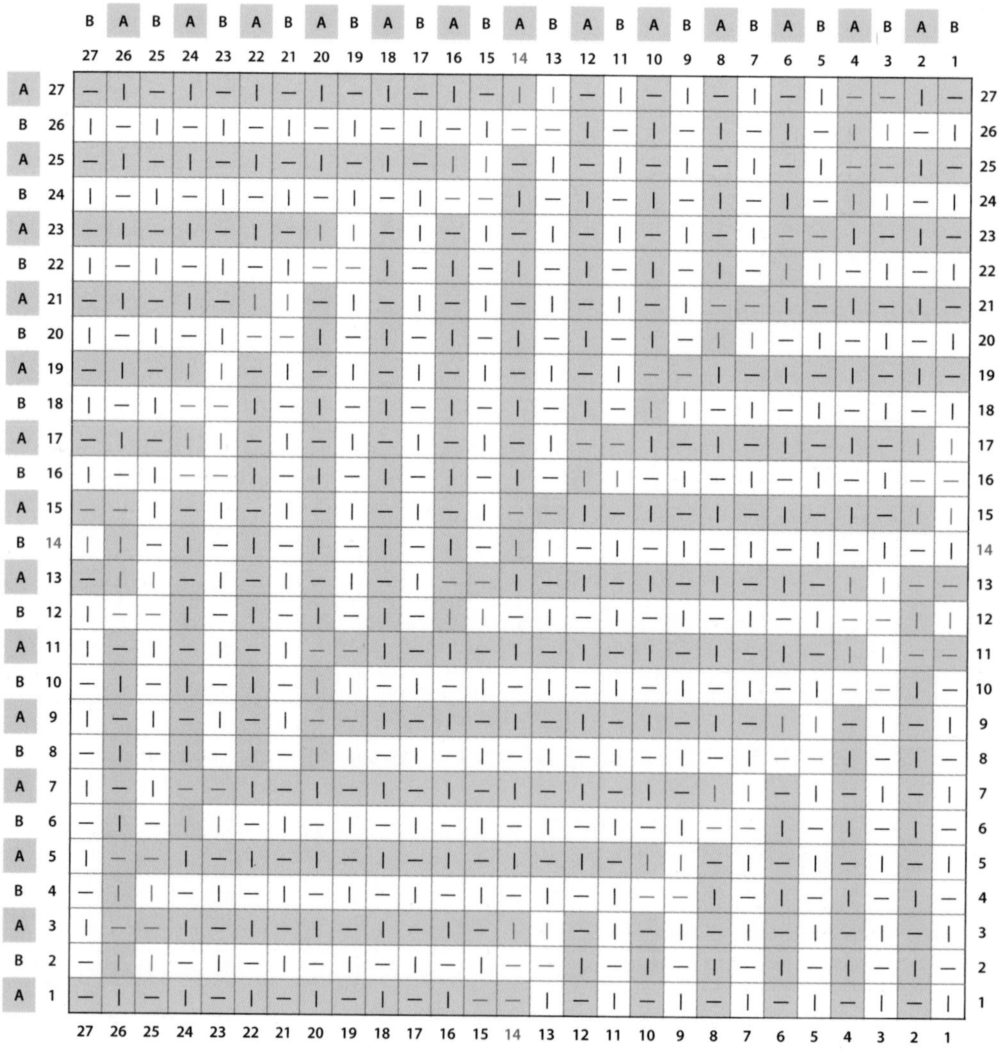

		B	A	B	A	B	A	B	A	B	A	B	A	B	A	B	A	B	A	B	A	B	A	B	A	B	A	B		
		27	26	25	24	23	22	21	20	19	18	17	16	15	14	13	12	11	10	9	8	7	6	5	4	3	2	1		
A	27																												27
B	26																												26

The original draft pattern continues across a 27 × 27 grid of interlacement symbols.

SHADOW SEAWEED

Draft charted by Deborah Jean Cohen

		B	A	B	A	B	A	B	A	B	A	B	A	B	A	B	A	B	A	
		18	17	16	15	14	13	12	11	10	9	8	7	6	5	4	3	2	1	
B	18	—	I	—	I	—	I	—	I	—	I	I	—	—	I	—	—	—	I	18
A	17	I	—	I	—	I	—	I	—	I	I	—	I	I	—	—	I	I	—	17
B	16	I	—	I	—	—	I	I	—	—	I	I	—	I	—	I	—	I	—	16
A	15	—	I	—	I	—	I	—	—	I	I	—	I	—	I	—	I	—	I	15
B	14	—	I	—	I	—	I	I	—	—	I	—	I	—	I	—	I	—	I	14
A	13	I	—	—	I	—	I	—	I	I	—	I	—	I	—	I	—	I	—	13
B	12	I	—	—	I	—	I	I	—	—	I	I	—	I	—	I	—	I	—	12
A	11	—	I	—	I	—	I	—	I	I	—	I	—	I	—	I	—	I	—	11
B	10	—	I	—	I	—	I	I	—	I	—	I	—	I	—	I	—	—	I	10
A	9	I	—	—	I	—	I	—	I	I	—	I	—	I	—	I	—	I	—	9
B	8	—	I	I	—	I	—	I	—	I	—	I	—	I	—	I	—	—	I	8
A	7	I	—	—	I	—	I	—	I	I	—	I	—	I	—	I	—	I	—	7
B	6	—	I	—	I	—	I	—	I	I	—	I	—	I	—	I	—	—	I	6
A	5	I	—	I	—	I	—	I	—	I	—	—	I	I	—	I	—	I	—	5
B	4	—	I	—	I	—	I	—	I	I	—	I	—	I	—	I	—	—	I	4
A	3	I	—	—	I	—	I	—	I	I	—	I	—	I	—	I	—	I	—	3
B	2	—	I	—	I	—	I	—	I	I	—	I	—	I	—	I	—	—	I	2
A	1	I	—	I	—	I	—	I	—	I	—	—	I	I	—	I	—	I	—	1
		18	17	16	15	14	13	12	11	10	9	8	7	6	5	4	3	2	1	

SHADOW KELP

Draft charted by Deborah Jean Cohen

		B	A	B	A	B	A	B	A	B	A	B	A	B	A	B	A	B	A	
		18	17	16	15	14	13	12	11	10	9	8	7	6	5	4	3	2	1	
B	18	—	I	—	I	I	—	I	—	—	I	—	I	I	—	I	—	—	I	18
A	17	I	—	I	—	—	I	—	I	I	—	I	—	—	I	—	I	I	—	17
B	16	I	—	—	I	—	I	I	—	—	I	—	I	I	—	I	—	I	—	16
A	15	—	I	I	—	I	—	—	I	—	I	I	—	I	—	—	I	—	I	15
B	14	I	—	I	—	—	I	—	I	I	—	I	—	—	I	—	I	I	—	14
A	13	—	I	—	I	I	—	I	—	—	I	—	I	I	—	I	—	—	I	13
B	12	I	—	I	—	—	I	—	I	I	—	I	—	—	I	—	I	I	—	12
A	11	I	—	—	I	—	I	I	—	—	I	—	I	I	—	I	—	I	—	11
B	10	—	I	—	I	I	—	I	—	—	I	—	I	I	—	I	—	—	I	10
A	9	I	—	I	—	—	I	—	I	I	—	I	—	—	I	—	I	I	—	9
B	8	I	—	—	I	—	I	I	—	—	I	—	I	I	—	I	—	I	—	8
A	7	—	I	I	—	I	—	—	I	—	I	I	—	—	I	—	I	—	I	7
B	6	I	—	I	—	—	I	—	I	I	—	I	—	—	I	—	I	I	—	6
A	5	—	I	—	I	I	—	I	—	—	I	—	I	I	—	I	—	—	I	5
B	4	—	I	—	I	I	—	I	—	—	I	—	I	I	—	I	—	—	I	4
A	3	I	—	—	I	—	I	I	—	—	I	—	I	I	—	I	—	I	—	3
B	2	—	I	—	I	I	—	I	—	—	I	—	I	I	—	I	—	—	I	2
A	1	I	—	I	—	—	I	—	I	I	—	I	—	—	I	—	I	I	—	1
		18	17	16	15	14	13	12	11	10	9	8	7	6	5	4	3	2	1	

X

From an Op Art painting, charted by Deborah Jean Cohen

SPIDER WOMAN'S CROSS

Draft charted by Deborah Jean Cohen

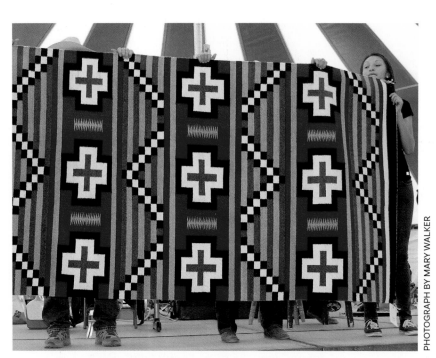

Spider Woman's Cross at the Hubbell auction

PHOTOGRAPH BY MARY WALKER

Spider Woman exists in different forms among Southwest Native American nations. To the Navajo Nation, she is Na'shjélii Asdzáá, who taught the Diné to use wool and weave. But she is much more than that: she was the first to weave the web of the universe.

This is a difficult design to weave, maybe the most difficult in this book. The many 2-floats that accommodate the pattern's angles require loops that have been tugged as much as they'll bear. Radical blocking helps (wet your weave thoroughly, and leave on the loom to dry overnight), and a mix of Friendly Loom loops with a sturdier loop (Solmate or Wool Novelty) stabilizes the structure. All of these techniques mitigate the draw-in that naturally occurs when there are 2 or more floats.

INSET SERIES: DIAMOND

Draft charted by Deborah Jean Cohen

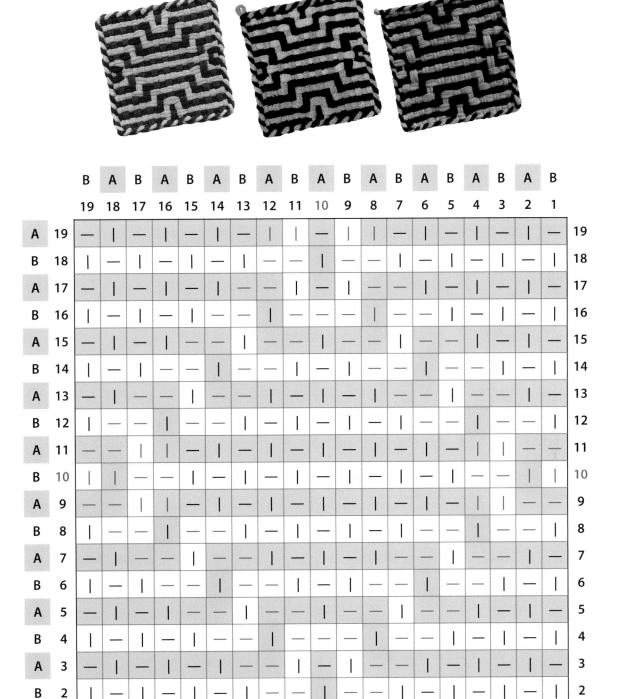

Original schematic. I changed the overall piece into the 19-peg (red outline) and 27-peg (yellow outline) charts.

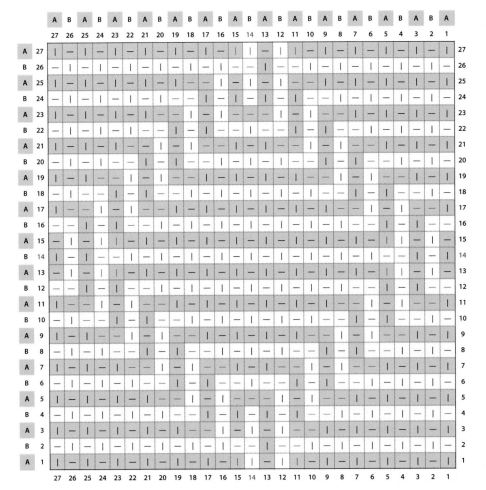

WALL DRAWING: TRIANGLE

Inspired by Sol LeWitt's Wall Drawing No. 370, 1982

Original design: Deborah Jean Cohen

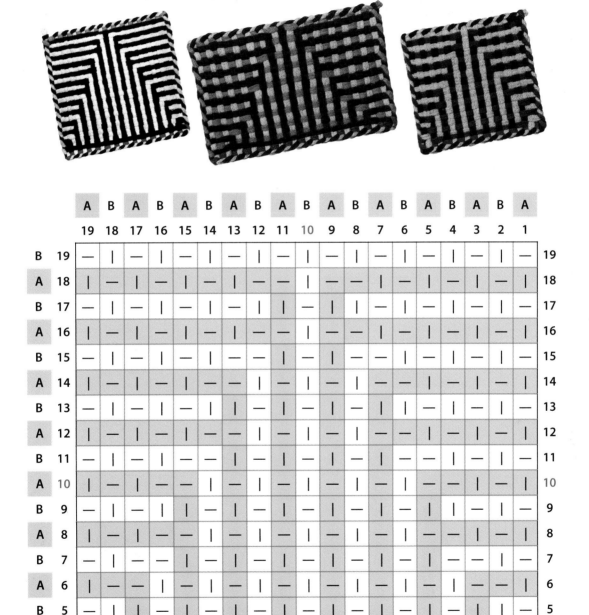

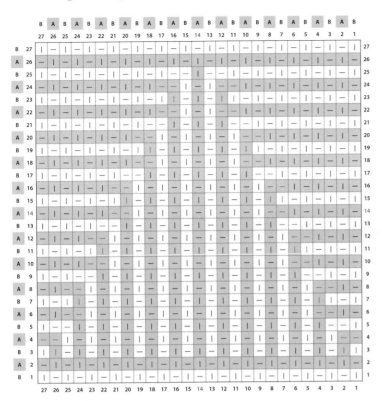

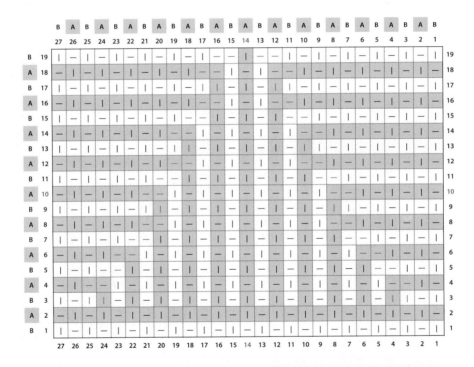

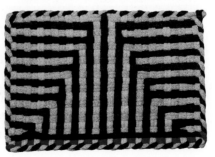

RESURRECTION

Original design: Deborah Jean Cohen

I began Resurrection in the fall of 2020, when I was just beginning to develop my charting method and hadn't charted many designs, either original or as draft adaptations. I wanted a cross for my aunt Jean but had difficulty with both design and stable structure. Resurrection was on and off the back burner until January 2022, when I finally was satisfied. This design is dedicated to Jean Boice.

		A	B	A	B	A	B	A	B	A	B	A	B	A	B	A	B	A	B	A	
		19	18	17	16	15	14	13	12	11	10	9	8	7	6	5	4	3	2	1	
A	19	|	—	—	|	—	|	—	—	|	—	|	—	—	|	—	|	—	—	|	19
B	18	—	|	—	—	|	—	|	—	—	|	—	—	|	—	|	—	—	|	—	18
A	17	—	—	|	—	—	|	—	|	—	—	—	|	—	|	—	—	|	—	—	17
B	16	|	—	—	|	—	—	|	—	|	—	|	—	|	—	—	|	—	—	|	16
A	15	—	|	—	—	|	—	—	|	—	|	—	|	—	—	|	—	—	|	—	15
B	14	|	—	|	—	—	|	—	—	|	—	|	—	—	|	—	—	|	—	|	14
A	13	—	|	—	|	|	—	|	—	—	|	|	—	|	—	|	|	—	|	—	13
B	12	|	—	|	—	|	|	—	|	—	—	—	|	—	|	|	—	|	—	|	12
A	11	—	|	—	|	—	—	|	—	|	|	—	—	|	—	—	|	—	|	—	11
B	10	|	—	|	—	—	|	—	—	|	—	|	—	—	|	—	—	|	—	|	10
A	9	—	|	—	—	|	—	—	|	—	|	—	|	—	—	|	—	—	|	—	9
B	8	|	—	—	|	—	—	|	—	|	—	|	—	|	—	—	|	—	—	|	8
A	7	—	—	|	—	—	|	—	|	—	|	—	|	—	|	—	—	|	—	—	7
B	6	—	|	—	—	|	—	|	—	|	—	|	—	|	—	|	—	—	|	—	6
A	5	|	—	—	|	—	|	—	|	—	|	—	|	—	|	—	|	—	—	|	5
B	4	—	—	|	—	|	—	|	—	|	—	|	—	|	—	|	—	|	—	—	4
A	3	|	|	—	|	—	|		|	—	|	—	|	—	|	—	|	—	|	|	3
B	2	|	—	|	—	|	—	|	—	|	—	|	—	|	—	|	—	|	—	|	2
A	1	—	|	—	|	—	|	—	|	—	—	—	|	—	|	—	|	—	|	—	1
		19	18	17	16	15	14	13	12	11	10	9	8	7	6	5	4	3	2	1	

POTHOLDER PATTERNS: TWILL AND TWILL-LIKE STRUCTURES

Twill is a weaving structure in which the weft passes over or under one or more threads, then over or under two or more threads, and so on, with an offset between rows. This method creates the distinguishing diagonal look of twill that you can see in your denim blue jeans. Blue jeans are also an example of a basic twill, in which the warp is one color (in blue jeans, white) and the weft another (in blue jeans, indigo). Check out your frayed jeans!

Because of the floats, twill will draw in more than plain weave and form a denser, stronger fabric: a reason why denim, a sturdy working fabric, is woven in this way. This characteristic also means that a twill potholder will be thicker and smaller than its plain weave counterpart woven on the same loom.

Twill weave is at least 5,000 years old. Minoan Crete frescoes of the Bronze Age (3000 BCE to 1500 BCE) showed women wearing various textile patterns, including allover patterns resembling twills and rose path twills. (Please reference E. J. W. Barber's *Prehistoric Textiles*, a fascinating book.)

Figure 6.1.
A twill draft

SPIRAL MAZE

Draft charted by Deborah Jean Cohen

	B	A	B	A	B	A	B	A	B	A	B	A	B	A	B	A	B	A	B	
	19	18	17	16	15	14	13	12	11	10	9	8	7	6	5	4	3	2	1	
A 19	I	I	—	—	I	I	—	I	I	—	—	I	I	—	—	I	I	—	—	19
B 18	—	I	I	—	—	I	I	—	—	I	—	—	I	I	—	—	I	I	—	—	18
A 17	—	—	I	I	—	—	I	I	—	—	I	I	—	—	I	I	—	—	I	17
B 16	I	—	—	I	I	—	—	I	I	—	I	—	—	I	I	—	—	I	I	16
A 15	I	I	—	—	I	I	—	—	I	I	—	—	I	I	—	—	I	I	—	15
B 14	—	I	I	—	—	I	I	—	—	I	I	—	—	I	I	—	—	I	I	—	14
A 13	—	—	I	I	—	—	I	I	—	—	I	I	—	—	I	I	—	—	I	13
B 12	I	—	—	I	I	—	—	I	I	—	I	—	—	I	I	—	—	I	I	12
A 11	I	I	—	—	I	I	—	—	I	I	—	—	I	I	—	—	I	I	—	11
B 10	—	I	I	—	—	I	I	—	—	I	I	—	—	I	I	—	—	I	I	10
A 9	—	I	—	I	—	—	I	I	—	—	I	I	—	—	I	I	—	—	I	9
B 8	I	I	—	—	I	I	—	—	I	I	—	—	I	I	—	—	I	I	—	8
A 7	I	—	—	I	I	—	—	I	I	—	—	I	I	—	—	I	I	—	I	7
B 6	—	—	I	I	—	—	I	I	—	—	I	I	—	—	I	I	—	—	I	6
A 5	—	I	I	—	—	I	I	—	—	I	—	I	I	—	—	I	I	—	—	5
B 4	I	I	—	—	I	I	—	—	I	I	—	—	I	I	—	—	I	I	—	4
A 3	I	—	—	I	I	—	—	I	I	—	I	—	—	I	I	—	—	I	I	3
B 2	—	—	I	I	—	—	I	I	—	—	I	I	—	—	I	I	—	—	I	2
A 1	—	I	I	—	—	I	I	—	—	I	I	—	—	I	I	—	—	I	I	1
	19	18	17	16	15	14	13	12	11	10	9	8	7	6	5	4	3	2	1	

		B	A	B	A	B	A	B	A	B	A	B	A	B	A	B	A	B	A	B	A	B	A	B	A	B	A	B	
		27	26	25	24	23	22	21	20	19	18	17	16	15	14	13	12	11	10	9	8	7	6	5	4	3	2	1	

B	27
A	26
B	25
A	24
B	23
A	22
B	21
A	20
B	19
A	18
B	17
A	16
B	15
A	14
B	13
A	12
B	11
A	10
B	9
A	8
B	7
A	6
B	5
A	4
B	3
A	2
B	1

27 26 25 24 23 22 21 20 19 18 17 16 15 14 13 12 11 10 9 8 7 6 5 4 3 2 1

DIAMOND BURST

Draft charted by Deborah Jean Cohen

Weave **UNDER** gray. Weave **OVER** white.

LEAF

Draft charted by Deborah Jean Cohen

Weave **UNDER** white and **OVER** gray, except where noted.

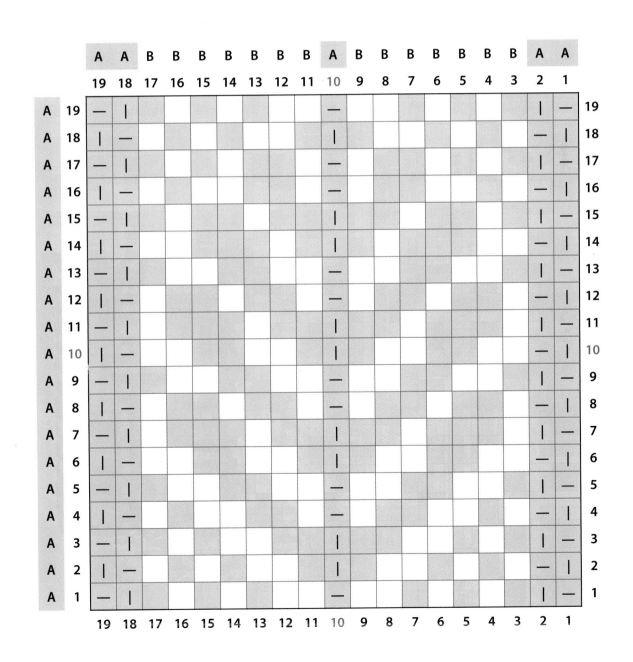

DIAMOND MIX
Draft charted by Christine Olsen Reis

Weave **UNDER** gray and **OVER** white.

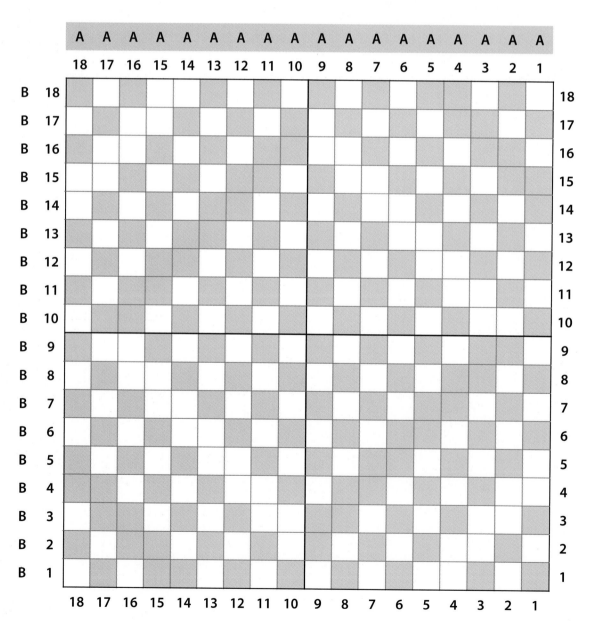

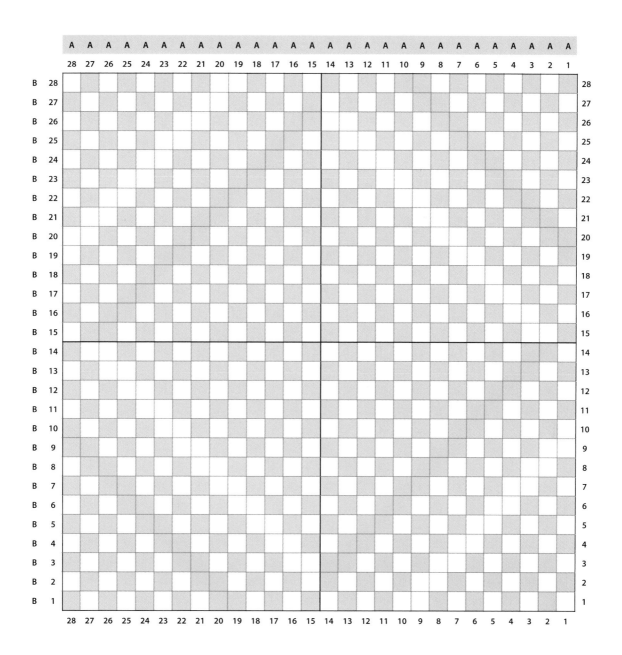

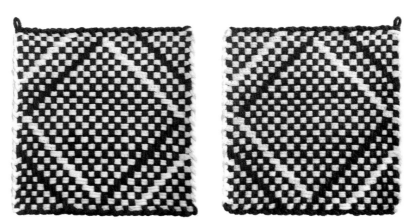

Front and back are the same!

DIAMOND REPEAT

Draft charted by Deborah Jean Cohen

Weave **UNDER** gray and **OVER** white.

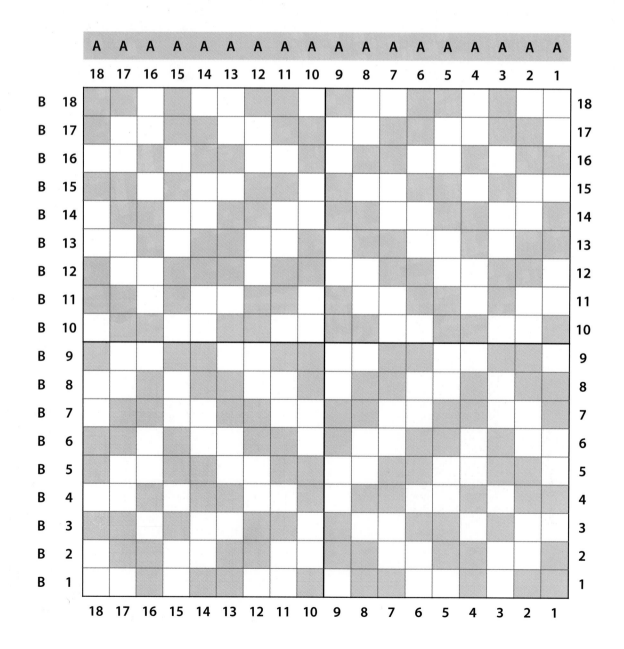

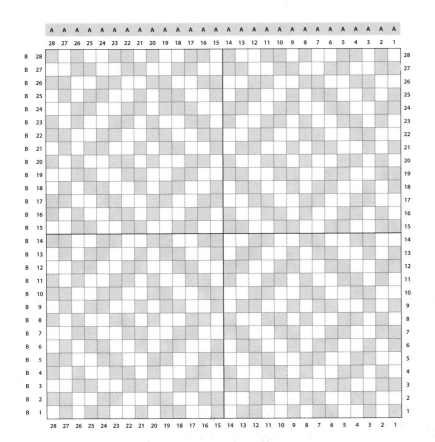

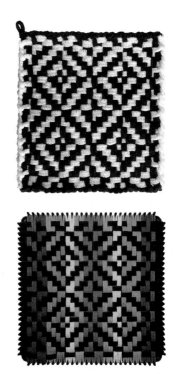

DIAMOND ROSE

Handweaving.net #4174, charted by Christine Olsen Reis

Weave **UNDER** gray and **OVER** white.

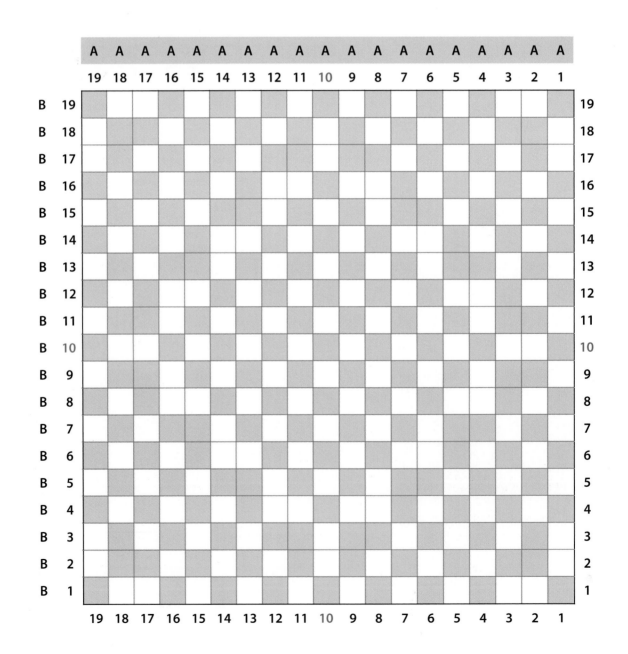

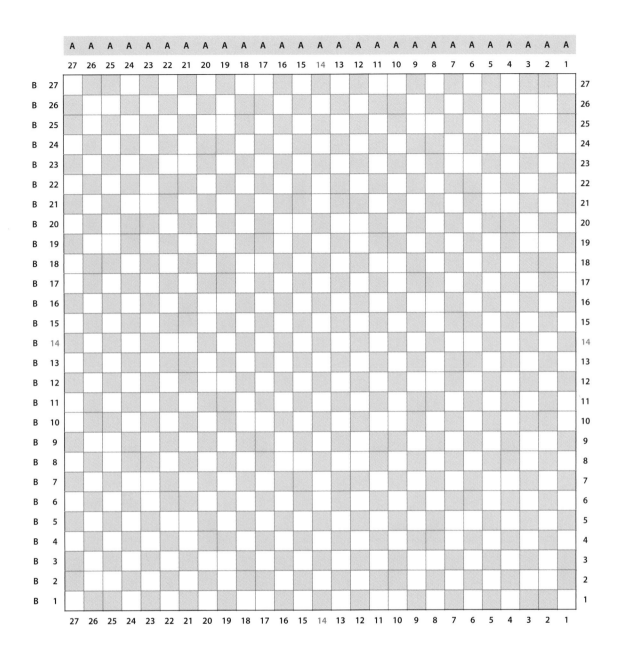

DIAMOND TWILL

Weave **UNDER** gray and **OVER** white.

The second potholder from the left shows the back side of this pattern.

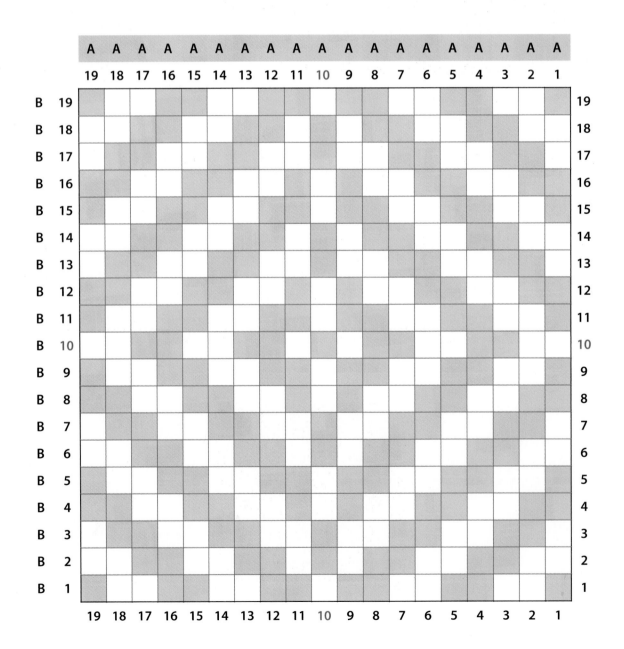

27 26 25 24 23 22 21 20 19 18 17 16 15 14 13 12 11 10 9 8 7 6 5 4 3 2 1

B	27	27
B	26	26
B	25	25
B	24	24
B	23	23
B	22	22
B	21	21
B	20	20
B	19	19
B	18	18
B	17	17
B	16	16
B	15	15
B	14	14
B	13	13
B	12	12
B	11	11
B	10	10
B	9	9
B	8	8
B	7	7
B	6	6
B	5	5
B	4	4
B	3	3
B	2	2
B	1	1

27 26 25 24 23 22 21 20 19 18 17 16 15 14 13 12 11 10 9 8 7 6 5 4 3 2 1

FLOWERS FOR JEAN

Original design: Andréa Scheidler

		C	B	A	A	B	B	A	A	B	B	A	A	B	B	A	A	B	C	
		18	17	16	15	14	13	12	11	10	9	8	7	6	5	4	3	2	1	
C	18																			18
B	17																			17
A	16																			16
A	15																			15
B	14																			14
B	13																			13
A	12																			12
A	11																			11
B	10																			10
B	9																			9
A	8																			8
A	7																			7
B	6																			6
B	5																			5
A	4																			4
A	3																			3
B	2																			2
C	1																			1
		18	17	16	15	14	13	12	11	10	9	8	7	6	5	4	3	2	1	

Andréa's design is lovely plain or with embroidered French knots for flower centers. This is a fast, easy weave, a lot of fun, and relaxing.

RUFFLES

Original design: Andréa Scheidler

The second potholder from the left shows the back side of this pattern.

		B	B	A	A	A	B	C	B	A	A	A	B	C	B	A	A	A	B	B	
		19	18	17	16	15	14	13	12	11	10	9	8	7	6	5	4	3	2	1	
B	19	—	I	—	I	—	I	—	I	—	I	—	I	—	I	—	I	—	I	—	19
B	18	I	—	I	—	I	—	I	—	I	—	I	—	I	—	I	—	I	—	I	18
B	17	—	—	I	—	I	—	I	—	I	—	I	—	I	—	I	—	I	—	—	17
B	16	I	I	—	I	—	I	—	I	—	I	—	I	—	I	—	I	—	I	I	16
B	15	I	—	I	—	I	—	I	—	I	—	I	—	I	—	I	—	I	—	I	15
B	14	I	—	I	—	I	—	I	—	I	—	I	—	I	—	I	—	I	—	I	14
B	13	—	I	—	I	—	I	—	I	—	I	—	I	—	I	—	I	—	I	—	13
B	12	I	—	I	—	I	—	I	—	I	—	I	—	I	—	I	—	I	—	I	12
B	11	I	—	I	—	I	—	I	—	I	—	I	—	I	—	I	—	I	—	I	11
B	10	I	I	—	I	—	I	—	I	—	I	—	I	—	I	—	I	—	I	I	10
B	9	—	—	I	—	I	—	I	—	I	—	I	—	I	—	I	—	I	—	—	9
B	8	I	—	I	—	I	—	I	—	I	—	I	—	I	—	I	—	I	—	I	8
B	7	—	I	—	I	—	I	—	I	—	I	—	I	—	I	—	I	—	I	—	7
B	6	I	—	I	—	I	—	I	—	I	—	I	—	I	—	I	—	I	—	I	6
B	5	—	—	I	—	I	—	I	—	I	—	I	—	I	—	I	—	I	—	—	5
B	4	I	I	—	I	—	I	—	I	—	I	—	I	—	I	—	I	—	I	I	4
B	3	—	—	I	—	I	—	I	—	I	—	I	—	I	—	I	—	I	—	—	3
B	2	I	—	I	—	I	—	I	—	I	—	I	—	I	—	I	—	I	—	I	2
B	1	—	I	—	I	—	I	—	I	—	I	—	I	—	I	—	I	—	I	—	1
		19	18	17	16	15	14	13	12	11	10	9	8	7	6	5	4	3	2	1	

DESERT BORDERED DIAMOND

Original design: Christine Olsen Reis

Weave **OVER** gray and **UNDER** white, except where noted.

	A	A	A	B	B	B	B	B	B	B	B	B	B	B	B	B	A	A	A	
	19	18	17	16	15	14	13	12	11	10	9	8	7	6	5	4	3	2	1	
A 19	—			—															—			—	19
A 18			—			—														—			—			18
A 17	—			—															—			—	17
A 16			—			—	—										—	—			—			16
A 15	—			—															—			—	15
A 14			—																			—			14
A 13	—			—															—			—	13
A 12			—			—	—										—	—			—			12
A 11			—																			—	11
A 10			—																				—			10
A 9	—																			—			—	9
A 8			—														—			—			8
A 7	—			—															—			—	7
A 6			—																			—			6
A 5	—			—															—			—	5
A 4			—			—	—										—	—			—			4
A 3	—			—															—			—	3
A 2			—			—															—			2
A 1				—																—			1
	19	18	17	16	15	14	13	12	11	10	9	8	7	6	5	4	3	2	1	

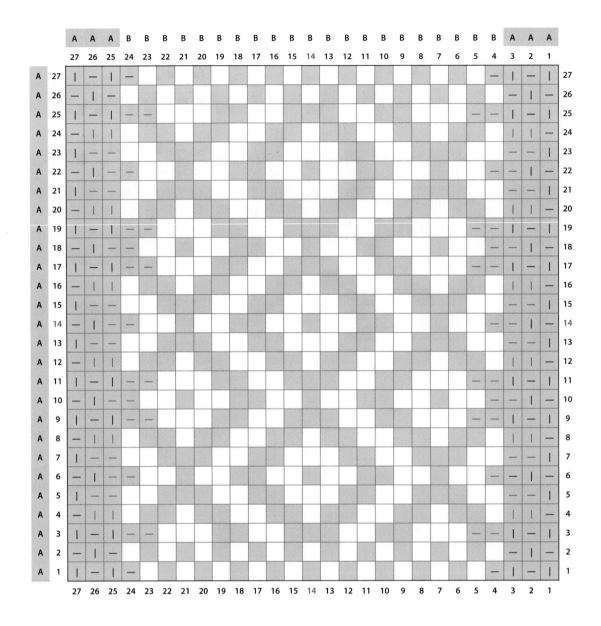

INSPO

Draft charted by Christine Olsen Reis

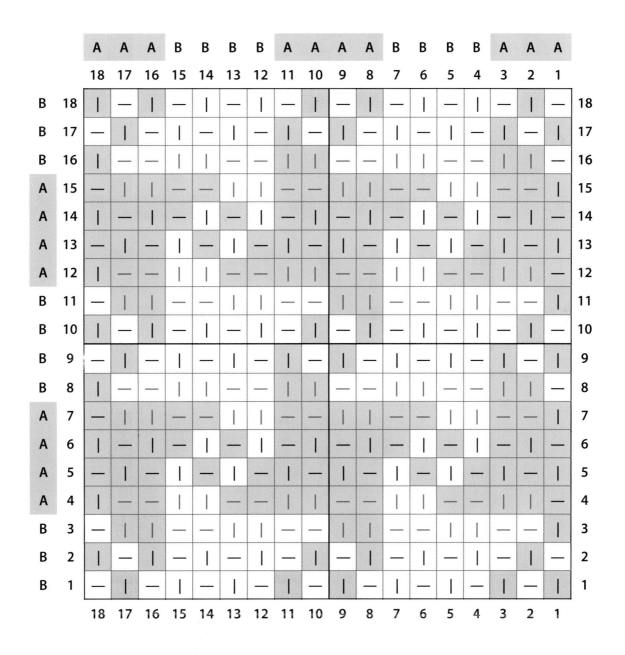

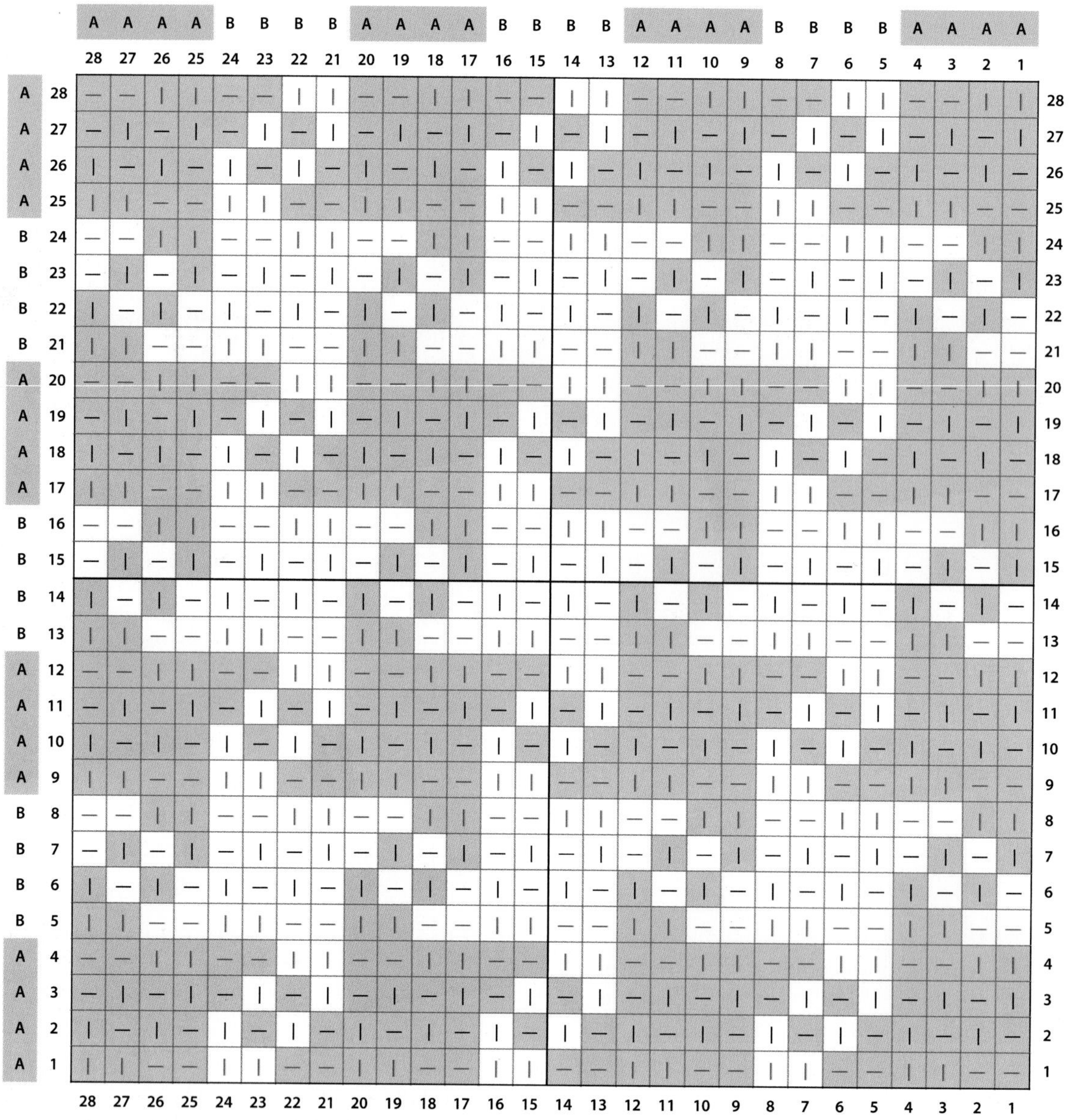
A A A A B B B B A A A A B B B B A A A A B B B B A A A A
28 27 26 25 24 23 22 21 20 19 18 17 16 15 14 13 12 11 10 9 8 7 6 5 4 3 2 1
A 28
A 27
A 26
A 25
B 24
B 23
B 22
B 21
A 20
A 19
A 18
A 17
B 16
B 15
B 14
B 13
A 12
A 11
A 10
A 9
B 8
B 7
B 6
B 5
A 4
A 3
A 2
A 1

BRANCHING
Original design: Christine Olsen Reis

Weave **UNDER** gray and **OVER** white.

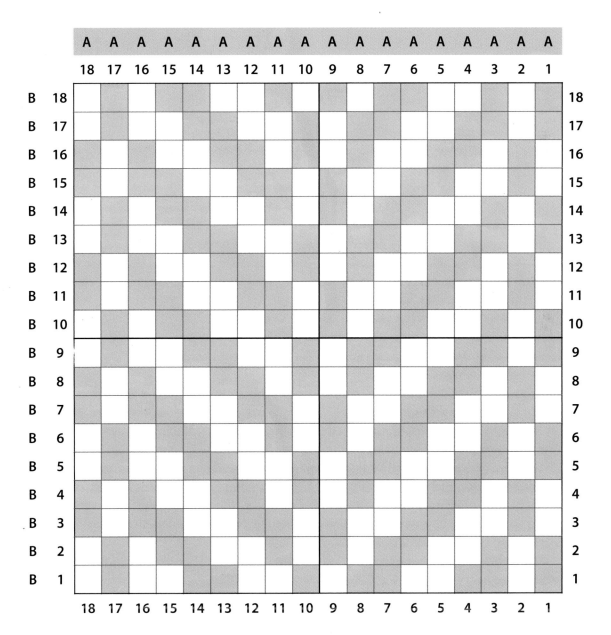

MOD

Original design: Christine Olsen Reis

		B	A	B	A	B	A	B	A	B	A	B	A	B	A	B	A	B	A	
		18	17	16	15	14	13	12	11	10	9	8	7	6	5	4	3	2	1	
A	18	—	│	│	—	—	│	│	—	│	│	—	—	│	│	—	—	│	18
A	17	—	—	│	—	│	│	—	│	—	│	—	│	│	—	│	—	—	17
A	16	│	—	—	│	│	—	│	│	—	—	│	│	—	—	│	│	—	16
B	15	│	│	—	│	—	—	│	—	│	—	│	—	—	│	—	│	│	15
B	14	—	│	│	—	—	│	│	—	—	│	│	—	—	│	—	—	│	14
B	13	—	—	│	—	│	│	—	│	—	│	—	│	—	—	│	—	—	13
B	12	│	—	—	│	│	—	│	│	—	│	—	│	—	—	│	│	—	12
A	11	│	—	—	│	—	—	│	—	│	—	│	—	—	│	—	│	│	11
A	10	—	│	│	—	—	│	│	—	│	—	—	—	│	—	—	—	│	10
A	9	—	—	│	—	—	—	│	│	—	│	—	—	—	│	—	—	│	9
A	8	│	—	—	│	│	—	│	│	—	—	│	—	—	│	│	—	│	8
B	7	│	│	—	│	—	—	│	—	│	—	│	—	—	│	—	│	│	7
B	6	—	│	│	—	—	│	│	—	│	│	—	—	│	—	—	—	│	6
B	5	│	—	│	—	│	—	│	—	│	—	│	—	│	—	│	—	—	5
B	4	│	—	—	│	—	│	—	│	│	—	│	—	—	│	│	—	—	4
A	3	│	│	—	│	—	│	—	│	—	│	—	│	—	—	│	│	│	3
A	2	—	│	│	—	│	│	—	│	—	│	│	—	—	│	—	—	│	2
A	1	—	—	│	—	│	│	—	│	—	│	—	│	—	—	│	—	—	1
		18	17	16	15	14	13	12	11	10	9	8	7	6	5	4	3	2	1	

Mod continued

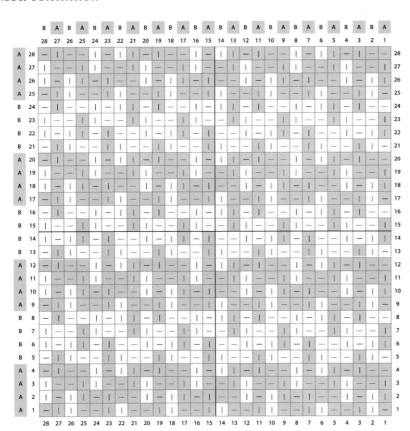

CIRCLE 1

Handweaving.net #6351, charted by Deborah Jean Cohen

Weave **UNDER** gray and **OVER** white.

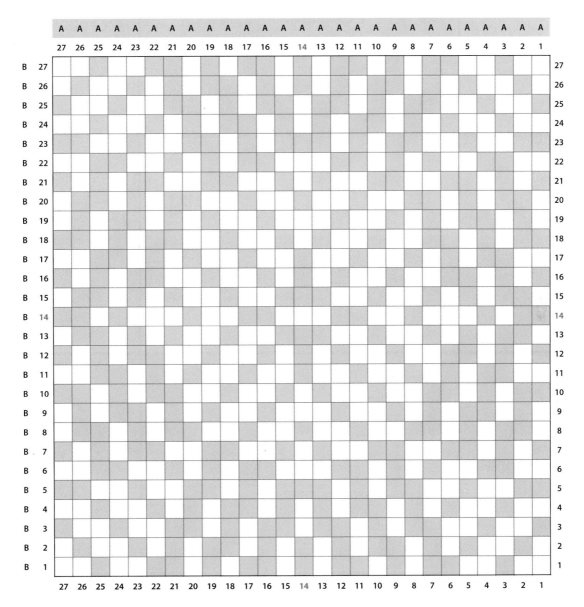

CIRCLE 2

Handweaving.net #6351, adapted by Deborah Jean Cohen

Weave **UNDER** gray and **OVER** white.

TWILL X

Draft charted by Deborah Jean Cohen

Weave **UNDER** gray and **OVER** white.

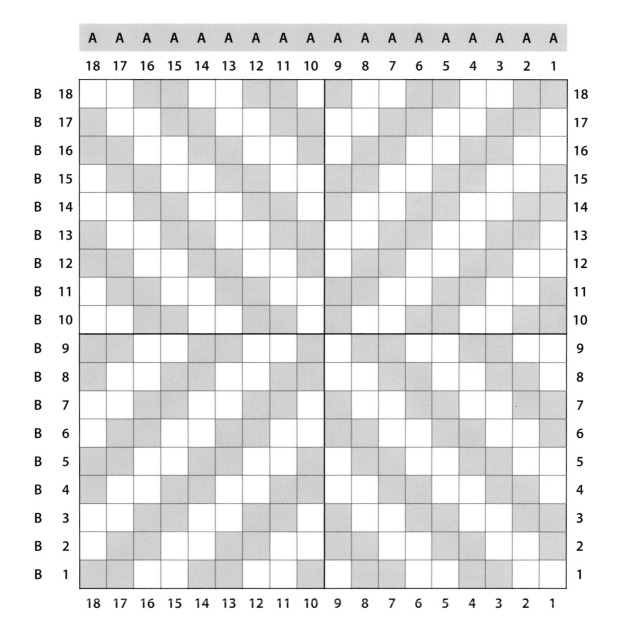

SHURIKEN

Draft charted by Deborah Jean Cohen

<table>
<tr><td></td><td></td><td>A</td><td>A</td><td>A</td><td>B</td><td>B</td><td>B</td><td>B</td><td>A</td><td>A</td><td>A</td><td>A</td><td>B</td><td>B</td><td>B</td><td>B</td><td>A</td><td>A</td><td>A</td><td></td></tr>
<tr><td></td><td></td><td>18</td><td>17</td><td>16</td><td>15</td><td>14</td><td>13</td><td>12</td><td>11</td><td>10</td><td>9</td><td>8</td><td>7</td><td>6</td><td>5</td><td>4</td><td>3</td><td>2</td><td>1</td><td></td></tr>
<tr><td>A</td><td>18</td><td>—</td><td>—</td><td>|</td><td>—</td><td>|</td><td>|</td><td>—</td><td>|</td><td>—</td><td>—</td><td>|</td><td>—</td><td>|</td><td>|</td><td>—</td><td>|</td><td>—</td><td>—</td><td>18</td></tr>
<tr><td>A</td><td>17</td><td>|</td><td>—</td><td>—</td><td>|</td><td>|</td><td>—</td><td>—</td><td>|</td><td>|</td><td>—</td><td>—</td><td>|</td><td>|</td><td>—</td><td>—</td><td>|</td><td>|</td><td>—</td><td>17</td></tr>
<tr><td>A</td><td>16</td><td>|</td><td>|</td><td>—</td><td>|</td><td>—</td><td>—</td><td>|</td><td>—</td><td>|</td><td>|</td><td>—</td><td>|</td><td>—</td><td>—</td><td>|</td><td>—</td><td>|</td><td>|</td><td>16</td></tr>
<tr><td>B</td><td>15</td><td>—</td><td>|</td><td>|</td><td>—</td><td>—</td><td>|</td><td>|</td><td>—</td><td>—</td><td>|</td><td>|</td><td>—</td><td>—</td><td>|</td><td>|</td><td>—</td><td>—</td><td>|</td><td>15</td></tr>
<tr><td>B</td><td>14</td><td>—</td><td>—</td><td>|</td><td>—</td><td>|</td><td>|</td><td>—</td><td>|</td><td>—</td><td>—</td><td>|</td><td>—</td><td>|</td><td>|</td><td>—</td><td>|</td><td>—</td><td>—</td><td>14</td></tr>
<tr><td>B</td><td>13</td><td>|</td><td>—</td><td>—</td><td>|</td><td>|</td><td>—</td><td>—</td><td>|</td><td>|</td><td>—</td><td>—</td><td>|</td><td>|</td><td>—</td><td>—</td><td>|</td><td>|</td><td>—</td><td>13</td></tr>
<tr><td>B</td><td>12</td><td>|</td><td>|</td><td>—</td><td>|</td><td>—</td><td>—</td><td>|</td><td>—</td><td>|</td><td>|</td><td>—</td><td>|</td><td>—</td><td>—</td><td>|</td><td>—</td><td>|</td><td>|</td><td>12</td></tr>
<tr><td>A</td><td>11</td><td>—</td><td>|</td><td>|</td><td>—</td><td>—</td><td>|</td><td>|</td><td>—</td><td>—</td><td>|</td><td>|</td><td>—</td><td>—</td><td>|</td><td>|</td><td>—</td><td>—</td><td>|</td><td>11</td></tr>
<tr><td>A</td><td>10</td><td>—</td><td>—</td><td>|</td><td>—</td><td>|</td><td>|</td><td>—</td><td>|</td><td>—</td><td>—</td><td>|</td><td>—</td><td>|</td><td>|</td><td>—</td><td>|</td><td>—</td><td>—</td><td>10</td></tr>
<tr><td>A</td><td>9</td><td>|</td><td>—</td><td>—</td><td>|</td><td>|</td><td>—</td><td>—</td><td>|</td><td>|</td><td>—</td><td>—</td><td>|</td><td>|</td><td>—</td><td>—</td><td>|</td><td>|</td><td>—</td><td>9</td></tr>
<tr><td>A</td><td>8</td><td>|</td><td>|</td><td>—</td><td>|</td><td>—</td><td>—</td><td>|</td><td>—</td><td>|</td><td>|</td><td>—</td><td>|</td><td>—</td><td>—</td><td>|</td><td>—</td><td>|</td><td>|</td><td>8</td></tr>
<tr><td>B</td><td>7</td><td>—</td><td>|</td><td>|</td><td>—</td><td>—</td><td>|</td><td>|</td><td>—</td><td>—</td><td>|</td><td>|</td><td>—</td><td>—</td><td>|</td><td>|</td><td>—</td><td>—</td><td>|</td><td>7</td></tr>
<tr><td>B</td><td>6</td><td>—</td><td>—</td><td>|</td><td>—</td><td>|</td><td>|</td><td>—</td><td>|</td><td>—</td><td>—</td><td>|</td><td>—</td><td>|</td><td>|</td><td>—</td><td>|</td><td>—</td><td>—</td><td>6</td></tr>
<tr><td>B</td><td>5</td><td>|</td><td>—</td><td>—</td><td>|</td><td>|</td><td>—</td><td>—</td><td>|</td><td>|</td><td>—</td><td>—</td><td>|</td><td>|</td><td>—</td><td>—</td><td>|</td><td>|</td><td>—</td><td>5</td></tr>
<tr><td>B</td><td>4</td><td>|</td><td>|</td><td>—</td><td>|</td><td>—</td><td>—</td><td>|</td><td>—</td><td>|</td><td>|</td><td>—</td><td>|</td><td>—</td><td>—</td><td>|</td><td>—</td><td>|</td><td>|</td><td>4</td></tr>
<tr><td>A</td><td>3</td><td>—</td><td>|</td><td>|</td><td>—</td><td>—</td><td>|</td><td>|</td><td>—</td><td>—</td><td>|</td><td>|</td><td>—</td><td>—</td><td>|</td><td>|</td><td>—</td><td>—</td><td>|</td><td>3</td></tr>
<tr><td>A</td><td>2</td><td>—</td><td>—</td><td>|</td><td>—</td><td>|</td><td>|</td><td>—</td><td>|</td><td>—</td><td>—</td><td>|</td><td>—</td><td>|</td><td>|</td><td>—</td><td>|</td><td>—</td><td>—</td><td>2</td></tr>
<tr><td>A</td><td>1</td><td>|</td><td>—</td><td>—</td><td>|</td><td>|</td><td>—</td><td>—</td><td>|</td><td>|</td><td>—</td><td>—</td><td>|</td><td>|</td><td>—</td><td>—</td><td>|</td><td>|</td><td>—</td><td>1</td></tr>
<tr><td></td><td></td><td>18</td><td>17</td><td>16</td><td>15</td><td>14</td><td>13</td><td>12</td><td>11</td><td>10</td><td>9</td><td>8</td><td>7</td><td>6</td><td>5</td><td>4</td><td>3</td><td>2</td><td>1</td><td></td></tr>
</table>

Chart 1 (top):

Top color sequence: A A A A | B B B B | A A A A A | B B B B B | A A A A A | B B B B | A A A

	27	26	25	24	23	22	21	20	19	18	17	16	15	14	13	12	11	10	9	8	7	6	5	4	3	2	1	
A 27																												27
A 26																												26
A 25																												25
A 24																												24
B 23																												23
B 22																												22
B 21																												21
B 20																												20
A 19																												19
A 18																												18
A 17																												17
A 16																												16
B 15																												15
B 14																												14
B 13																												13
B 12																												12
A 11																												11
A 10																												10
A 9																												9
A 8																												8
B 7																												7
B 6																												6
B 5																												5
B 4																												4
A 3																												3
A 2																												2
A 1																												1

Bottom: 27 26 25 24 23 22 21 20 19 18 17 16 15 14 13 12 11 10 9 8 7 6 5 4 3 2 1

Chart 2 (bottom):

Top color sequence: A A A | B B B B | A A A A | B B B B | A A A

	18	17	16	15	14	13	12	11	10	9	8	7	6	5	4	3	2	1	
A 27																			27
A 26																			26
A 25																			25
A 24																			24
B 23																			23
B 22																			22
B 21																			21
B 20																			20
A 19																			19
A 18																			18
A 17																			17
A 16																			16
B 15																			15
B 14																			14
B 13																			13
B 12																			12
A 11																			11
A 10																			10
A 9																			9
A 8																			8
B 7																			7
B 6																			6
B 5																			5
B 4																			4
A 3																			3
A 2																			2
A 1																			1

Bottom: 18 17 16 15 14 13 12 11 10 9 8 7 6 5 4 3 2 1

INSET SERIES: SQUARE

2 x 2 twill, inset in different directions

Original design: Deborah Jean Cohen

Weave **UNDER** gray and **OVER** white.

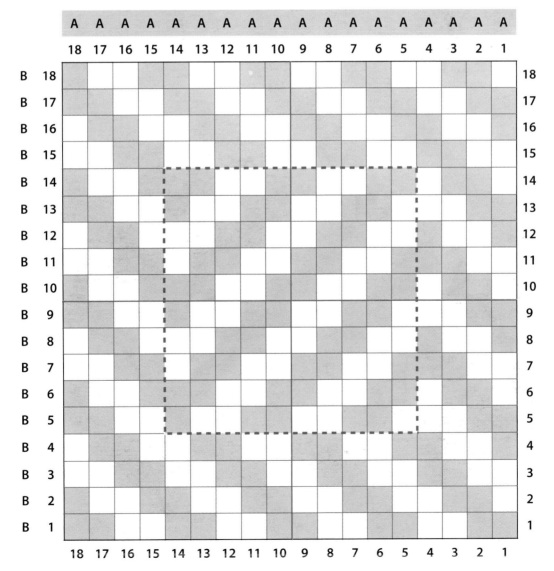

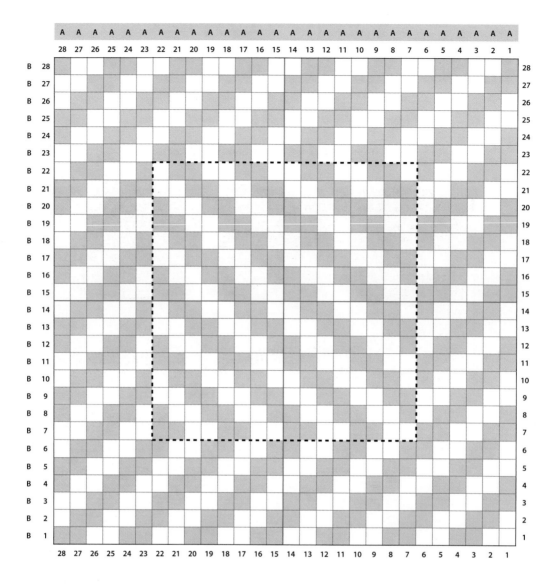

INSET SERIES: TWO RECTANGLES

2 x 2 twill, inset in different directions

Original design: Deborah Jean Cohen

Weave **UNDER** gray and **OVER** white.

INSET SERIES:
FOUR SQUARES

2 x 2 twill, inset in different directions

Original design: Deborah Jean Cohen

Weave **UNDER** gray and **OVER** white.

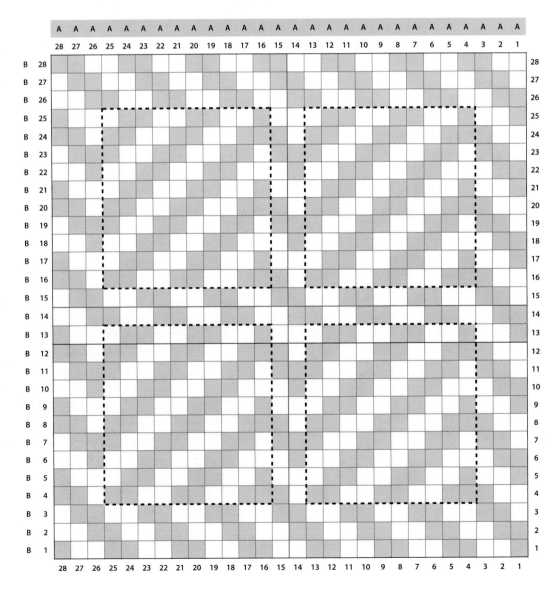

WAVY CHEVRON TWILL

Weave **OVER** gray and **UNDER** white.

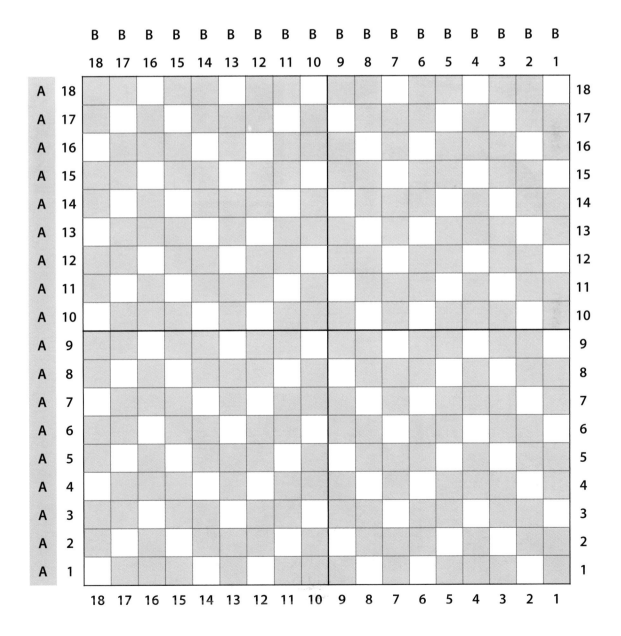

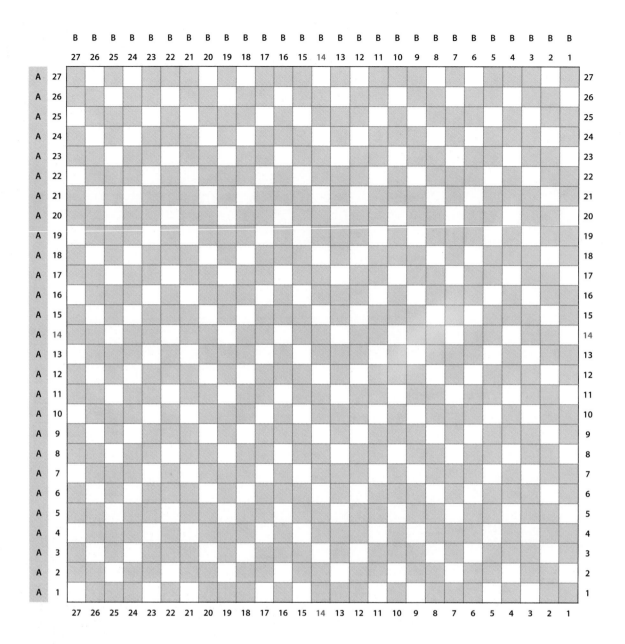

SCATTERED TWILL (BROKEN TWILL)

Original design: Deborah Jean Cohen

Weave **UNDER** gray and **OVER** white.

REFLECTIONS

Draft charted by Christine Olsen Reis

Weave **UNDER** gray and **OVER** white.

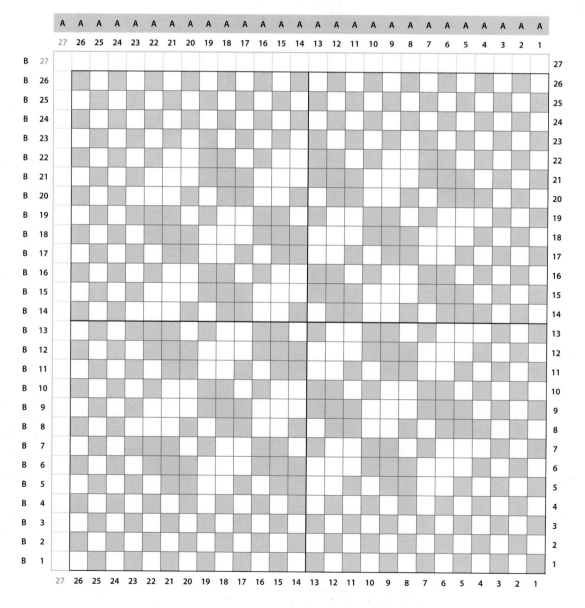

BIRDS FLYING HIGH

Original design: Angela West

<table>
<tr><td></td><td></td><td>A</td><td>B</td><td>A</td><td>B</td><td>A</td><td>B</td><td>A</td><td>B</td><td>A</td><td>B</td><td>A</td><td>B</td><td>A</td><td>B</td><td>A</td><td>B</td><td>A</td><td>B</td><td>A</td><td></td></tr>
<tr><td></td><td></td><td>19</td><td>18</td><td>17</td><td>16</td><td>15</td><td>14</td><td>13</td><td>12</td><td>11</td><td>10</td><td>9</td><td>8</td><td>7</td><td>6</td><td>5</td><td>4</td><td>3</td><td>2</td><td>1</td><td></td></tr>
<tr><td>A</td><td>19</td><td>|</td><td>—</td><td>|</td><td>|</td><td>—</td><td>|</td><td>—</td><td>—</td><td>|</td><td>|</td><td>—</td><td>|</td><td>—</td><td>—</td><td>|</td><td>|</td><td>—</td><td>|</td><td>—</td><td>19</td></tr>
<tr><td>B</td><td>18</td><td>—</td><td>|</td><td>|</td><td>—</td><td>|</td><td>—</td><td>—</td><td>|</td><td>|</td><td>—</td><td>|</td><td>—</td><td>—</td><td>|</td><td>|</td><td>—</td><td>|</td><td>—</td><td>—</td><td>18</td></tr>
<tr><td>A</td><td>17</td><td>|</td><td>|</td><td>—</td><td>—</td><td>|</td><td>—</td><td>|</td><td>|</td><td>—</td><td>—</td><td>|</td><td>—</td><td>|</td><td>|</td><td>—</td><td>—</td><td>|</td><td>—</td><td>|</td><td>17</td></tr>
<tr><td>B</td><td>16</td><td>|</td><td>—</td><td>—</td><td>|</td><td>—</td><td>|</td><td>|</td><td>—</td><td>—</td><td>|</td><td>—</td><td>|</td><td>|</td><td>—</td><td>—</td><td>|</td><td>—</td><td>|</td><td>|</td><td>16</td></tr>
<tr><td>A</td><td>15</td><td>—</td><td>—</td><td>|</td><td>—</td><td>—</td><td>|</td><td>—</td><td>—</td><td>|</td><td>—</td><td>—</td><td>|</td><td>—</td><td>—</td><td>|</td><td>—</td><td>—</td><td>|</td><td>—</td><td>15</td></tr>
<tr><td>B</td><td>14</td><td>|</td><td>|</td><td>—</td><td>|</td><td>|</td><td>—</td><td>|</td><td>|</td><td>—</td><td>|</td><td>|</td><td>—</td><td>|</td><td>|</td><td>—</td><td>|</td><td>|</td><td>—</td><td>|</td><td>14</td></tr>
<tr><td>A</td><td>13</td><td>—</td><td>—</td><td>|</td><td>|</td><td>—</td><td>|</td><td>—</td><td>—</td><td>|</td><td>|</td><td>—</td><td>|</td><td>—</td><td>—</td><td>|</td><td>|</td><td>—</td><td>|</td><td>—</td><td>13</td></tr>
<tr><td>B</td><td>12</td><td>—</td><td>|</td><td>|</td><td>—</td><td>|</td><td>—</td><td>—</td><td>|</td><td>|</td><td>—</td><td>|</td><td>—</td><td>—</td><td>|</td><td>|</td><td>—</td><td>|</td><td>—</td><td>—</td><td>12</td></tr>
<tr><td>A</td><td>11</td><td>|</td><td>|</td><td>—</td><td>—</td><td>|</td><td>—</td><td>|</td><td>|</td><td>—</td><td>—</td><td>|</td><td>—</td><td>|</td><td>|</td><td>—</td><td>—</td><td>|</td><td>—</td><td>|</td><td>11</td></tr>
<tr><td>B</td><td>10</td><td>|</td><td>—</td><td>—</td><td>|</td><td>—</td><td>|</td><td>|</td><td>—</td><td>—</td><td>|</td><td>—</td><td>|</td><td>|</td><td>—</td><td>—</td><td>|</td><td>—</td><td>|</td><td>|</td><td>10</td></tr>
<tr><td>A</td><td>9</td><td>—</td><td>—</td><td>|</td><td>—</td><td>—</td><td>|</td><td>—</td><td>—</td><td>|</td><td>—</td><td>—</td><td>|</td><td>—</td><td>—</td><td>|</td><td>—</td><td>—</td><td>|</td><td>—</td><td>9</td></tr>
<tr><td>B</td><td>8</td><td>|</td><td>|</td><td>—</td><td>|</td><td>|</td><td>—</td><td>|</td><td>|</td><td>—</td><td>|</td><td>|</td><td>—</td><td>|</td><td>|</td><td>—</td><td>|</td><td>|</td><td>—</td><td>|</td><td>8</td></tr>
<tr><td>A</td><td>7</td><td>—</td><td>—</td><td>|</td><td>|</td><td>—</td><td>|</td><td>—</td><td>—</td><td>|</td><td>|</td><td>—</td><td>|</td><td>—</td><td>—</td><td>|</td><td>|</td><td>—</td><td>|</td><td>—</td><td>7</td></tr>
<tr><td>B</td><td>6</td><td>—</td><td>|</td><td>|</td><td>—</td><td>|</td><td>—</td><td>—</td><td>|</td><td>|</td><td>—</td><td>|</td><td>—</td><td>—</td><td>|</td><td>|</td><td>—</td><td>|</td><td>—</td><td>—</td><td>6</td></tr>
<tr><td>A</td><td>5</td><td>|</td><td>|</td><td>—</td><td>—</td><td>|</td><td>—</td><td>|</td><td>|</td><td>—</td><td>—</td><td>|</td><td>—</td><td>|</td><td>|</td><td>—</td><td>—</td><td>|</td><td>—</td><td>|</td><td>5</td></tr>
<tr><td>B</td><td>4</td><td>|</td><td>—</td><td>—</td><td>|</td><td>—</td><td>|</td><td>|</td><td>—</td><td>—</td><td>|</td><td>—</td><td>|</td><td>|</td><td>—</td><td>—</td><td>|</td><td>—</td><td>|</td><td>|</td><td>4</td></tr>
<tr><td>A</td><td>3</td><td>—</td><td>—</td><td>|</td><td>—</td><td>—</td><td>|</td><td>—</td><td>—</td><td>|</td><td>—</td><td>—</td><td>|</td><td>—</td><td>—</td><td>|</td><td>—</td><td>—</td><td>|</td><td>—</td><td>3</td></tr>
<tr><td>B</td><td>2</td><td>|</td><td>|</td><td>—</td><td>|</td><td>|</td><td>—</td><td>|</td><td>|</td><td>—</td><td>|</td><td>|</td><td>—</td><td>|</td><td>|</td><td>—</td><td>|</td><td>|</td><td>—</td><td>|</td><td>2</td></tr>
<tr><td>A</td><td>1</td><td>—</td><td>—</td><td>|</td><td>|</td><td>—</td><td>|</td><td>—</td><td>—</td><td>|</td><td>|</td><td>—</td><td>|</td><td>—</td><td>—</td><td>|</td><td>|</td><td>—</td><td>|</td><td>—</td><td>1</td></tr>
<tr><td></td><td></td><td>19</td><td>18</td><td>17</td><td>16</td><td>15</td><td>14</td><td>13</td><td>12</td><td>11</td><td>10</td><td>9</td><td>8</td><td>7</td><td>6</td><td>5</td><td>4</td><td>3</td><td>2</td><td>1</td><td></td></tr>
</table>

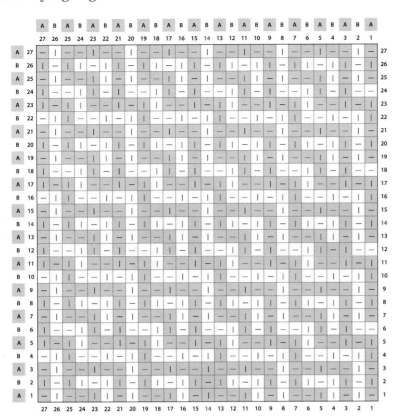

UKRAINIAN EIGHT-POINTED STAR

Traditional motif: Malia Jackson

Weave **UNDER** gray and **OVER** white.

Left: 27-peg trivet woven using the 19-peg chart with added tabby rows

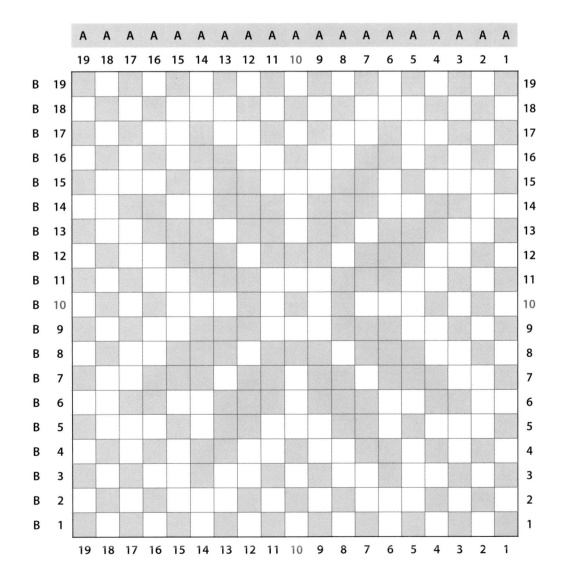

STAR VARIATION 1

Adapted and charted by Deborah Jean Cohen
Weave **UNDER** gray and **OVER** white.

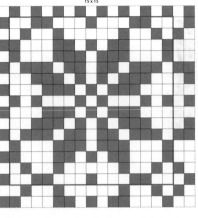

15 x 15

The draft cutout from which the three Star Variations are adapted

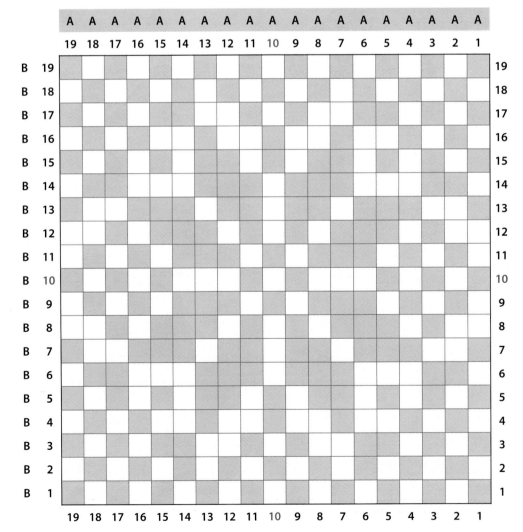

STAR VARIATION 2

Adapted and charted by Deborah Jean Cohen

Weave **UNDER** gray and **OVER** white.

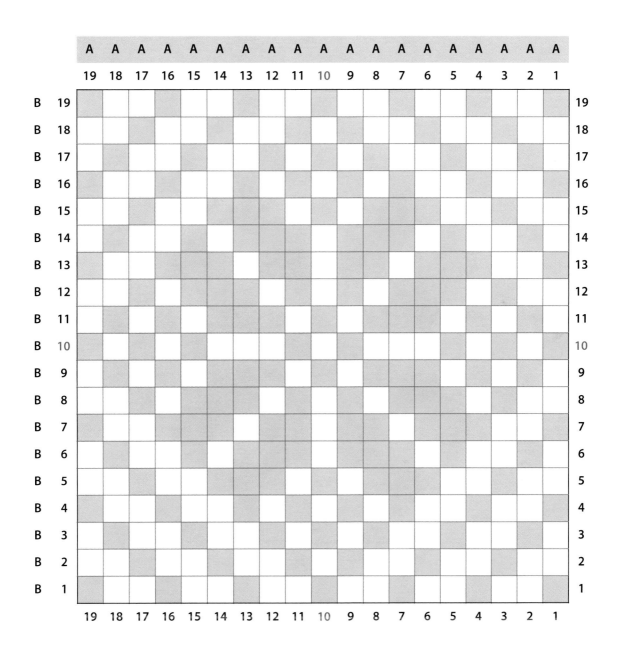

STAR VARIATION 3

Adapted and charted by Deborah Jean Cohen

Weave **UNDER** gray and **OVER** white.

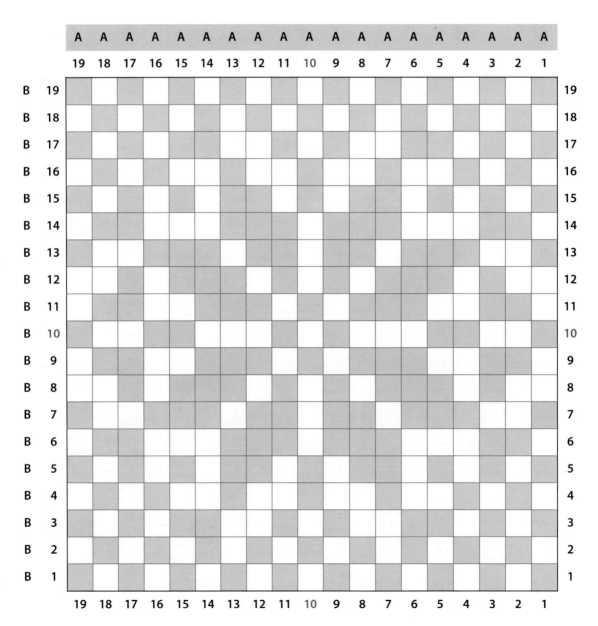

MALIA'S HONEYCOMB

Original design: Malia Jackson

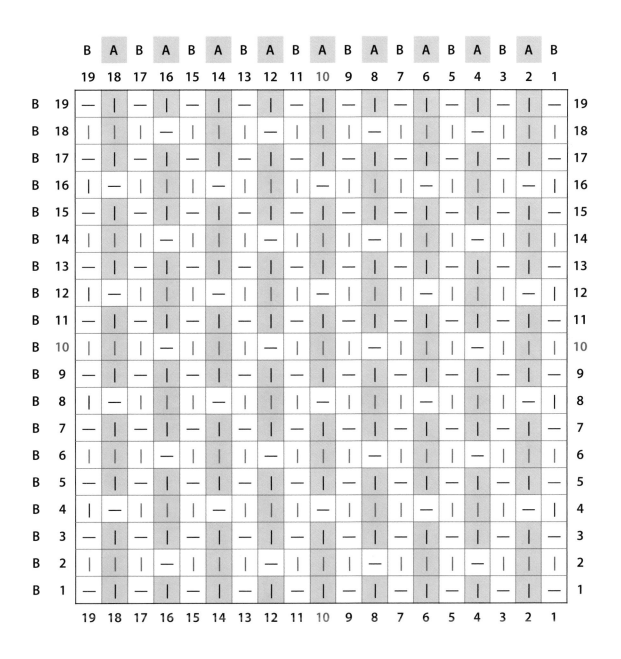

	B	A	B	A	B	A	B	A	B	A	B	A	B	A	B	A	B	A	B	A	B	A	B	A	B	A	B	
	27	26	25	24	23	22	21	20	19	18	17	16	15	14	13	12	11	10	9	8	7	6	5	4	3	2	1	
B 27	—	I	—	I	—	I	—	I	—	I	—	I	—	I	—	I	—	I	—	I	—	I	—	I	—	I	—	27
B 26	I	I	I	—	I	I	I	—	I	I	I	—	I	I	I	—	I	I	I	—	I	I	I	—	I	I	I	26
B 25	—	I	—	I	—	I	—	I	—	I	—	I	—	I	—	I	—	I	—	I	—	I	—	I	—	I	—	25
B 24	I	—	I	I	I	—	I	I	I	—	I	I	I	—	I	I	I	—	I	I	I	—	I	I	I	—	I	24
B 23	—	I	—	I	—	I	—	I	—	I	—	I	—	I	—	I	—	I	—	I	—	I	—	I	—	I	—	23
B 22	I	I	I	—	I	I	I	—	I	I	I	—	I	I	I	—	I	I	I	—	I	I	I	—	I	I	I	22
B 21	—	I	—	I	—	I	—	I	—	I	—	I	—	I	—	I	—	I	—	I	—	I	—	I	—	I	—	21
B 20	I	—	I	I	I	—	I	I	I	—	I	I	I	—	I	I	I	—	I	I	I	—	I	I	I	—	I	20
B 19	—	I	—	I	—	I	—	I	—	I	—	I	—	I	—	I	—	I	—	I	—	I	—	I	—	I	—	19
B 18	I	I	I	—	I	I	I	—	I	I	I	—	I	I	I	—	I	I	I	—	I	I	I	—	I	I	I	18
B 17	—	I	—	I	—	I	—	I	—	I	—	I	—	I	—	I	—	I	—	I	—	I	—	I	—	I	—	17
B 16	I	—	I	I	I	—	I	I	I	—	I	I	I	—	I	I	I	—	I	I	I	—	I	I	I	—	I	16
B 15	—	I	—	I	—	I	—	I	—	I	—	I	—	I	—	I	—	I	—	I	—	I	—	I	—	I	—	15
B 14	I	I	I	—	I	I	I	—	I	I	I	—	I	I	I	—	I	I	I	—	I	I	I	—	I	I	I	14
B 13	—	I	—	I	—	I	—	I	—	I	—	I	—	I	—	I	—	I	—	I	—	I	—	I	—	I	—	13
B 12	I	—	I	I	I	—	I	I	I	—	I	I	I	—	I	I	I	—	I	I	I	—	I	I	I	—	I	12
B 11	—	I	—	I	—	I	—	I	—	I	—	I	—	I	—	I	—	I	—	I	—	I	—	I	—	I	—	11
B 10	I	I	I	—	I	I	I	—	I	I	I	—	I	I	I	—	I	I	I	—	I	I	I	—	I	I	I	10
B 9	—	I	—	I	—	I	—	I	—	I	—	I	—	I	—	I	—	I	—	I	—	I	—	I	—	I	—	9
B 8	I	—	I	I	I	—	I	I	I	—	I	I	I	—	I	I	I	—	I	I	I	—	I	I	I	—	I	8
B 7	—	I	—	I	—	I	—	I	—	I	—	I	—	I	—	I	—	I	—	I	—	I	—	I	—	I	—	7
B 6	I	I	I	—	I	I	I	—	I	I	I	—	I	I	I	—	I	I	I	—	I	I	I	—	I	I	I	6
B 5	—	I	—	I	—	I	—	I	—	I	—	I	—	I	—	I	—	I	—	I	—	I	—	I	—	I	—	5
B 4	I	—	I	I	I	—	I	I	I	—	I	I	I	—	I	I	I	—	I	I	I	—	I	I	I	—	I	4
B 3	—	I	—	I	—	I	—	I	—	I	—	I	—	I	—	I	—	I	—	I	—	I	—	I	—	I	—	3
B 2	I	I	I	—	I	I	I	—	I	I	I	—	I	I	I	—	I	I	I	—	I	I	I	—	I	I	I	2
B 1	—	I	—	I	—	I	—	I	—	I	—	I	—	I	—	I	—	I	—	I	—	I	—	I	—	I	—	1
	27	26	25	24	23	22	21	20	19	18	17	16	15	14	13	12	11	10	9	8	7	6	5	4	3	2	1	

MALIA'S HONEYCOMB: ARGUS

Original design: Malia Jackson

Argus, or Argos Panoptes (All-Seeing Argos), is a many-eyed giant in Greek mythology—the honeycomb pattern can resemble eyes if you choose the right colors. Below are the front and back sides of two really striking Argus motifs. The 27-peg textile is woven by Christine Olsen Reis, and the 19-peg variation is woven by Andréa Scheidler. The last small "artholder" can be imagined not only as fanciful honeybees, with delicate flaxen wings, but also as honey in the comb.

MALIA'S HEART
Original design: Malia Jackson

		B	A	B	A	B	A	B	A	B	A	B	A	B	A	B	A	B	A	B
		19	18	17	16	15	14	13	12	11	10	9	8	7	6	5	4	3	2	1
B	19	—	|	—	|	—	|	—	|	—	|	—	|	—	|	—	|	—	|	—	19
B	18	|	—	|	—	|	—	|	—	|	—	|	—	|	—	|	—	|	—	|	18
B	17	—	|	—	|	—	|	—	|	—	|	—	|	—	|	—	|	—	|	—	17
B	16	|	—	|	—	|	—	|	—	|	—	|	—	|	—	|	—	|	—	|	16
B	15	—	|	—	|	—	|	—	|	—	|	—	|	—	|	—	|	—	|	—	15
B	14	|	—	|	—	|	—	|	—	|	—	|	—	|	—	|	—	|	—	|	14
B	13	—	|	—	|	—	|	—	|	—	|	—	|	—	|	—	|	—	|	—	13
B	12	|	—	|	—	|	—	|	—	|	—	|	—	|	—	|	—	|	—	|	12
B	11	—	|	—	|	—	|	—	|	—	|	—	|	—	|	—	|	—	|	—	11
B	10	|	—	|	—	|	—	|	—	|	—	|	—	|	—	|	—	|	—	|	10
B	9	—	|	—	|	—	|	—	|	—	|	—	|	—	|	—	|	—	|	—	9
B	8	|	—	|	—	|	—	|	—	|	—	|	—	|	—	|	—	|	—	|	8
B	7	—	|	—	|	—	|	—	|	—	|	—	|	—	|	—	|	—	|	—	7
B	6	|	—	|	—	|	—	|	—	|	—	|	—	|	—	|	—	|	—	|	6
B	5	—	|	—	|	—	|	—	|	—	|	—	|	—	|	—	|	—	|	—	5
B	4	|	—	|	—	|	—	|	—	|	—	|	—	|	—	|	—	|	—	|	4
B	3	—	|	—	|	—	|	—	|	—	|	—	|	—	|	—	|	—	|	—	3
B	2	|	—	|	—	|	—	|	—	|	—	|	—	|	—	|	—	|	—	|	2
B	1	—	|	—	|	—	|	—	|	—	|	—	|	—	|	—	|	—	|	—	1
		19	18	17	16	15	14	13	12	11	10	9	8	7	6	5	4	3	2	1

B A B A B A B A B A B A B A B A B A B A B A B A B A B

27 26 25 24 23 22 21 20 19 18 17 16 15 14 13 12 11 10 9 8 7 6 5 4 3 2 1

B 27	pattern	27
B 26	pattern	26
B 25	pattern	25
B 24	pattern	24
B 23	pattern	23
B 22	pattern	22
B 21	pattern	21
B 20	pattern	20
B 19	pattern	19
B 18	pattern	18
B 17	pattern	17
B 16	pattern	16
B 15	pattern	15
B 14	pattern	14
B 13	pattern	13
B 12	pattern	12
B 11	pattern	11
B 10	pattern	10
B 9	pattern	9
B 8	pattern	8
B 7	pattern	7
B 6	pattern	6
B 5	pattern	5
B 4	pattern	4
B 3	pattern	3
B 2	pattern	2
B 1	pattern	1

27 26 25 24 23 22 21 20 19 18 17 16 15 14 13 12 11 10 9 8 7 6 5 4 3 2 1

The 19-peg pattern is set
within the 27-peg loom.

Argus eyes are inside the heart.

Potholder Patterns: Twill and Twill-like Structures **187**

ONE HEART
(FOR JIM)

Original design: Christine Olsen Reis

Weave **UNDER** gray and **OVER** white.

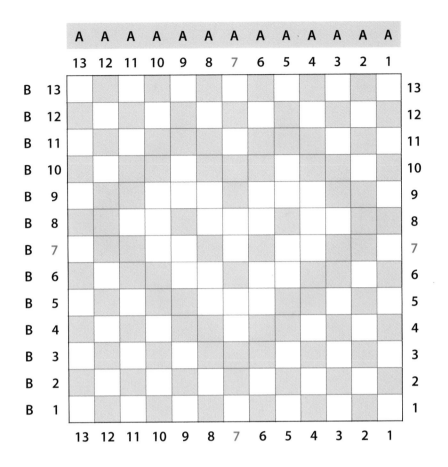

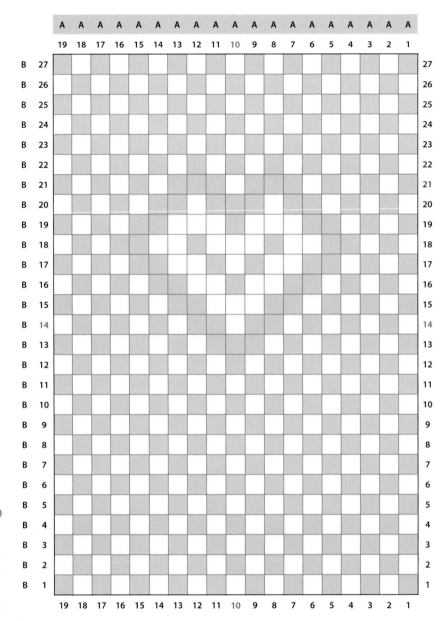

CHRISTINE'S CROSS

Original design: Christine Olsen Reis

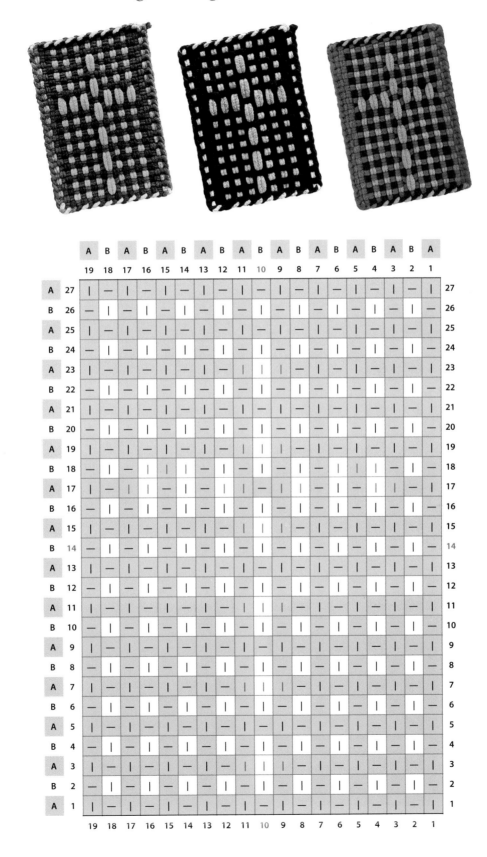

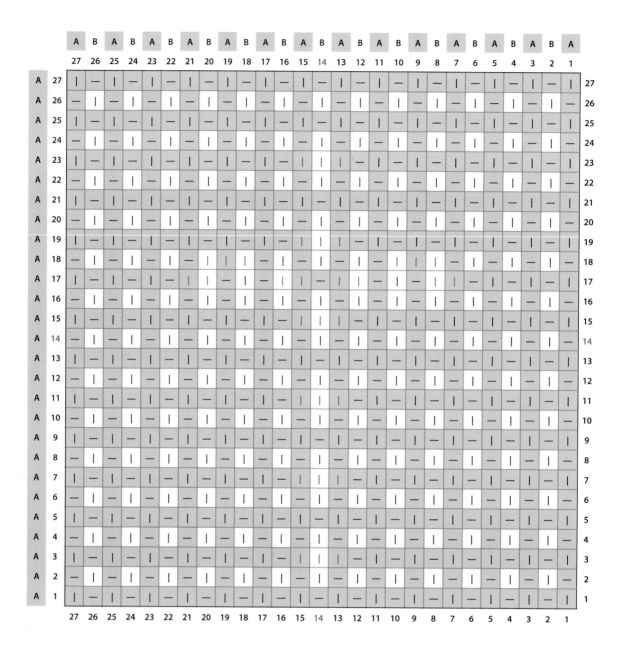

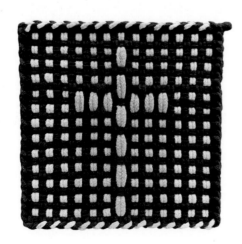

This weaving loom and the method of weaving thereon is protected by U. S. Pat. No. 2,186,692
Manufactured and Distributed by:

Nelly Bee Products   *Hickory, North Carolina*

NELLY BEE SPLIT-LOOP INDIAN WEAVES

Mary Clarke was responsible for setting off a flurry of split-loop Indian Weave variations in the weaving community when she discovered Nelly Bee's 1940s Indian Weave pattern. The Nelly Bee instructions had a completely mind-boggling error in the center row, so Mary fixed it. I charted it and posted it in Radical Potholder Weavers on Facebook. The lovely way the design fades in and out captured everyone's imagination, and people wove it and then began to riff on the original with their own variations. This small section gives charts for the original Indian Weave and four of the variations inspired by it.

Nelly Bee was Nell E. Boyer, and besides holding the patent for her potholder loom, all we know about her is what's found in her book *The Nelly Bee Loom Weaving Designs, vol. 3.* (I can't find volumes 1 or 2.) I guess that the photo to the right shows Nell among the young weavers.

Nelly Bee Weaving Class

Courtesy of the
St. Elizabeth's Day Nursery, Chicago

PAGE SIXTEEN

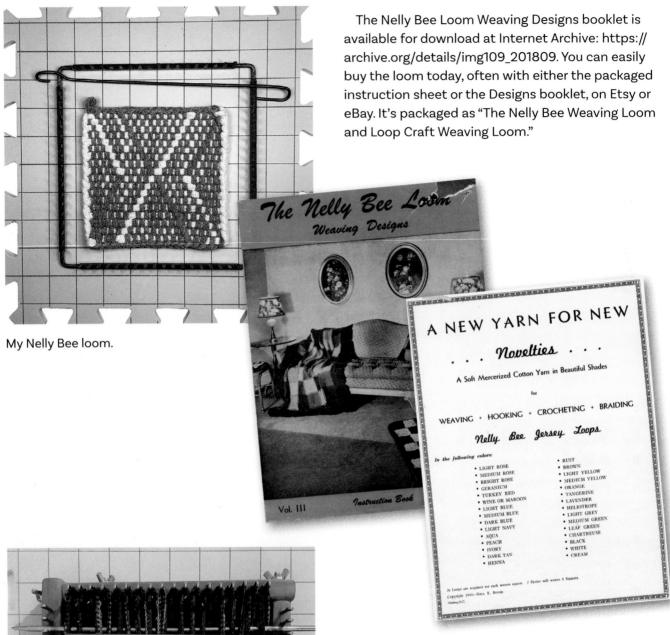

My Nelly Bee loom.

Figure 7.1

The Nelly Bee Loom Weaving Designs booklet is available for download at Internet Archive: https://archive.org/details/img109_201809. You can easily buy the loom today, often with either the packaged instruction sheet or the Designs booklet, on Etsy or eBay. It's packaged as "The Nelly Bee Weaving Loom and Loop Craft Weaving Loom."

Indian Weave is a bit tricky to weave—it works best when you choose loops that match in thickness and elasticity. Beat down each row very well before moving on, and straighten the weft spacing. It's a tight weave, so I put a firm base at the bottom by sliding a knitting needle in, securing it with a rubber band (figure 7.1). A sturdy wide-toothed comb makes a good beater.

The result is a potholder with a wonderful hand, more supple than other weaves, yet effective in the kitchen. The weaves that follow are my favorite kitchen potholders.

INDIAN WEAVE
Original design: Nell E. Boyer

In these charts, follow the pick notation. The gray is a guide to weave structure rather than color; refer to the photos for examples.

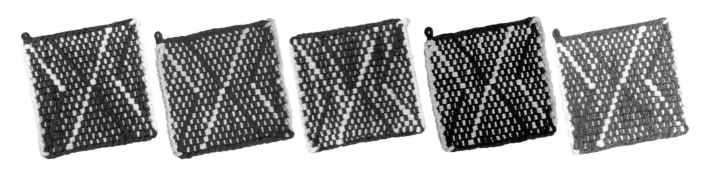

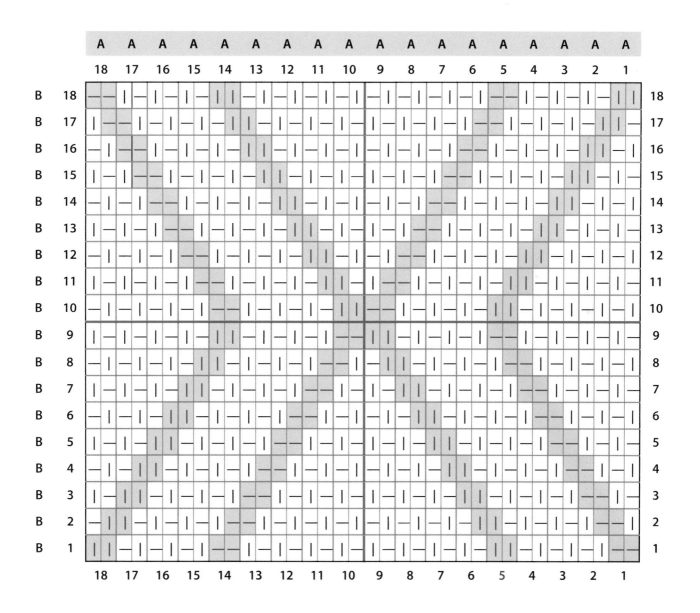

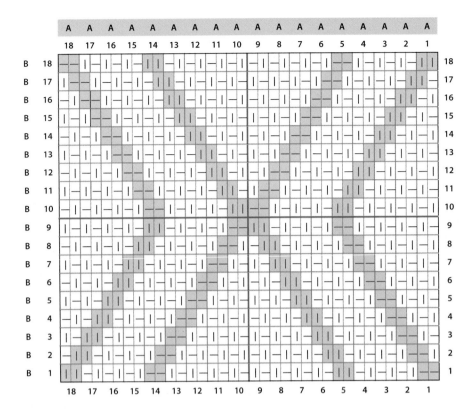

Indian Weave No. 5

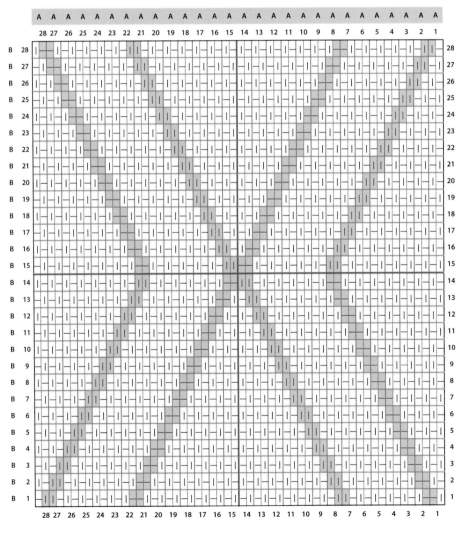

This is a 28-peg, very tight weave. Christine wove it, and she recommends weaving it over 26 pegs on a 27-peg loom, dropping the outer rows and columns. If you decide to be adventurous and weave the 28, we admire you!

MARY'S INSIDE-OUT INDIAN WEAVE

Nelly Bee–inspired original design: Mary Clarke

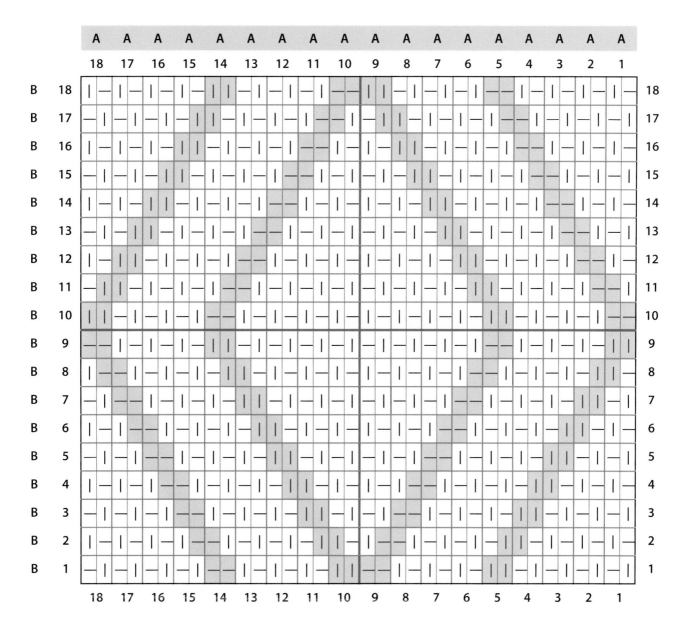

DECONSTRUCTED INDIAN WEAVE

Nelly Bee–inspired original design: Mary Clarke

Deconstructed is an asymmetrical inside-out. Weave it, flip it sideways, and bind off.

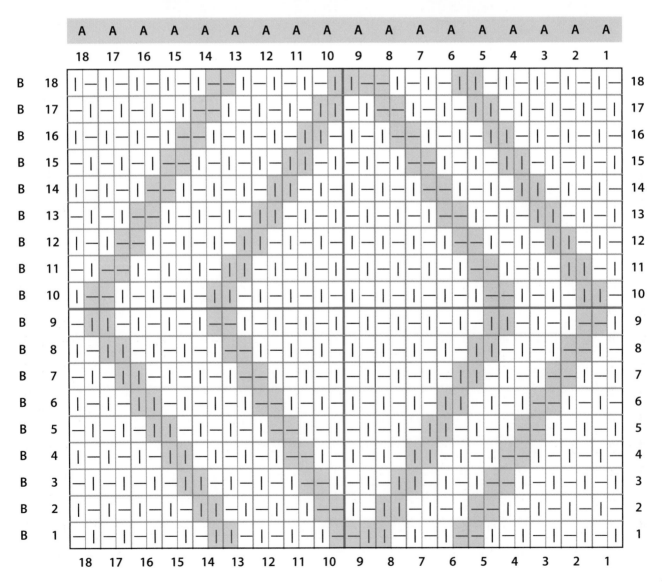

INTERWOVEN INDIAN WEAVE

Nelly Bee–inspired original design: Deborah Jean Cohen

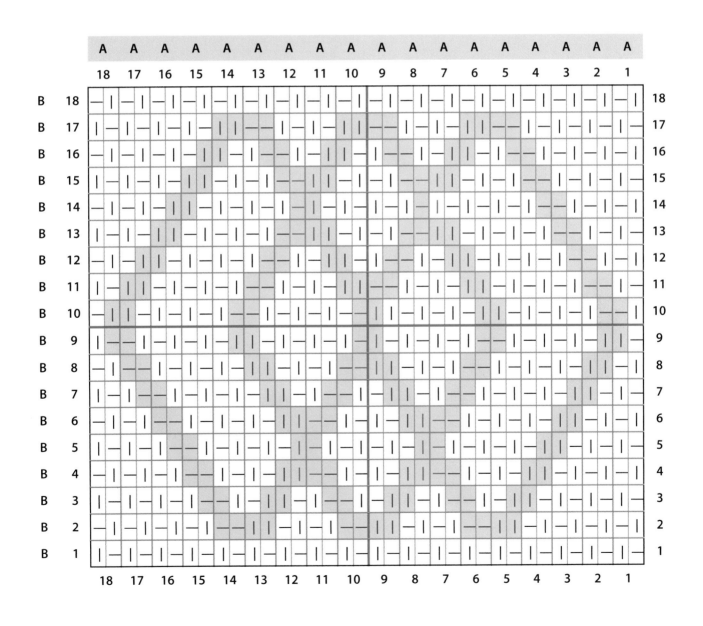

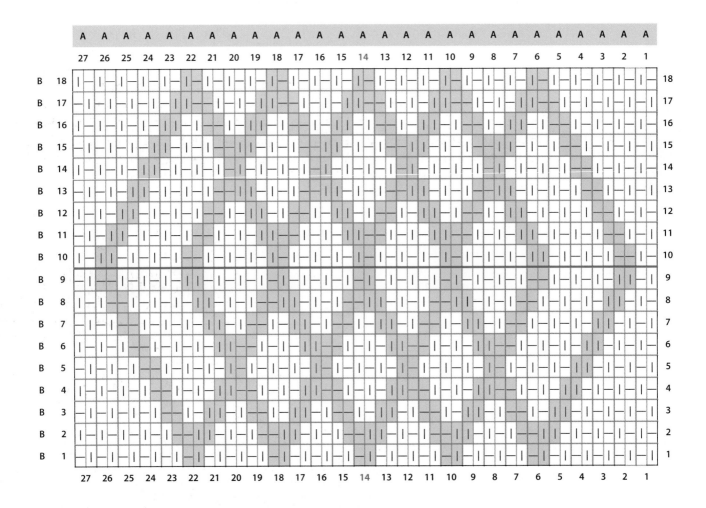

DOUBLE INDIAN WEAVE

Nelly Bee–inspired original design: Deborah Jean Cohen

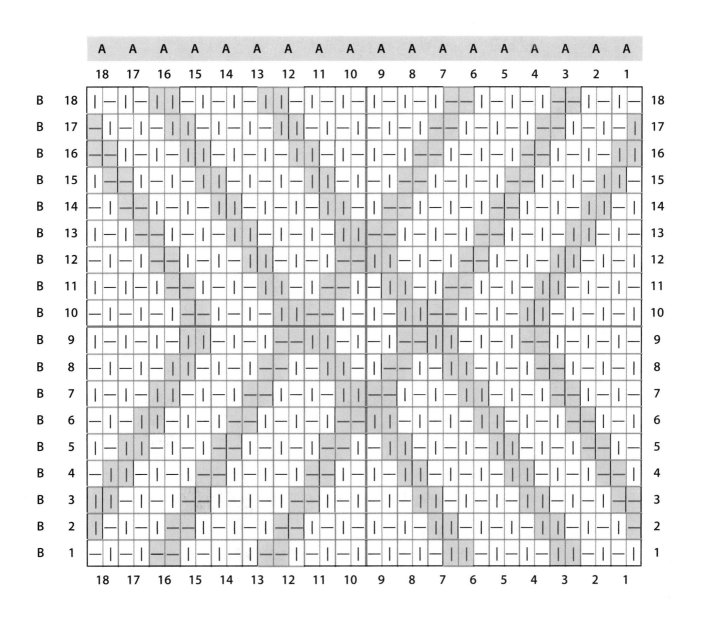

CHAPTER 8

A SOMEWHAT NERDY LOG CABIN STUDY

The history of Log Cabin goes back at least as far as Neolithic central and western Europe (4500 to 500 BCE), where an example of the pattern was found in a pile dweller's archeological site (reference: E. J. W. Barber, *Prehistoric Textiles*). I couldn't find a photo of the textile fragment and would love to see it! We weave the traditional Log Cabin by warping a sequence of two alternating colors, repeating the sequence reversed, and repeating the whole for the width of your loom. Weft then follows the warp sequence. From this rule have come some of our strongest classic patterns: all the variations of Pinwheel (also known as Puppytooth), the Log Cabin itself, and more.

In mathematics, one way to find out how many ways to arrange objects in a given number (n) of places is a simple permutation. The Log Cabin rule uses two colors: light and dark. So we'd use the formula 2 (for the colors A and B) to the power of n: 2^n.

What happens if you systematically permute the light and dark colors of the Log Cabin pattern from 2 places through 5 places, and then apply the rule? A sequence of repeating motifs come and go, are rotated, or displaced up, down, to the right or to the left. Take a look at figure 8.1: you might find a new favorite.

Figure 8.1

LOG CABIN 2²

2² = 4: There are four permutations of A and B in two places: AA, BB, AB, and BA. For each, we first write the sequence and then reverse it.

Since AA/AA and BB/BB don't meet the two-color requirement, they're eliminated as Log Cabin. We're left with AB/BA and BA/AB—but these are the same:

AB/BA —> ABBAABBAABBAABBAAB

BA/AB —> BAABBAABBAABBAAB

If you look closely, you'll see that if BA/AB is turned upside down (rotated 180 degrees), you get AB/BA.

We get three distinct potholders from four permutations, and we get one potholder that meets the Log Cabin rule. This is Pinwheel, also known as Puppytooth, because it is the most basic form of the Houndstooth pattern.

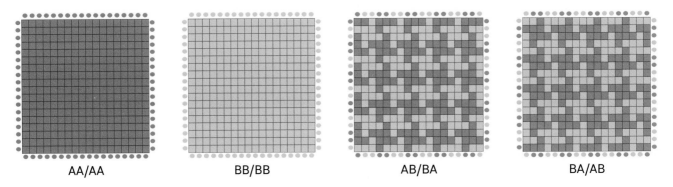

AA/AA BB/BB AB/BA BA/AB

LOG CABIN 2³

2³ = 8: There are eight permutations of A and B in three places: AAA, BBB, AAB, BAA, ABB, BBA, ABA, and BAB.

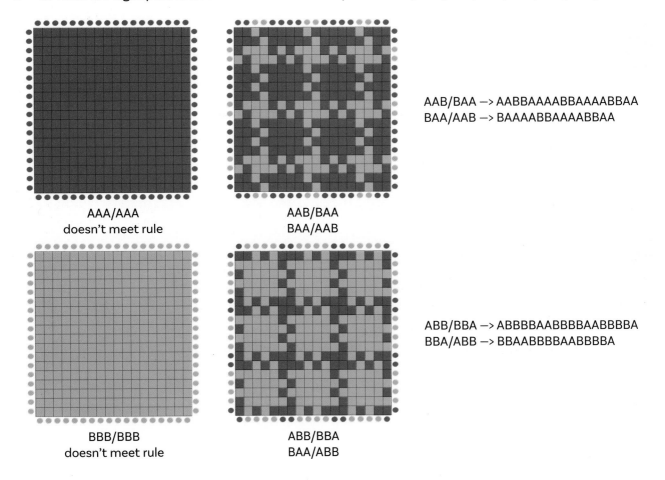

AAA/AAA
doesn't meet rule

AAB/BAA
BAA/AAB

AAB/BAA —> AABBAAAABBAAAABBAA
BAA/AAB —> BAAAABBAAAABBAA

BBB/BBB
doesn't meet rule

ABB/BBA
BBA/ABB

ABB/BBA —> ABBBBAABBBBAABBBBA
BBA/ABB —> BBAABBBBAABBBBA

This is AAB/BAA, with a color reversal and a shift—it's centered.

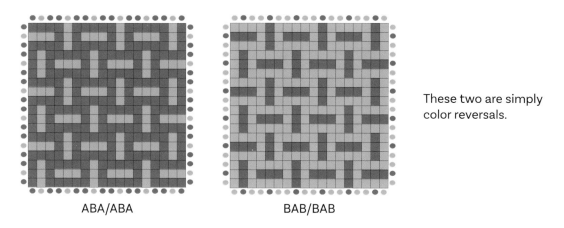

These two are simply color reversals.

ABA/ABA   BAB/BAB

Again, we eliminate AAA and BBB. Two sets of permutations are the same, and another two are color reversals. We get six distinct potholders from eight permutations, and we get three Log Cabin patterns.

LOG CABIN 2⁴

2^4 = 16: There are 16 permutations of A and B in four places: AAAA, BBBB, ABAA, AABA, BABB, BBAB, AAAB, BAAA, ABBB, BBBA, AABB, BBAA, ABBA, BAAB, ABAB, and BABA.

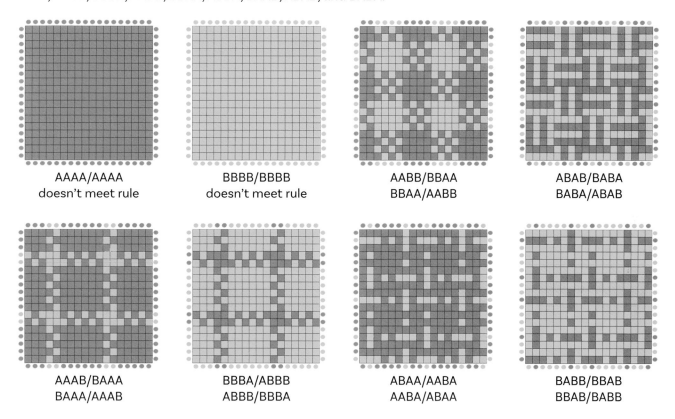

AAAA/AAAA
doesn't meet rule

BBBB/BBBB
doesn't meet rule

AABB/BBAA
BBAA/AABB

ABAB/BABA
BABA/ABAB

AAAB/BAAA
BAAA/AAAB

BBBA/ABBB
ABBB/BBBA

ABAA/AABA
AABA/ABAA

BABB/BBAB
BBAB/BABB

These are color reversals.   These are color reversals.

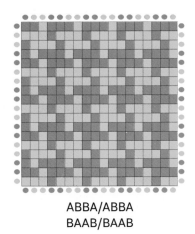

ABBA/ABBA —> ABBAABBAABBAABBAAB
BAAB/BAAB —> BAABBAABBAABBAAB
AB/BA —> ABBAABBAABBAAB

This is the same as AB/BA, Pinwheel, so we won't count it twice.

ABBA/ABBA
BAAB/BAAB

We get nine distinct potholders from 16 permutations, and we get five Log Cabin patterns.

LOG CABIN 2⁵

2^5 = 32: There are 32 permutations of A and B in five places: AAAAA, BBBBB, AAAAB, BAAAA, BBBBA, ABBBB, AAABA, ABAAA, BBBAB, BABBB, AABAA, BBABB, AAABB, BBAAA, AABBB, BBBAA, AABAB, BABAA, BBABA, ABABB, BABBA, ABBAB, AABBA, ABBAA, BBABB, BAABB, ABBBA, BAAAB, ABABA, BABAB, ABAAB, and BAABA.

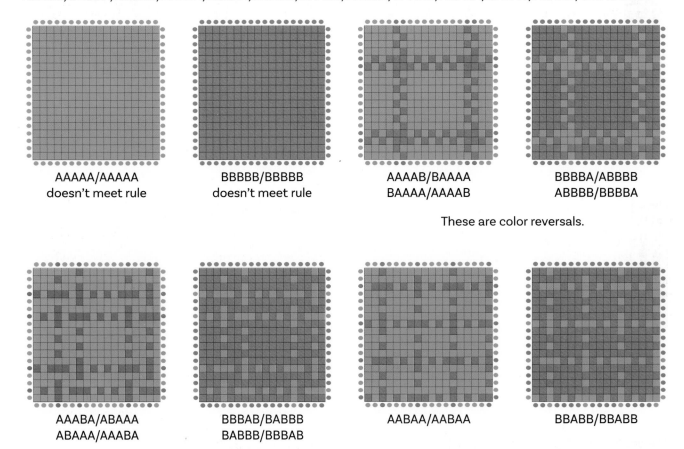

AAAAA/AAAAA
doesn't meet rule

BBBBB/BBBBB
doesn't meet rule

AAAAB/BAAAA
BAAAA/AAAAB

BBBBA/ABBBB
ABBBB/BBBBA

These are color reversals.

AAABA/ABAAA
ABAAA/AAABA

These are color reversals.

BBBAB/BABBB
BABBB/BBBAB

AABAA/AABAA

These are color reversals.

BBABB/BBABB

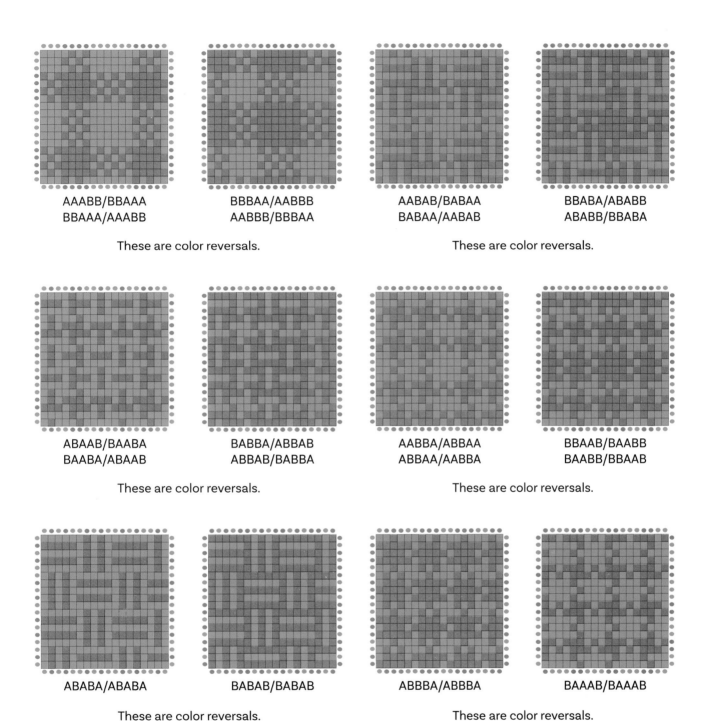

AAABB/BBAAA
BBAAA/AAABB

These are color reversals.

BBBAA/AABBB
AABBB/BBBAA

AABAB/BABAA
BABAA/AABAB

These are color reversals.

BBABA/ABABB
ABABB/BBABA

ABAAB/BAABA
BAABA/ABAAB

These are color reversals.

BABBA/ABBAB
ABBAB/BABBA

AABBA/ABBAA
ABBAA/AABBA

These are color reversals.

BBAAB/BAABB
BAABB/BBAAB

ABABA/ABABA

BABAB/BABAB

ABBBA/ABBBA

These are color reversals.

BAAAB/BAAAB

These are color reversals.

We get 19 distinct potholders from 32 permutations, and we get nine Log Cabin patterns.

But where are the logs?

…you might ask. The most common Log Cabin looks like stacked logs and is warped (and woven) with alternating light/dark colors. So the notation would be written ABAB for as far as you like and then reversed, per the Log Cabin rule. As the length of the sequence increases past five, the logs become more recognizable.

Here are those from the above permutation sets:

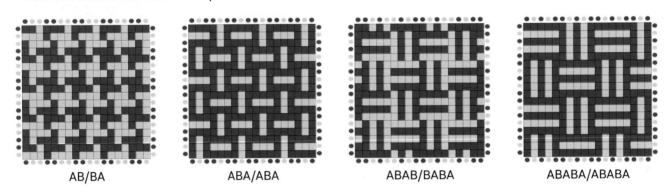

AB/BA   ABA/ABA   ABAB/BABA   ABABA/ABABA

Here are the others, up to the limit of an 18-peg loom:

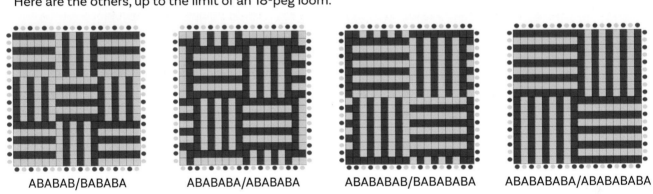

ABABAB/BABABA   ABABABA/ABABABA   ABABABAB/BABABABA   ABABABABA/ABABABABA

The Log Cabin Rule: Log Cabin is woven by warping a sequence of two alternating colors, repeating the sequence reversed, and repeating the whole for the width of your loom. Weft follows the warp sequence.

CHAPTER 9

POTHOLDER WEAVERS

There are no potholders without potholder weavers. And there are no potholders that catch your eye, startle you, make you want to hang them up on the wall, and change your mind about what a potholder is and can be, without potholder weavers with vision. These potholder weavers look at a simple loom and see possibility; they take the loom in hand and weave a transformation. From our most cherished traditional patterns to the completely original, potholder weavers move this most simple, practical craft forward, exploring color and structure.

It's both a small adventure and a large one. People like potholders, it seems. A strong pattern is continually pleasant to look at, and, since a potholder has a necessary, practical use in the kitchen as a hand protection or trivet, it's always there to brighten a moment. Weaving these small textiles is relaxing, simple, interesting, fairly quick, and fun. Working with color and weave structure is fascinating and expressive: something inside is released into freedom as you explore the possibilities. Every person has creativity to access, and using it makes weaving potholders so satisfying. Then you can give them away and make other people happy.

The weavers in this chapter are those who have helped with this book or who have supported this crazy effort: they converted patterns from 4-harness loom drafts, invented original patterns, test wove them, had encouraging words to say, and together inspired creative breakthrough. I hope they inspire you and that their work sparks your own innate creativity.

MARY CLARKE
Instagram: @maryksee

Back when I was at Rhode Island School of Design, a Freshman Foundation teacher suggested I major in textile design. Instead, I went into painting and soon switched to photography. So much for weaving. Still, my photo degree served me well. I've spent most of my working life toiling in the editorial and photo-shoot trenches as a beauty and fashion editor at magazines including *Seventeen*, *Ladies' Home Journal*, *Redbook*, and *Modern Bride* (RIP, all). I even clawed my way up to creative director at legendary *Sassy* magazine and, along the way, contributed to *Vogue*, *T—the New York Times* style magazine, and *Harper's Bazaar* and was a contributing editor at the late great *INDEX* magazine. While at *Modern Bride*, I got the urge to revisit potholder making, something I'd done on and off—mostly off—since childhood. At that time, circa 1999, potholder-making supplies were limited to 18-peg looms and loops in kindergarten brights. So much has changed since then. Potholder-weaving communities are thriving across social media. We can work with bigger looms in an expanded palette of loop colors. And these days, potholders are just as likely to be called handweavings or fiber art. For now, I'm sticking to 18- and 19-peg looms for my potholders, er, handweavings. However you choose to work and whatever you choose to call it, enjoy this book—and weave on!

I was idly walking up Madison Avenue one afternoon when I spotted an incredible vintage overshot coverlet in a shop window. The weave was stunning, of course, but the colors were what really caught my eye: dead ringers for my newest batch of Great Northern Weaving loopers!

5 Days Only!

Cloth made more interesting by people

Feature Inc.

131 Allen St NY NY 10002 212.675.7772
featureinc.com featureinc@featureinc.com

Magic Flying Carpets of the Berber Kingdom of Morocco ◆ Jhola Bags by 5 Year Plan ◆ T-Shirts by Deli Grocery Specialty Products ◆ Pot Holders by Mary Clarke

Reception Tuesday 4 June 6-8 pm

Wednesday thru Sunday, 5 thru 9 June 12-6 pm

When my artist husband, Bill Komoski, told his gallerist, Hudson, that I made potholders, he lit up. It turns out Hudson appreciated woven potholders as much as I do—he was keen on having me show them at the gallery's upcoming annual five-day pop-up show. What a thrill seeing my potholders on an actual gallery wall!

Collect Pond Park
Book/Record Sale
Saturday, May 15th, 11 -6pm

Bunk Club, Your Other Left Ear, VorteXity Books, all.uPINIT Hassla Books, Fenrick Books, Sequence Press, PERADAM Press, May68, Boo-Hooray, Matthew Higgs, RATSTAR, Fugitive Materials, Straight to Hell, Whatever's Clever, Mary Clarke, Branded Pen ++more

130 Leonard St. NY, NY.   ALL WELCOME!!

Uh oh. It was a very dedicated bunch of book collectors and music heads at Collect Pond, organized by artist Ryan Foerster. Would anyone even be interested in potholders? After a bit of a slow start, all was revealed. Just about everyone loves a good potholder.

My writer/curator pal Bob Nickas asked whether I'd be interested in having some potholders on his display table at artist Rob Pruitt's flea market. The place was jammed, and every last potholder sold.

Fillet gumbo

CHRISTINE OLSEN REIS
Instagram: @creiscreate

Textiles and patterns have always captivated me. They still do. Multiple generations of farmers, fishermen, and fiber artisans in my family influenced how I look at the world.

As a child in southeast Alaska, I was mesmerized by morphing tide lines and wave-etched markings in the sand. We lived above a beach where shells, kelp, logs, stray icebergs, and gravel sifted into organic shapes along the shore. During my summer visits to my uncle's farm in Southern California, I saw the more geometric rows of crops and trees and flowers.

My visual world also included strong textures—coils of line and skeins of rope packed in the Alaskan boathouses, mosses on the muskeg, bark on the trees, and, above it all, the stark silhouettes of mountains against sky. In the south, oranges dotting green trees, waving stalks of grain, and explosions of floral colors softened the linear crop rows. Inside, my mother's, aunties', and grandmother's knitted and embroidered creations fascinated me, as did the tactile joy of our fresh bedsheets, warm sweaters and hats, handmade mittens, afghans, doilies, and colorful dresses.

I began weaving in my late teens. Captivated and inspired by excellent teachers and that love for finding rhythms and patterns, my early work was with Northwest Coastal Indian textiles and basketry as well as Swedish loom weaving. I studied at California College of the Arts after graduating with an art and art history degree from Western Washington University. Later I received an MFA from the University of Washington in fiber arts.

After some years of weaving and teaching art and design, I stepped away from the formal textile world. Thankfully, the advent of this dynamic group of little loom designers and artists has rekindled my interest in art and weaving. They have inspired me to develop and weave new patterns. My current passion is seeking out and creating repeat patterns that work structurally and have personal resonance and meaning.

DEBORAH JEAN COHEN

I remember weaving potholders in Brownies, most vividly the difficult last row, on a little metal loom. Loops would pop off in a most frustrating way. Never would I have imagined today's involvement with loops, looms, design, and the process of putting a book together. I'm a retired coder/analyst, living with my husband and two dogs in west-central Arkansas. The 10- to 12-hour workdays vanished at retirement, and I got a small spinner's flock of Jacob, Navajo-Churro, and Border Leicester sheep, plus two llamas and one alpaca. I learned to care for the animals and process their fiber from shearing to yarn; to spin, dye, and weave. Now too old to care for a flock, I'm exploring the possibilities of the small loom, astonished at the satisfaction in opening a creative door (much different from the logical creativity of coding).

I hope you enjoy this book and opening your own creative door.

Test weaving
for the book

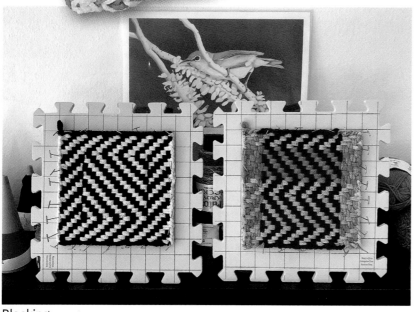

Blocking

ANDRÉA SCHEIDLER

As an artist, I paint outside the lines. As a career educator of children whose intelligence and learning needs begged for a nontraditional approach, I reached across the desk and drew them into the art room and onto the stage.

In 2021, a distracted driver plowed into the rear of my stopped car at a speed of over 50 miles per hour. I survived thanks to the skills of a world-class brain surgeon at Brigham and Women's Hospital.

Following recovery from surgery, I began therapy at the Cantu Concussion Center. On my own, I decided to weave on a square potholder loom to strengthen my ocular/motor skills and to challenge my cognitive abilities.

At Harrisville Designs in nearby Harrisville, New Hampshire, I found not only necessary loops and looms but also a copy of Deborah Jean Cohen's *In the Loop: Radical Potholder Patterns & Techniques.*

I found Deborah's site on Facebook, discovered patterns online, and became a loop weaver. As I experimented with patterns and colors, I soon felt like I was "painting" with loops. Members of the FB weaving community reached out to me. I found myself testing the limits of what I could do. My hands became steadier, my ideas more complex. I felt welcomed and inspired by the weavers in this richly skilled and varied community.

A new pattern for me is like a page in a coloring book. A strong pattern provides serious possibilities for "painting with loops." Painting with loops can be a fine art. I am still an oil painter in my thinking, but even as I tool up to paint on canvas again, I remain grateful for this new medium and the craft community that has embraced this decades-old practice of weaving squares with cotton loops. I'm also honored to be part of a worthwhile endeavor that benefits others. I will eventually return to my easel, but I don't see an end to my affection for this charming and challenging craft.

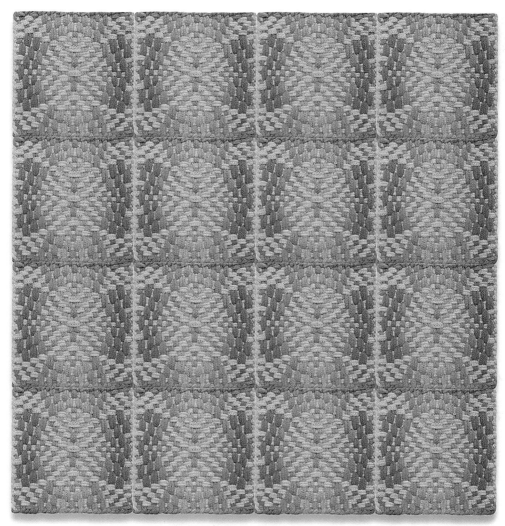

Centering by Andréa Scheidler

PAULA ROYSE

I am a wife, mother, and grandmother. I retired from social service many years ago and live in the northern lakes region of Indiana. I started weaving on Christmas Day 2021, after being gifted two looms and a supply of loops. It has been a rare day since that I have not held a loom in my hands.

I love every aspect of this craft and hope that I will always feel the slight feeling of astonishment at looking at a beautiful little textile that began with a humble pile of loops and a very basic loom.

My interests, aside from weaving, include anything antique or vintage: architecture, homes, interior design, fashion, and jewelry. Vintage color motifs have inspired many of my color choices for potholders. I feel strongly that though many of my pieces are functional, some are purely art pieces to be displayed and enjoyed as such.

Happy weaving!

KENDAL ROSENBERGER

I was born and raised and to this day live in northwest Ohio. In my midforties, after many years of volunteer work and helping my mother run her gift shop, I returned to school. There I discovered that I loved learning new things, obtained a master's degree in clinical social work, and had a rewarding career for almost 20 years. Since retiring in 2020, I still love learning new things and take classes online or at one of our local universities. I also enjoy being outside in nature, walking my dog at one of the beautiful metro-parks near our home. Along with needlework and weaving on small looms, sewing has been a hobby of mine from a very young age. My mother taught sewing, and by the age of 12, I was making a lot of my own clothing. My life as an adult got busy; there was no time to sew, and my machine sat patiently in the closet. Shortly after retiring, I reconnected with my old friend and started sewing again. I'm not sure why but I've always loved aprons, vintage and new, and started making them. Inspired by the potholders woven by my daughter and grandsons, I decided that reconnecting with my little loom was the next step. As a novice weaver and someone who loves to learn new things, it was exciting to discover all the beautiful new patterns. Even after three years, every time I complete a pattern I'm in awe of the design and its beauty.

So I welcome you to this wonderful world of radical potholder patterns. It has been my honor to contribute my work to this book and be a part of this amazing group of artisans. Personally I have grown as a novice weaver, learned so many new things, and been inspired by everyone who has contributed. As someone who believes strongly in the importance of volunteering, I'm honored to be part of the fundraising effort for the monastery Thegtse Sangyé Chöling.

MALIA JACKSON

Malia has been captivated by the fiber arts ever since learning to crochet on the playground during recess. Since then, she's branched out considerably. Like many, a desire to reconnect to childhood joy in the early days of the COVID-19 pandemic led her back to potholder weaving. While she loves a traditional potholder, she's also interested in what other materials and techniques the potholder loom can support. Originally from the Adirondack Mountains of New York, she lives with her husband in Bloomington, Indiana.

KAREN BROILES D'ANGELO

Karen is a lifelong New Yorker and visual artist living on Manhattan's Upper West Side and working at Pratt Institute as director of marketing in the School of Continuing and Professional Studies. Karen's interest in drawing, watercolors, and handweaving was noticed by age three or four, and she developed a strong color sense before starting school.

Today Karen's creative portfolio includes a visual focus on bold designs, grid patterns, and elements of the world (both natural and handmade), using complementary colors as a base for mixing and creating. Her wish is that all people, especially our elders, can participate in handweaving because the results can be beautiful and feel very good in our hands.

KATE KILMURRAY
Instagram: @katekilmurray • www.katekilmurray.com

I had been practicing and teaching yoga and meditation for more than 30 years before unearthing a forgotten item from my childhood that sparked an immediate connection between my meditative practice and using my hands in craft. Holding a simple 7 x 7-inch metal handloom, I remembered my grandmother's hands teaching me to weave, and I realized that my introduction to meditation had happened as a child, weaving on a handloom.

When I rediscovered weaving through these evocative memories, I remembered something that we, as a culture, have forgotten: that we can always access inner stillness and peace through simple, embodied practices. Handweaving as meditation has been a way of life for me ever since.

Understanding this connection has allowed me to be part of a community of women who are pioneering a new terrain of weaving, transforming something that has previously been thought of as an activity for children into a medium that has depth and presence for the 21st century.

By using our hands in craft and contemplation, we can quiet the mind and reconnect with ourselves, something that is sorely needed in our technology-saturated world.

In 2020, I created The Weaving Way Community, an online group of now over 80 members across the United States who all share a passion and interest for this style of weaving. This connection with my fellow members helps to drive my innovation in handweaving, and my designs emerge from spacious and quiet communion with the colors, textures, and patterns of the natural world. Weaving in this way has led me to running a successful business selling my weaving designs across the world, as well as teaching others to weave as a meditative experience.

I believe that by incorporating handweavings in our homes, we bring more depth, beauty, and meaning to our daily lives. Weaving as meditation is a process of remembering who we are.

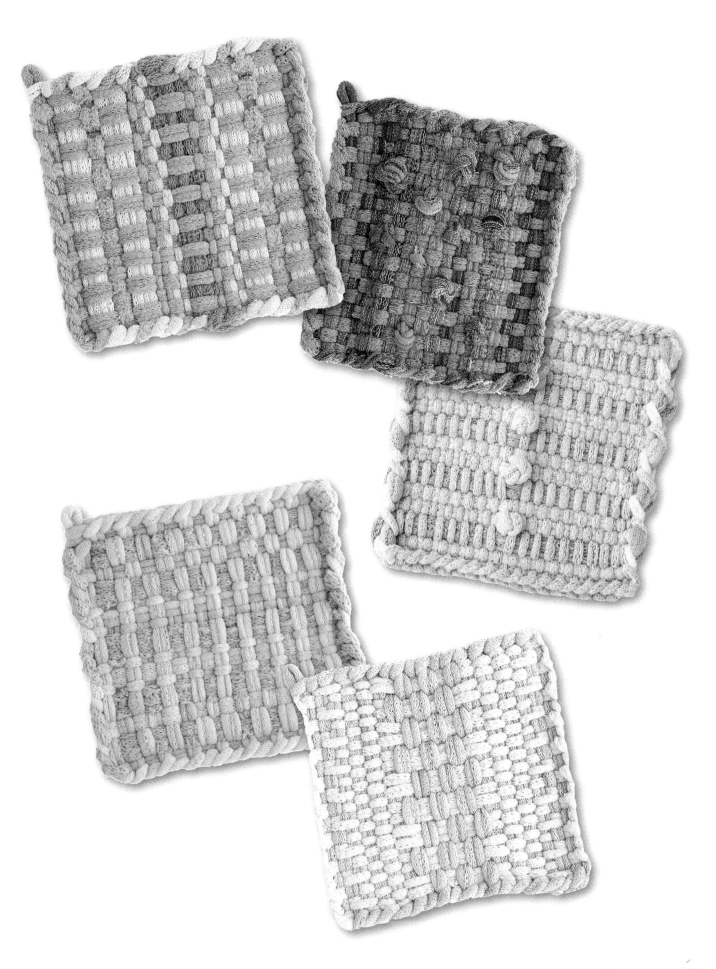

H. MICHELLE SPAULDING
www.Craftydivacottage.com

I am a certified dream coach, teacher, expressive arts facilitator, visionary artist, author, and storyteller. I express myself through the textile and fiber arts. I teach workshops to women who want to express their creativity through crafting and art making. I left the corporate world after 20 years as founder and CEO of a high-tech firm in the government contracting arena to pursue a second career in expressive arts education.

My latest crafting obsession is weaving potholders and making baskets and journals out of them. My weaving style is "freestyle," or intuitive. I don't follow patterns. I look at patterns for inspiration, but when I sit down to weave I go with the flow. Weaving is a spiritual practice for me. I weave as a form of active meditation. Making and creating allow me to tap into the Divine creativity of our Universal force. I find making baskets, totes, purses, journals, and more from handwoven potholders spiritually rewarding.

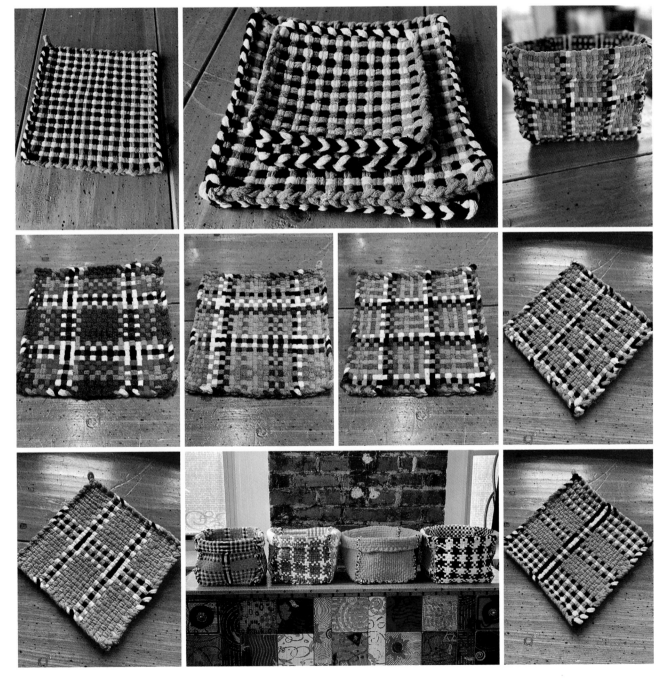

YAVIA MIREZ

I am Yavia Mirez, and I live in the unique village of Hell, Michigan. Yes, that is its real name! Before you ask, yes, it does freeze over. I have the best job ever. I am the official minister of Hell's Chapel of Love and officiate wedding ceremonies all year round. Your marriage license will actually say "Married in Hell."

We have a lot of fun with the village's name and promote a fun, family-friendly community filled with lakes, hiking trails, and year-round events.

I am a crocheter, circular knitter, and rock painter. I've recently added loom potholder maker to my list after a 52-year hiatus! I have rekindled the happiness that making these items brings! The designs and colors are much more fascinating and kicked up than when I was eight and learned to make them.

GLOSSARY

 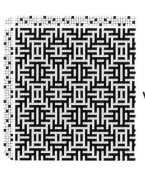 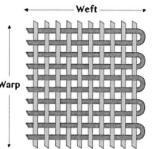 

clasped weft: a weaving technique in which the warp/weft loops are folded over each other, resulting in two or more different weaving areas within your loom.

color-and-weave: a broad classification in which the pattern effect is a result of both a weave structure and the sequence of contrasting warp and weft loops.

Log Cabin: the most basic shadow weave effect, in which the alternating sequence of dark and light loops look like logs. Log Cabin is woven by warping a sequence of two alternating colors, repeating the sequence reversed, and repeating the whole for the width of your loom. Weft follows the warp sequence.

pick: (a) moving the weft loop over or under a warp loop; (b) properly, one pass of the weft through the shed.

plain weave: a basic weave structure in which the weft alternates over and under the warp. It's also called tabby.

shadow weave: a color-and-weave effect with a combination structure of plain weave and a twill step at pattern changes. Two adjacent colors shadow each other.

shed: the gap that occurs when you separate your warp loops into upper and lower.

shrinkage: how much the fabric shrinks after washing. As a rule of thumb, cotton shrinks 10%, wool 15%, and synthetics (in general) 10%.

split loop: a weaving technique in which the weft loop is woven over or under each strand of the warp loop separately, instead of the usual both strands together.

take-up, or draw-in: how much the fabric rebounds after being removed from the loom. If your weft loops lie fairly loosely across the loom, tension will be less, and take-up will be less: your potholder will lie flatter. Tug your loops.

twill: a weave structure in which the weft passes over or under one or more warp loops, then over or under two or more warp loops, and so on, with a "step" or offset, between rows. The offset creates the diagonal look of a twill.

warp: the vertical loops on a loom.

weave structure: the manner in which the warp and weft interlace, as in plain weave, twill, basket weave, satin weave, and so on.

weaving draft: a graphic representation of how to set your loom up to weave the pattern shown on the draft. The parts of the draft—threading, treadling, tie-up, and drawdown—tell the weaver how to warp the loom, and what the pattern will look like.

weft: the horizontal loops that are woven over and under the warp loops.

PATTERN INDEX